NELSON'S ANNUAL

Children's Ministry Sourcebook

2006 EDITION

NELSON'S ANNUAL
Children's Ministry Sourcebook

2006 EDITION

Vicki Wiley, Editor

NELSON REFERENCE & ELECTRONIC
A Division of Thomas Nelson Publishers
Since 1798

www.thomasnelson.com

Nelson's Annual Children's Sourcebook, 2006 Edition
Copyright © 2005 by Thomas Nelson, Inc.
Published in Nashville, Tennessee, by Thomas Nelson, Inc.

Unless otherwise indicated, Scripture quotations are from International Children's Bible, copyright © 1986, 1988, 1999 by Tommy Nelson™, a division of Thomas Nelson, Inc., Nashville, Tennessee, 37214. Used by permission.

Weekly alternative versions of the memory verses, and verses marked NKJV, are from the New King James Version, copyright © 1979, 1980, 1982, 1990 by Thomas Nelson, Inc., Publishers.

Book design and composition by Kristy L. Morell, Smyrna, Tennessee

Wiley, Vicki (ed.)
Nelson's annual children's ministry sourcebook, 2006 edition

ISBN 1-4185-0546-3

Printed in the United States of America.
1 2 3 – 07 06 05

Dedication

To my dad, my encourager, my buddy
Kenneth Taylor
Who went to be with the Lord this year.

Contents

Feature Articles

Preface

You have responded to God's call to teach children—Congratulations! You have answered the greatest calling!

In your classroom you will find a variety of children; all who have a different style of learning. We have designed this book to meet the challenges that you will face. Each lesson contains many different activities to involve all the children into the lesson.

How to Use This Book:

This book has been designed to provide flexibility for the teacher.

The 52 dated weekly segment include two main parts: The first part may be used for midweek services and introduces the subject for the following Sunday. The second part contains the Sunday lesson.

If you do not have a midweek program, the two parts of the lesson can be combined for one extended Children's Church time.

Each lesson comes with several components; all of which work together to incorporate all learning styles.

Scripture: The Bible text from which the lesson is drawn.

Lesson Aim: The "target" of the lesson, the one thing that we want the children to remember and take away with them.

Bible lesson/Sermon: The meat of the lesson, a lesson taken from a Bible passage. If you are also using the Pastor's Sourcebook, the passage will be the same.

Supply List: To help you prepare for your activities, we have listed all items necessary at the beginning of the section.

Song Suggestions: Songs that will enhance the lesson.

Bible Activities: Activities that involve learning more about the Scripture passage.

Enrichment Activities: Activities that come from culture, history, or other sources to bring the Bible story to life.

Crafts: Craft activities for the children to make and take home.

Snack: A lesson-related snack to help the children remember the point of the lesson as well as refresh them.

Memory Verse: A verse taken from the passage chosen for children to memorize.

Memory Verse Activity: Using that same passage, we have provided an activity to help with the memorization process as well as make it fun.

Prayer Focus: A prayer "starter" to use as you pray for the children.

My prayer is that you will feel encouraged in your teaching and equipped to do the best job you can—that is your task. Let God do the rest!

—Vicki Wiley
General editor

Contributors

Rev. Barney Kinard is the President and full-time Children's Evangelist with Creative Children's Ministries in Buena Park, California. Barney holds degrees from Moody Bible Institute, Azusa Pacific University and Fuller Theological Seminary. Barney is an accomplished teacher and mentor to children's leaders and is much in demand as a national speaker to children using creative methods like puppetry, ventriloquism, gospel illusions and object lessons. You can find him at his Web site *www.Kidhelper.com*.

Tina Houser has been involved in children's ministry for 26 years and is presently the Minister of Children at First Church of God in Kokomo, Indiana. For the past 16 years she has greatly enjoyed writing early elementary curriculum for Warner Press. Recently, her commitments have expanded to include speaking engagements for both children and adults, along with mentoring young people just starting out in children's ministry. (Jan. 4, 11, 18, 25, Feb. 1, 8, 15, 22, March 1, 8, 15, 22, 26, 29, April 5, 12, 19, 26, May 3, 10, 14, 17, 24, 31, June 7, 14, 21, 28, July 5, 9, 12, 19, 26, August 2, 9, 16, 23, 30, Sept. 6, 13, 20, 27, Oct. 4, 11, 15, 18, 22, 25, Nov. 1, 5, 8, 12, 15, 19, 22, 26, 29, Dec. 3, 6, 10, 13, 17, 20, 24, 27)

Ivy Beckwith has served churches in Boston, Chicago, and Minnesota and holds a Ph.D. in Education from Trinity International University. Ivy has worked also for two curriculum publishers as a consultant and editor. She is the author of *Postmodern Children's Ministry: Ministry to Children In the 21st Century*. (Jan. 1, Jan. 22, Feb. 12, Feb. 26, April 23, May 28, July 30, Aug. 13, Aug. 20, Aug. 27, Sept. 3, Sept. 10, Sept. 17, Oct. 1)

Graham Bingham is a retired pastor, editor, and traveler currently living in St. Augustine, Florida. He has a great heart for children and loves writing children's sermons. (July 23)

Rev. Eric J. Titus is a minister with the Reformed Church in America. He has served congregations in California and New York for the past ten years. Recently he has accepted an appointment with RCA Missions Services to teach theology at the Evangelical Theological Seminary in Osijek, Croatia and work with the Reformed Christian Church in Croatia. Rev. Titus completed his Bachelor of Arts and Master of Arts Degree in Biblical Literature at Oral Roberts University and his Master of Divinity at Yale University. Throughout the course of his professional ministry Rev. Titus has been a pastoral advocate for children's ministry and children's education in the Church (March 5, March 19)

Rev. Jim Miller is a pastor at the First Presbyterian Church of Honolulu and freelance writer. He received his M.Div. from Princeton Theological Seminary and his B.A. from U.C. Berkeley. He and his wife, Yolanda, have been serving in ministry for ten years and are proud new parents of a baby daughter, Sonoma. (June 4, June 11, June 18, Dec. 31)

Pat Verbal is the founder of Ministry to Today's Child and an inspirational guest speaker in churches, conferences, and the media. Pat holds a Master's Degree in Pastoral Studies and is a best-selling author who served 20 years as Pastor of Children and Christian Education. (Jan. 15, Jan. 29, Feb. 5, Feb. 19, March 12, May 21)

Vicki Wiley, General editor, is the Director of Children's Ministries at First Presbyterian Church in Honolulu, Hawaii. She is a graduate of Fuller Seminary and on the faculty of the Bible Institute of Hawaii. (Jan. 8, April 2, April 9, April 16, April 30, May 7, June 25, July 2, July 16, Aug. 6. Sept. 24, Oct. 8, Oct. 29)

Sammy Renauro is founder and executive director of By His Side Ministries. An organization dedicated to encouraging bringing truth to God's people. This is being accomplished through seminars and workshops in cities and colleges around the world. He is the author of the book "By His Side" You can learn more of By His Side Ministries and Samuel Renauro at www.byhisside.com.

Karl Bastian is a Children's Pastor at the Village Church of Barrington, Illinois. Karl holds a Bachelors degree in Bible Theology from Moody Bible Institute, and a Masters in Children's Ministry from the Trinity Evangelical Divinity School. Karl is the founder of Kidology Inc., a non-profit ministry dedicated to equipping and encouraging children's workers. Kidology ministers through the KidologyWeb, a powerful interactive online database of creative ideas and resources. Karl wrote articles for this year's sourcebook.

2006 Calendar

January 1	**New Year's Day**
January 6	Epiphany
January 8	
January 15	**Sanctity of Human Life Sunday**
January 16	Martin Luther King, Jr. Day
January 22	
January 26	Australia Day
January 29	
February 1–28	Black History Month
February 1	National Freedom Day
February 2	Groundhog Day
February 5	**Super Bowl Sunday**
February 12	**Lincoln's Birthday**
February 14	Valentine's Day
February 19	
February 20	President's Day
February 22	Washington's Birthday
February 26	**30 Hour Famine-World Vision**
March 1	Ash Wednesday
March 5	**First Sunday of Lent; Cinco de Mayo**
March 12	**Second Sunday of Lent**
March 17	St. Patrick's Day
March 19	**Third Sunday of Lent**
March 20	Spring Begins
March 26	**Fourth Sunday of Lent**
April 2	**Fifth Sunday of Lent;**
	Daylight Savings Time Begins
April 9	**Palm Sunday**

April 13	Maundy Thursday; Jefferson's Birthday; Passover
April 14	Good Friday
April 16	**Easter Sunday**
April 22	Earth Day
April 23	
April 25	Holocaust Remembrance Day
April 26	Administrative Professional's Day
April 30	
May 4	National Day of Prayer
May 7	
May 14	**Mother's Day**
May 20	Armed Forces Day
May 21	
May 25	Ascension Day
May 28	
May 29	Memorial Day
June 4	**Pentecost**
June 11	**Trinity Sunday**
June 14	Flag Day
June 18	**Father's Day**
June 21	Summer Begins
June 25	
July 1	Canada Day
July 2	
July 4	Independence Day
July 9	
July 16	
July 23	**Parent's Day**
July 30	
August 6	**Transfiguration Day; Friendship Day**
August 13	

August 20	
August 27	
September 3	
September 4	Labor Day
September 10	**Grandparent's Day**
September 17	
September 20	See You At the Pole
September 22	Native American Day
September 23	Autumn Begins; Rosh Hashanah Begins
September 24	
October 1–31	Pastor Appreciation Month
October 1	
October 2	Yom Kippur Begins
October 8	**Clergy Appreciation Day**
October 9	Columbus Day
October 15	
October 16	Bosses' Day
October 22	**Mother-in-Law Day**
October 29	**Reformation Sunday;**
	Daylight Savings Time Ends
October 31	Halloween
November 1	All Saints' Day
November 5	
November 11	Veterans' Day
November 12	**International Day of Prayer for the**
	Persecuted Church
November 19	
November 23	Thanksgiving Day
November 26	
December 3	**First Sunday of Advent**
December 7	Pearl Harbor Remembrance Day
December 10	**Second Sunday of Advent**

December 16	Hanukkah Begins
December 17	**Third Sunday of Advent**
December 22	Winter Begins
December 24	**Fourth Sunday of Advent; Christmas Eve**
December 25	Christmas Day
December 26	Boxing Day; Kwanzaa Begins
December 31	**New Year's Eve**

Weekly Suggestions for 53 Weeks

Epiphany

By Ivy Beckwith

Scripture: Matthew 2:1–12

Lesson Aim: Children will learn how the three kings brought special gifts to Jesus and identify gifts they can give to Jesus.

Memory Verse: Matthew 2:10

Preparation

○ WRAP A MEDIUM SIZED PACKAGE IN COLORFUL WRAPPING PAPER. (Wrapping paper with stars on it will help to enhance the Epiphany theme.)
○ LARGE STAR FROM YELLOW POSTER BOARD

Show children the wrapped present. **Who likes to get presents?** (Wait for response.) **When do we give and get presents?** (Take several responses such as birthdays, Christmas, when a baby is born, when someone gets married.)

Today we have a story about some men who brought special presents to Jesus when He was a little boy. The Bible tells us King Herod, who didn't like the baby Jesus, sent three men called the Magi to search for Jesus. Herod told the men when they found Jesus they needed to tell him right away. So the three Magi went out to find Jesus. They saw a special star up in the eastern sky. (Show children the star.) They followed the star hoping it would lead them to Jesus. One day the star stopped right over the house where Jesus, Mary, and Joseph were living. The three men walked up to the house and knocked on the door. When they were invited into the house they found Jesus with His mother Mary. The three Magi bowed down and worshiped Jesus immediately. **Why do you think they did that?** (Wait for a few responses.) They worshiped Jesus because they knew that Jesus was a very special baby. They knew Jesus would grow up to be a king.

After the Magi bowed down to Jesus they opened the special presents they brought for Him. They brought Jesus gold which is a metal worth lots of money and they brought Jesus some very special spices and incense. These were very extravagant gifts during the time that Jesus lived. These were gifts fit for a king.

We know Jesus is God's Son. We know Jesus is a king because He came to earth to bring God's kingdom to earth. And like the three Magi, we can give gifts to Jesus the King, too. In fact, this is a special Sunday at church called Epiphany when we think about the kinds of gifts we can give to Jesus. So let's think for a minute about the kinds of gifts we can give to Jesus. **What kinds of gifts would you like to give to Jesus?** (Wait for a few responses.) I can think of two gifts Jesus would really like us to give Him. Just like the

Magi worshiped Jesus—Jesus likes it when we worship Him. **How can we worship Jesus?** (Wait for several responses.) When we thank Jesus for loving us we are worshipping Him. When we sing songs to Jesus in church and Sunday school we're worshiping Him. When we obey Jesus' words we are worshiping Him.

Another gift we can give Jesus is our service. **What are some ways we can serve Jesus?** (Wait for a few responses.) When we love our neighbor, when we're kind to others, when we help other people, we are serving Jesus. Serving Jesus is a gift Jesus really likes. So just like the three kings who came to see Jesus when He was a child, we can give gifts to Jesus, too.

Song Suggestions

"We Three Kings" (Traditional)
"Follow that Star" by Mary Rice Hopkins from *Mary Christmas* (Big Steps 4 U, 1993)
"I Open My Heart" by Mark Thompson from *Yes Yes Yes!* (Markarts, 2000)
"Day by Day" by Jana Alayra from *Jump into the Light* (Montjoy Music, 1995)

Craft for Younger Children: Star Light!

○ CRAFT FOAM   ○ SHORT DOWEL RODS   ○ GLITTER   ○ GLUE

Before class, cut a star shape out of craft foam (white or yellow), and glue to the dowel. Demonstrate to the children how to put a thin film of glue onto the star and sprinkle with glitter.

Say: **The kings followed a star to where Jesus was living. Let's pretend that this is the star that they followed.** Lead children around the room holding up their stars.

Craft for Older Children: Gift for the King

○ BABY FOOD OR SMALL JARS   ○ WHOLE CLOVES   ○ POTPOURRI   ○ BABY OIL

Myrrh was one of the gifts that the Kings brought to the child Jesus. We are going to make something that is similar to myrrh today.

Show children how to fill the baby food jar about 1/3 full with baby oil. Add a clove and a small amount of potpourri to the jar and shake it up well.

Have children sit with their jars. Say: **Now open your jar carefully and get a little of the oil on your finger. How does that smell?** (*good!*) **In Bible times, they had to make everything themselves and this may be the way they made perfumed oil and myrrh.**

 **Snack:** King Cake

○ ONE CAKE LARGE ENOUGH FOR YOUR GROUP   ○ ONE ALMOND   ○ ONE CROWN

Before class, place the almond into the cake in such a way that the kids will not be able to see it.

Serve the cake to the children and say: **In some countries, Epiphany is celebrated by serving a "Kings Cake" which is what this is. One of you will find an almond in your piece. Whoever finds it will be the king!**

Give the crown to the child who gets the almond and let them have some special attention or privilege.

Memory Verse: Matthew 2:10 (ICB)

"When the wise men saw the star, they were filled with joy!"

Alternate Version: Matthew 2:10 (NKJV)
"When they saw the star, they rejoiced with exceedingly great joy."

Memory Verse Activity: Follow That Star!

○ POSTER BOARD   ○ MARKERS

Draw a star shape and cut out of poster board. Write the verse on the star and cut into a puzzle. Let children work the puzzle as they say the verse.

Prayer Focus

Dear God help me to always look for You and worship You. You are a wonderful God! Amen

Baptism of Jesus:
The Start of a New Season of Life

By Tina Houser

Scripture: Matthew 3:13–17

Lesson Aim: The children will understand how Jesus started His ministry.

Memory Verse: Matthew 3:17

☞ **Bible Activity for Younger Children:** How Do We Start?

The children will take their shoes off of their feet and put their hands in them instead. Line up the children with their shoes on their hands on one side of the room.

The teacher will give one of the following actions and the children will tell what the first step is in accomplishing that task. If the group agrees with the answer, then they all take one step toward the other side of the room with their hands in their shoes.

Example: Teacher: Starting a car; Students: Put the key in the ignition.

Fixing a bowl of cereal	Using the computer
Painting a picture	Feeding the dog
Washing your hair	Playing a soccer game
Making a bed	Building a sand castle
Riding a bike	Jesus starting His ministry

When it was time for Jesus to choose His disciples and start His ministry, the first step He took was to be baptized by John the Baptist. This was His first action as He started a whole new part of His life.

☞ **Bible Activity for Older Children:** Choices!
○ PLAIN CUPCAKES   ○ TOOTHPASTE   ○ WHITE CREAM CHEESE ICING   ○ CRAFT STICKS

Give each child a plain cupcake and tell them that they will be able to ice their cupcakes with one of two things. Bring out the cream cheese icing as their first choice. Then, show them that their second choice is a tube of toothpaste. Both will spread easily on cupcakes. Provide craft sticks as their spreading utensils and allow them time to ice their cupcakes.

Say: **Which of the two did you feel was the better choice? Is toothpaste a bad thing? Of course not, but this isn't the time to use toothpaste.**
Jesus made a choice when He was about 30 years old to begin His ministry. **What was the first thing He chose to do?** *(be baptized)* **What else could He have chosen to do?** *(stay at the carpenter shop, travel)* **Are those bad things? No, but He chose to do what God wanted Him to do at that time.**

Enrichment for Younger Children: All About Doves

The Bible says that Jesus saw the Holy Spirit come down like a dove when He was baptized. **What is a dove?** *(a bird)* **What do you think a dove looks like? Is it a big bird or a little bird?** *(little)* Some birds, like owls, are known for hunting down mice for the farmers. Pelicans are known for catching fish in their beaks. Eagles are known for being able to see tiny little critters from very high. **What are doves like?**

Doves are often seen on Christmas cards carrying a ribbon that says "Peace." They make a very soft little sound called a coo. **Can you sound like a dove?** Doves are very gentle birds and do not like to fight, even when their nest is being attacked. Because they are so calm and innocent they have become a symbol for peace. When the dove came down to Jesus when He was baptized, a voice from heaven said, "This is my Son and I love him. I am very pleased with him." **Does that sound like a peaceful thing to say?** It was one way that Jesus was reminded that His heavenly Father was happy with this first step in His ministry.

Enrichment for Older Children: Seasons Change

We identify different seasons by certain ways the trees around us look, by the foods we eat, by the holidays we celebrate. Each season has its own purpose in the year-long cycle. Place a sign on one wall that says *Summer,* on another wall a sign that says *Autumn, Winter,* and *Spring.* Divide the class into four groups—one for each of the seasons. Each group will draw pictures and post special words that help to identify that season. On the "Summer" wall they may put pictures of swimming at the pool, fireworks, watermelon and strawberries. They may also put words like "hot" and "too short."

Discuss the changes in seasons with the children. Say: **Name one thing that happens that tells you the season is about to change. As spring begins, you notice a few flowers coming up and the trees starting to turn green.** Discuss each season this way.

Share that Jesus was now 30 years old. He had spent the first "season" of His life growing up and learning about the people around Him. Now, His life was changing. The first thing He did to mark the change in His life was to be baptized. His baptism was one way to let everyone know that there was a change. Days of working at the carpenter shop and staying in the little town of Nazareth were over. Now, He would be traveling about the countryside gathering followers, healing people, teaching about His Father, and going about the business for which He had been sent. Jesus marked the beginning of a new season in His life with baptism.

Memory Verse: Matthew 3:17 (ICB)

"And a voice spoke from heaven. The voice said, 'This is my son and I love him. I am very pleased with him.'"

Alternate Version: Matthew 3:17 (NKJV)
"And suddenly a voice came from heaven, saying, 'This is my beloved Son, in whom I am well pleased.'"

Baptism of Jesus:
The Start of a New Season of Life

By Vicki Wiley

Scripture: Matthew 3:13–17

Lesson Aim: The children will understand how Jesus started his ministry.

Memory Verse: Matthew 3:17

Preparation

○ GRADUATION TYPE CAP   ○ BABY BOTTLE   ○ SIPPER CUP   ○ REGULAR GLASS

Show a baby bottle to the children and say: **Who drinks out of this? Yes, a baby! Do any of you still drink out of one?** (No, you don't!) (show sipper cup) **Who drinks out of one of these cups?** (Oh, some of you do… but most of you don't because you drink out of one of these) (show regular glass).

Everyone used to drink from one of these (show baby bottle) and then you changed and started drinking out of one of these. Now you all changed again and now you use these to drink out of. Each time, you were excited about the changes! Each time your mom let you change what you drink out of. It was a "new beginning" for you and you didn't go back to the old way.

Show the graduation-type cap. Say: **Do you know what this is?** It is a graduation cap. People wear this cap when they are graduating from college or high school. When they wear this cap, everyone knows that they have completed one part of their lives and are ready for another part. When you wear one of these you will show everyone that you are finished preparing for your career and ready to start your career.

Jesus had lived a good life, learning how to be a carpenter and at the same time, learning how to serve God. Jesus learned all about God. Now Jesus knew that it was time to start serving God. Jesus showed everyone else that it was time, by being baptized. When Jesus was baptized, He started a new part of His life—He was ready to begin His ministry.

Song Suggestions

Let the Lord Have His Way Songsheets published by CEF Press, P.O. Box 348, Warrenton, MO 63383

"I Will Obey You" by Cindy Rethmeier from *I Want to Be Like Jesus* (Mercy Vineyard, 1995)

"I Will Follow You" by Mary Rice Hopkins *15 Singable Songs* (Big Steps 4 U, 1985)

🐦 Craft for Younger Children: Doves
○ WHITE CRAFT PAINT ○ PAPER PLATE ○ BLUE CONSTRUCTION PAPER ○ FEATHERS

Put some white craft paint on a paper plate. Using a feather instead of a brush, the children will paint a dove on a piece of blue construction paper. They will enjoy painting with this unusual brush.

Make a label with the memory verse typed on it for the children to put on their papers. As the children leave, give them a clean feather as a reminder of today's lesson.

🐦 Craft for Older Children: Doves
○ REGULAR PAPER PLATES (1 PER CHILD) ○ PLASTIC SPOONS

Cut paper plates in half then cut one half into three equal parts. Show children how to form a dove in this manner. Use the half paper plate for the body, the spoon for the head and neck and the three parts for the wings and the tail. Glue all together to form a dove.

Say: The dove is a sign of peace and it is also the symbol of the Holy Spirit. When Jesus was baptized, the Holy Spirit came as a dove. **What do you think it would have been like to see that happen?**

🍿 Snack: Dove Cakes
○ WHITE DOUGHNUTS ○ WHITE DOUGHNUT HOLES ○ RAISINS FOR EYES

Let children make a "dove" snack by putting together the above ingredients. The doughnut can be used for the body and the hole for the head.

Say: **Have you ever seen a dove? Do they look like this?** No! Doves are very beautiful birds, but this will at least remind us of a dove!

✒️ Memory Verse: Matthew 3:17 (ICB)

"And a voice from heaven said,
'This is my Son, whom I love, and I am very pleased with him.'"

Alternate Version: Matthew 3:17 (NKJV)
"And suddenly a voice came from heaven, saying,
'This is my beloved Son, in whom I am well pleased.'"

Children's Ministry Sourcebook

Memory Verse Activity

Find a simple dove shape and copy it onto paper for each child. Let the children write the verse onto the dove shape. Read the verse together.

Prayer Focus

Dear God, thank You for Jesus and the example that He gave us. Thank You that we can always have new beginnings in our lives, too! Amen.

Sanctity of Life

By Tina Houser

Scripture: Psalm 139:13–16

Lesson Aim: The children will realize that God had a plan for them, even before they were born.

Memory Verse: Psalm 139:14

☞ **Bible Activity for Younger Children:** Plans for Building
○ SUPPLY OF SNAP-TOGETHER BLOCKS

Tell each child to think of something very simple they can build with their blocks. They will come up with a plan and a picture in their minds of what their creations are going to look like. Encourage them to use the blocks to build what they saw in their minds. Do not tell anyone what you are building. When everyone is done, share your creations with the rest of the group.

Say: You were just a picture in God's mind at one time, and then He decided to create you. He had a plan for you—exactly what He wanted you to be like. God can make anything He wants, and He wanted to make YOU!

☞ **Bible Activity for Older Children:** In the Beginning . . .
○ ULTRASOUND PICTURE OF A BABY ○ PHOTOGRAPH OF THE SAME BABY AFTER BIRTH

If you do not have access to an ultrasound picture, there are many available at *ultrasound.net*. The parents of the baby in the ultrasound and photograph may want to bring the items themselves and show them to the children. Ultrasounds can be quite difficult to understand unless someone tells you what you are viewing. Then, it seems so easy to see. Use a small pointer to help lessen the confusion. The parents of some of the children in your group may have ultrasound pictures of your students. It would be especially interesting to show how the two are related.

What kinds of things do you think babies can do before they are born? Did you know that they:
- have a heart beat
- can suck their thumb
- can kick hard enough that the mother might yelp
- have fingerprints
- can feel pain

Each baby is made special by God and is already a human being before he or she comes out into the world. Now show the picture of the same child after birth. Emphasize that the two are alive in both pictures.

Enrichment Activity for Younger Children: Can We Help?
- ○ SMALL GIFTS FOR A BABY ○ LARGE BASKET ○ BABY SHOWER GIFT WRAP
- ○ SCISSORS ○ TAPE

Before class, you may want to solicit help from an adult group to provide gifts for a mother at the local Crisis Pregnancy Center or the children could be instructed the week before to bring a small gift with them.

Explain to the children that a Crisis Pregnancy Center is a place where they take care of young women who are going to have a baby but do not have a husband or family that wants to help them. At this special center, the women are helped with medical attention so they can make sure the baby is healthy when he/she is born. They help the women find a place to live once the baby is born.

Say: Babies need lots of special "stuff" because they have to be taken care of in a special way. **What kinds of things do mothers need so they can take care of their babies?** *(diapers, car seat, clothes, lotion)*

We're going to have a baby shower in a basket for one of the new moms at the Crisis Pregnancy Center. Place all the gifts that have been collected on a table where everyone can see. Provide an assisting hand to any of the children who need help wrapping a baby shower gift. Place the gifts in the basket as they are completed. Make sure you include a card signed by all the children and what church you represent.

If you have time and the proper transportation, take the children with you to deliver the basket; otherwise, make sure the basket gets delivered before you meet with the children again.

Enrichment Activity for Older Children: Baby Beginnings

When the President of the United States begins his job, there are parades and speeches and parties. It's a very BIG beginning! When someone starts to build a house, they bring in a bulldozer to dig the basement and that's a really BIG beginning! Each and every person, though, has a very, very, very tiny beginning.

Place a dot on a piece of paper. You were no bigger than this dot when you began. Inside that little dot was all the information about what you would be like. God already had decided what color your hair would be, how big your feet would be, if you would be a boy or a girl, and if your eyes would be blue, brown, green, or grey. Let's look at what happened to you in the next nine months before you were born.

Your very first month: you had a heartbeat

Second month: fingers, feet, ears, nose, lips start

Third month: you have fingerprints that are unlike anyone else's

Fourth month: your heart is big enough now that the doctor can hear it and you've learned to suck your thumb—get that thumb out of your mouth!

Fifth month: you're kicking up a storm and your mom can really feel it!

Sixth month: you get the hiccups!

Seventh month: you can open and close your eyelids and look around

Eighth month: You are gaining strength and weight. It's almost time for you to be born.

Ninth month: Do you remember the one little dot (one cell) when we began? There are now 200 million of those little cells. You are the same person you were when it was that tiny dot, you're just a lot bigger now.

Memory Verse: Psalm 139:14 (ICB)

"I praise you because you made me in an amazing and wonderful way
What you have done is wonderful
I know this very well."

Alternate Version: Psalm 139:14 (NKJV)

"I will praise You, for I am fearfully and wonderfully made;
Marvelous are Your works,
And that my soul knows very well."

Sanctity of Life

By Pat Verbal

Scripture: 1 Corinthians 6:19-20

Lesson Aim: To help children understand that their bodies are a gift from God.

Memory Verse: Psalm 139:14

It's 7:00 AM at Sam Beller's house and he is watching cartoons with his brothers and sisters. They've all three piled onto Sam's bed before getting ready for school. After school they will go to soccer, ballet and piano lessons, but Sam won't go with them. Eleven-year-old Sam can't move at all. He can't talk either, but in his face his family finds inspiration. Sam is severely disabled with cerebral palsy. His days are filled with nurses, medicines, ventilators to help him breath and tube feedings to keep him nourished.

Do you think Sam ever gets discouraged and feels like giving up? Sure he does, but Sam is not alone. Most of us get frustrated sometimes with our bodies and wish we were smarter, faster, thinner, stronger, healthier or prettier. It's easy to forget that our bodies are gifts from God and He created each of us the way we are for a very important purpose.

The Apostle Paul wrote two letters to a church in the very worldly city of Corinth. Their culture taught them that their bodies had nothing to do with their spirits. Some pagan religions required people to cut their bodies and give human sacrifices to idols. Paul warned Christians to thank God for their bodies and use them for God's service. In 1 Corinthians 12, Paul reminded believers that God gave each of them spiritual gifts to build up Christ's body, the Church. He challenged them to honor God by respecting their bodies as God's earthly temple.

Sam knows he's special and his joy is not a secret—It's visible every day. His nurse says when Sam looks at you, his bright eyes express so much love. His mom says she gets to see a lot of good in people, because she has Sam in her life. Each evening, Sam's brothers and sisters share their day with him, because his smile makes life seem more precious.

Sam represents millions of children in our world who have disabilities, and God created each one of them for a divine purpose. Their lives are valuable because God said they were created in His image . . . "and it was very good." (Genesis 1:26–31).

 Song Suggestions

"Can You Hear My Heart?" by Jana Alayra from *Dig Down Deep* (Montjoy Music, 1997)
"A Dad Like You" by Mary Rice Hopkins from *Good Buddies* (Big Steps 4 U, 1994)
"It Started with an Egg" by Mary Rice Hopkins from *In My Garden* (Big Steps 4 U, 1995)
Less of Me, Mr. Bill, When I Grow Up (Mr. Bill Music, 1997)

Craft for Younger Children: God Loves Babies!
○ SMALL WOODEN SPOONS (1 PER CHILD)   ○ 4-INCH SQUARE OF FABRICE
○ MARKERS

Say: **When God made you, God made you exactly how He wanted you to be. Today you get to make a little baby exactly how you want it to be.**

Show the children how to draw a face on the spoon; then, wrap it in cloth. Say: **Do you have a younger brother or sister? Next time you are with them, remember how God made them so special!**

Craft for Older Children: Poster Making

Invite children to participate in the Sanctity of Human Life Week by making posters showing what this is all about. Since children hear these words on the 6:00 PM news, they are curious. It's not too early to help them understand that life is sacred. Children can write poems and songs, create posters, and distribute literature.

Snack: Masterpieces
○ GRAHAM CRACKER SQUARES   ○ ICING   ○ DECORATIONS

Let the children ice and decorate their square as they wish. Say: **Look at all of these beautiful cookies! Each one is different, just like each of you is completely different!**

Memory Verse: Psalm 139:14 (ICB)

"I praise you because you made me in an amazing and wonderful way.
What you have done is wonderful. I know this very well."

Alternate Version: Psalm 139:14 (NKJV)
"I will praise You, for I am fearfully and wonderfully made;
Marvelous are Your works, And that my soul knows very well."

Memory Verse Activity

Write the verse on a poster board or board so the children can easily see it. Read the verse to the class, one section at a time. Let them repeat the sections after you.

I praise you (I praise you)
because You made me (because You made me)
in an amazing and wonderful way. (in an amazing and wonderful way.)
What You have done is wonderful. (What You have done is wonderful.)
I know this very well. (I know this very well.)

Prayer Focus

Dear God we thank You and praise You for the way You made us! You are an awesome God! We love You. Amen

Prayer

By Tina Houser

Scripture: Matthew 6:9–13 (The Lord's Prayer)

Lesson Aim: The children will gain a new appreciation for prayer.

Memory Verse: Matthew 6:9

☞ Bible Activity for Younger Children: Breathing and Praying
○ STOPWATCH OR A WATCH WITH A SECOND HAND

Is breathing important? Let's see how important breathing really is. Let's time how long you can go without breathing. You may want the younger children to pinch their noses and lips tightly. This will keep them from sneaking little breaths. Record the times.

What happens when we stop breathing completely? Breathing is pretty important, isn't it? Breathing is like praying. Praying is pretty important, too. Breathing keeps our bodies alive, and prayer keeps our souls alive. Our bodies won't forget to breathe, but we sometimes forget to pray. When we start forgetting to pray, we get further and further away from God. It's as if we don't know God anymore. Pray often, and keep your soul breathing.

☞ Bible Activity for Older Children: Prayer Takes Time!
○ TIMER

Instruct the children to greet every single person in the room before the timer goes off. (Set the timer for some ridiculously short amount of time, depending on the size of your group.) During that time they must shake hands, say "good morning", and tell their names to each one they greet. If you complete your greetings before the timer goes off, then sit down. Encourage any adults in the room to participate, also.

Did you learn anything that you didn't already know about anyone? (couldn't because we were too hurried)
Did anyone make you feel really special? (there wasn't time)
How did it make you feel to be greeted this way?
How is the way we greeted each other like the way we pray sometimes? (we are told what to say; we get in a hurry; we only say what we have to say)

How do you think God feels when we rush through our prayer time?
God doesn't want us to pray because someone else told us what to say. He wants us to talk to Him from the things that our heart is speaking. Take a deep breath; don't look at the clock; and just relax and tell God the things that are on your mind and heart.

How does it make you feel when someone hurries through being with you so they can go do something else? If the only attention we give to God is hurried time, then it sends God the message that He isn't special to us or worthy of our love and time.

Enrichment Activity for Younger Children: Daily Bread
- ○ A VARIETY OF BREADS
- ○ TOPPINGS LIKE HONEY, CHEESE SPREAD, SQUIRT MARGARINE AND/OR JELLY

One of the things Jesus told us to pray for was our "daily bread," thanking God for providing the food necessary for us each day. Different people around the world eat different types of bread. Bread can pull apart in flakey layers like a biscuit, be flat like a tortilla, have a strange shape like a pretzel, be dry and hard like a cracker, or just right for a peanut butter and jelly sandwich.

Check the bakery of the local grocery store. Provide a variety of types of bread for the children to taste. Also, bring a few items they could use to enhance their bread. Invite the children to join you in saying a prayer together before sampling: "Thank You, God, for giving us our daily bread."

The local public library will most likely have some lower elementary books describing breads from around the world. Bring one of the books to read to the children or for them to look at the pictures.

Enrichment Activity for Older Children: Daily Bread
- ○ SUGAR, GALLON ZIP-LOCK BAG   ○ LUKEWARM WATER (100 DEGREES)
- ○ ENVELOPE OF RAPID RISING ACTIVE DRY YEAST   ○ CONTAINERS FOR MIXING

There are few things nicer than the smell of bread baking, the feel of the nice soft center, and the taste of a big warm slice. Jesus gave His followers a sample prayer, so they would know how to pray to God. In His prayer, He prayed that God would provide food, or "daily bread." He told His followers to ask God for what they needed for that day. People all over the world eat bread. It may have different things added to it or it may have a unique shape, but everyone has some sort of bread.

We're going to do an experiment today that will help us understand how bread gets so nice and fluffy. Write these instructions somewhere visible to all the children.

1. Mix an envelope of yeast with 1 cup of lukewarm water.

2. Add in 1/2 cup of sugar.

3. Put this mixture in the plastic bag. Before you seal it, push out as much air as possible, so the plastic is down around the mixture.

4. Place the bag in a warm place. You can make a warm place by preheating your oven to 150 degrees. Turn the oven off. Place the bag on a cookie sheet or in a shallow pan and set it in the closed oven.

In an hour, go back to the oven to view the bag. The yeast should have created a gas known as carbon dioxide. That gas should fill the bag and make the bag puffy. Leave the bag in the oven longer and the difference will become even more noticeable.

If your time is limited and you can't wait the full hour, prepare a bag a couple of hours ahead of time to show the children what will happen.

Think about how puffy the bag became. The yeast will do the same thing to the bread dough. Aren't you glad God made yeast? That's what makes bread light and airy—and yummy!

Memory Verse: Matthew 6:9 (ICB)

"So when you pray, you should pray like this:
'Our Father in heaven,
we pray that your name will always be kept holy.'"

Alternate Version: Matthew 6:9 (NKJV)
"In this manner, therefore, pray:
Our Father in heaven,
Hallowed be Your name."

Prayer

By Ivy Beckwith

Scripture: Matthew 6:9–13

Lesson Aim: Children will understand the different parts of prayer as modeled and illustrated in the Lord's Prayer.

Memory Verse: Matthew 6:9

Preparation

Make four signs with the words from the Lord's Prayer printed on them ("Our Father in heaven," "Give us today our daily bread," "Forgive us our debts," "And lead us not into temptation, but deliver us from the evil one").

Ask: **Who can tell me what prayer is?** (Wait for several responses.) Prayer is talking to God. Just like we can talk with our friends and our families, we can talk to God anytime about anything. But not everyone knows what prayer is or, even, how to pray. Jesus wanted all His friends to understand how to pray, so one day when He was out teaching the people, He taught them how to pray. He gave them a special prayer they could use to help them pray.

Today we call that prayer the Lord's Prayer because it shows us, too, how we should pray. I'm going to read you the prayer Jesus taught His friends. We find it in our Bible in the gospel of Matthew. (Show kids where the verses are in your Bible and read the Lord's Prayer to them.) Now let's talk about some of the parts of this prayer and how it helps us know how to talk to God.

Show the "Our Father in Heaven" sign. Read it out loud and ask: **What do you think that means?** (Wait for several responses.) This part of the prayer tells us who we are talking to. The first part of the prayer reminds us we are talking to God, and it reminds us that God acts like a father to us. We don't have to start our prayers like this all the time, but Jesus wanted us to remember always we are talking to God.

Show the "Give us today our daily bread" sign. Read it out loud and ask: **What do you think these words mean?** (Wait for several responses.) This part of the prayer reminds us God wants to give us good things and that it is OK to ask for things from God. **What kinds of things can we ask God for when we pray?** (Wait for several responses.) Just like we ask our parents for things and just like our parents want to give us good things, Jesus wanted us to remember that God does that, too.

Show the "Forgive us our debts" sign. Read it out loud and ask: **What do you think**

these words mean? (Wait for several responses.) This is the part of the prayer where we ask God to forgive us for the things we've done that make God unhappy and sad. "Debts" is another word for *sin.* In this part of the prayer we're asking God to forgive us for the sins we've done. Jesus wanted to remind His friends and us we should always ask God for forgiveness when we pray.

Show the "And lead us not into temptation, but deliver us from the evil one" sign. Read it out loud and ask: **What do you think these words mean?** (Wait for several responses.) This is the part of the prayer where we ask God to keep us safe from bad things, and also, to help us not to do bad things. Jesus wanted us to know that God has the power to protect us and He wanted us to remember to include the knowledge of that protection in our prayers.

Who can remember the four things Jesus teaches us about prayer in this special prayer called the Lord's Prayer? (Wait for several responses.) Jesus wanted us to remember we are talking to God when we pray. Jesus wanted us to remember God gives us all we have and that we can ask God for the things we need. Jesus wanted us to remember we should ask God for forgiveness of our sins when we pray and that we remember to ask God to protect us every time we pray. End with a short prayer for the children using the four elements of prayer.

 Song Suggestions

"No Need to Worry" by Jana Alayra from *Jump into the Light* (Montjoy Music, 1995)
"Pray, Pray, Pray" by Mary Rice Hopkins from *Good Buddies* (Big Steps 4 U, 1994)
Let the Lord Have His Way Songsheets published by CEF Press, P.O. Box 348, Warrenton, MO 63383
"I Will Obey You" by Cindy Rethmeier from *I Want To Be Like Jesus* (Mercy Vineyard, 1995)

Craft for Younger Children: Prayer Bracelets
○ CHENILLE STEMS   ○ BEADS—GOLD, CLEAR, AND BLUE

Show children how to put the beads onto the bracelet and twist ends together to form a bracelet. Explain that this bracelet will help us remember what to pray for. The gold bead will remind us to thank God for everything He has done for us because gold will remind us of Heaven where God lives. The clear bead will remind us to ask God to forgive us of our sin, which will give us a "clear and pure" heart. My favorite color is blue and this blue bead will remind us to pray for our friends who are our favorite people. When we pray we are talking to God!

Craft for Older Children: Prayer Journal
○ LARGE PIECES OF CRAFT FOAM   ○ PAPER TO FIT INSIDE "BOOK"   ○ PENCILS
○ CHENILLE WIRES CUT INTO THREE PIECES EACH

Fold craft foam in half making book cover. Punch holes in the paper with a hole punch. Line up the paper in the book cover and punch one piece of chenille wire through each hole, holding the paper in place. Decorate the book as you wish.

What do you think a prayer journal could be used for? (let them respond) When we write down what we pray for, we can come back and see how God answers our prayers. Knowing that God answers our prayers helps our faith to grow.

Snack: Prayer Biscuits

○ "FLAKEY" CANNED BISCUITS   ○ COOKIE SHEET

Bake enough biscuits for each child to have one. Give each child a flakey biscuit to use as a review of the four parts of the Lord's Prayer that we talked about earlier. **What was the first part?** (Pull out the sign of "Our Father in heaven.") Instruct the children to pull off one layer from their biscuits. You can eat each layer as you go, or you can wait and eat all four layers after the review. **What was the second part of the Lord's Prayer?** (Display the sign of "Give us today our daily bread.") Pull off one more layer from the biscuit. Continue this process with the third and fourth signs used previously.

Memory Verse: Matthew 6:9 (ICB)

"So when you pray, you should pray like this: 'Our Father in heaven, we pray that your name will always be kept holy.'"

Alternate Version: Matthew 6:9 (NKJV)
"In this manner, therefore, pray: Our Father in heaven, Hallowed be Your name."

Memory Verse Activity

Write the words to the memory verse on separate pieces of paper. Tape each piece of paper onto a piece of toast (daily bread). Place the pieces of toast at the other end of the room. Using a pair of kitchen tongs, the children will take turns retrieving one piece/word of the memory verse in the correct order. The other players will assemble the pieces of toast so the memory verse can be read when all the toast has been retrieved.

Prayer Focus

Dear God thank You for letting us talk to You! You are the almighty God and You are our Father! Thank You for all You do, we want to know You more. Amen.

Sabbath

By Tina Houser

Scripture: Mark 2:27

Lesson Aim: The children will recognize God's plan for a day of rest.

Memory Verse: Mark 2:27

☞ Bible Activity for Younger Children: Patterns for Life!
- ○ A SUPPLY OF CANDY-COATED CHOCOLATE CANDIES FOR EACH CHILD
- ○ STRIPS OF PAPER 2 INCHES WIDE

Give each child some candy-coated chocolate candies and a strip of paper. The leader will create a pattern line with some of the candies (such as 2 red, 4 green, 1 yellow, 2 red, 4 green, 1 yellow) on his or her strip of paper. The children will imitate the pattern the leader created. After a few patterns, invite one of the children to present the pattern to be imitated. End the session with this pattern (6 red, one brown, 6 green, one brown, 6 yellow, one brown, 6 orange). **What do you think will follow?** (of course, a brown)

God created a pattern for us to imitate in our daily lives. When God created the world, He worked on it for six days and then He rested on the seventh. The pattern was work six days, rest one day. That day has a special name; it's called the Sabbath. On our last pattern, it didn't matter what color we used six of, we knew the one that would follow would be brown. On that day, God expects us to rest and concentrate on Him.

☞ Bible Activity for Older Children: Prescription for Life!
- ○ EMPTY PRESCRIPTION BOTTLE   ○ MAILING LABELS   ○ STRIPS OF PAPER
- ○ BABY FOOD JARS

What is a prescription? (medicine that you take to get you healthy or to keep you healthy) Show the empty prescription bottle. God gave us a prescription to help keep us physically, mentally, emotionally and spiritually healthy. His prescription was to work for six days and then take a day of rest. That sixth day is a time to let our minds and bodies rest while we think about and enjoy our mighty God. If we don't rest, our bodies get worn out and we get sick more easily, so it's not good for us physically to go without a day of rest. When we are tired we don't think clearly and we're more likely to get angry. Keeping busy starts pushing God out of our lives, and that' definitely not a healthy thing. We need time to rest in God's goodness and soak it in, so that He can renew us. Working six days and resting one is God's prescription for a healthy life all the way around!

Give each child an empty, clean baby food jar and a mailing label. Before removing the label from its backing, write *Sabbath Prescription* on it. Put the sticker on the outside of the jars. (Pretend the baby food jar is a prescription bottle.) You will also want to type these sentences that follow so they can be cut apart into strips. Give each child a set of strips to roll up and place in their bottles. Pull one out each Sabbath day and do what the strip says. Maybe that will help you rest and worship.

Include on the strips:
> • Take a nice long walk with someone special.
> • Look at a picture book of God's wonderful creations.
> • Curl up with a parent and talk about your last vacation.
> • Look through some old photographs.
> • Call someone you haven't talked to in a long time.
> • Eat dessert first just this once!
> • Think of three things you've never thanked God for and thank Him now.

Enrichment Activity for Younger Children: Stop and Go!

Play a game with the children similar to "red light, green light." Let children line up along one wall and when you say "GO!" they run toward you but must stop when you say "Stop!"

Play for several minutes and then ask: **Would this game be more fun if we just got to go?** Yes, it might be more fun, but it wouldn't be much of a game, would it? That's the same with our lives—we would rather go, go, go! We don't like to rest, but we need to. Sometimes a day of rest is called a "Sabbath."

God knew that we needed a Sabbath so He told us to have a day each week that we would rest on. **Can you try to have a "Sabbath"?**

Enrichment Activity for Older Children: You Set the Rules!

From the time of Creation, God gave people the pattern of six days of work and one day of rest. He also gave us the Ten Commandments. One of those Commandments says to "Remember the Sabbath and keep it holy."

To make sure everyone knew exactly what it meant to "remember the Sabbath" people started adding to the law. They made many more rules to help define the one main rule. Jews could only walk a short distance on the Sabbath, because too much walking would be considered work, and there's no working on the seventh day. They wouldn't let their animals work. Preparing food was considered work, so all the food had to be prepared the day before the Sabbath. Sabbath went from sundown to sundown.

To make sure that people observe the Sabbath as a day of rest and worship, put together your own set of Sabbath rules. **Can you keep from getting carried away? Will your rules help people rest and worship or will they just be something people have to worry about doing right?**

Memory Verse: Mark 2:27 (ICB)

"Then Jesus said to the Pharisees, 'The Sabbath day was made to help people. They were not made to be ruled by the Sabbath day.'"

Alternate Version: Mark 2:27 (NKJV)
"And He said to them, 'The Sabbath was made for man, and not man for the Sabbath.'"

Sabbath

By Pat Verbal

Scripture: Mark 2:23–28, Exodus 20:8

Lesson Aim: To help children understand that Sunday is the best day of the week no matter where we worship.

Memory Verse: Mark 2:27

When my father was a little boy, he rode to church every Sunday on horseback or in a wagon. After church, he sat on the farm house porch or chased ducks around the barn yard. In the winter he played jacks by the wood-burning stove in the parlor. Every Sunday night his family read the Bible together by a gasoline lamp.

When I was a little girl, we drove to church in a car listening to Gospel music on the radio. We usually had guests over for a delicious lunch that my mom fixed on Saturday. We didn't shop or eat out because businesses were closed on Sunday. Afternoons were for quiet table games not boisterous play. Sunday nights meant a trip back to church for evening worship.

When my sons were young, we often went to church in two cars since one of us usually had to be there early to teach. On the way we popped a music cassette into the car tape player. Bike rides were big around our house on Sunday afternoons. Sunday nights included a youth service followed by a lively game of basketball in the church gym and treats from the snack shack. Sometimes we even had a movie at church.

What do you do on Sunday? Are your activities different? How?

Jesus didn't always do what other people thought He should do on the Sabbath.* He went to the temple for worship, but He also healed people telling them to carry their mats. Jesus allowed His disciples to pick grain from the fields on the Sabbath when they were hungry. Read Mark 2:23–27. When the Pharisees accused Jesus of breaking laws barring work on the Sabbath, He explained God's purpose for setting aside a special day. It was not a day of rules, but of worship, rest and good deeds.

God designed our bodies to work hard to provide for our daily needs. He gave us good minds to study and learn about our world. He knew we would get busy and tired. As a loving Father, He planned a day of rest so we could spend time with Him, our families and friends. Sunday should always be the best day of the week.

*Sabbath—The word means *rest*. The Jewish Sabbath is on Saturday because it was the seventh day of the week. After Jesus rose from the dead on the first day of the week, His followers observed Sunday as their Sabbath.

Song Suggestions:

One Step at a Time Songsheets published by CEF Press, P.O. Box 348, Warrenton, MO 63383
"Praise His Holy Name" by Norm Hewitt from *Ablaze with Praise!* (Revelation Generation Music, 2000)
"He Is God" by Jana Alayra from *Believin' On* (Montjoy Music, 2002)
"Little Is Much" by Mary Rice Hopkins from *15 Singable Songs* (Big Steps 4 U, 1988)

Craft for All Children: Holy Day Book
○ DRAWING PAPER AND CONSTRUCTION PAPER FOR COVER OF BOOK

For younger children: beforehand, make a book using the plain paper inside (about 4 pieces per child) and the construction paper for the cover.

For older children: let them make the book themselves.

When books are finished, lead the children to draw pictures of how they think Americans used to celebrate the Sabbath and how their families celebrate the Sabbath today.

Snack: Nehemiah's Favorite Food
○ NAPKINS   ○ CRACKERS   ○ SMALL PIECES OF FRUIT

In the Old Testament (Nehemiah 13:15–22), there is a story of a man named Nehemiah. It was the Sabbath day, a day when everyone was supposed to rest and worship God, and what Nehemiah saw made him very angry! People were loading up their donkeys to bring grapes, figs and all kinds of produce to the market to sell. Men from a different city were bringing fish in to sell at the market. The more Nehemiah saw, the angrier he got! He reminded the people that this was the day God wanted them to set aside to rest. The people wouldn't listen, so Nehemiah ordered the gates to be shut tight when the Sabbath started at sundown on Friday, and they weren't to be opened again until the Sabbath was over. He even sent men to stand guard at the gates, so no one would try to sneak in. Some of the merchants camped outside the gates, thinking that Nehemiah would soften and let them in to do business. Boy, were they wrong! Nehemiah went out to the merchants and told them if they didn't leave he would have them arrested. That was the last time they came on the Sabbath. Nehemiah knew that if the people were working at the market to sell their goods, then they were not resting and worshiping like God had told them to do. This was a man who wanted to obey God and who wanted his people to obey, also.

The children will help prepare the table for a little meal of crackers and fruit. Once the table is set and ready for all of them to sit down and enjoy, turn out the lights. Tell them that it is sundown and the Sabbath has begun. You have the food ready for the Sabbath day, so you don't have to do any work. Turn the lights back on and enjoy your meal together.

 Memory Verse: Mark 2:27 (ICB)

"Then Jesus said to the Pharisees, 'The Sabbath day was made to help people. They were not made to be ruled by the Sabbath day.'"

Alternate Version: Mark 2:27 (NKJV)
"And He said to them, 'The Sabbath was made for man, and not man for the Sabbath.'"

Memory Verse Activity: Eraser Verse

Write the verse on the board. Lead children in saying the verse. Erase two words (choose randomly) and say the verse again. Continue saying the verse and erasing words until the children have learned the entire verse.

Prayer Focus

Dear God, thank You for telling us to rest! Please help us to obey Your word and take a day of rest each week. Amen.

Stewardship

By Tina Houser

Scripture: 1 Peter 4:10

Lesson Aim: The children will realize that each believer has been given the responsibility of using the gift God gave them.

Memory Verse: 1 Peter 4:10

☞ **Bible Activity for Younger Children:** What's Your Gift?

○ 2 DOZEN WASH CLOTHS ○ WRAPPING PAPER ○ TAPE ○ SCISSORS ○ MASKING TAPE

Place the washcloths in an unfolded pile. Divide the children into groups of five.

Every member of each group will have a number: 1, 2, 3, 4, or 5. Assign jobs to the different numbers. All the children who are number *1* will fold three wash cloths in a nice stack. The number *2* children will roll the folded wash cloths and place a piece of masking tape around them to hold them in a bundle. All the number *3* children will cut a piece of wrapping paper that will be the right size to wrap the wash cloths. Numbers *4* and *5* will work together to wrap the cloths. Number *4* will pull the wrapping paper around the bundle, and number *5* will hold it secure with the tape. Repeat the tasks until all the wash cloths have been wrapped.

What would've happened if number 5 had said that he didn't want to use any of his tape to wrap the presents? What would've happened if number 2 rolled the washcloths but didn't tape them? What would've happened if number 3 showed up, but didn't want to cut the paper?

God has given each of us a special gift to be used in ministry. Our gift may help others in need so that they will know that God loves them. Our gift may be putting God's Word into sign language so people who are hearing impaired can understand. Our gift may be sitting with older people in their home for a visit. Think about the people you know and the gifts God has given them. **How are they using their gift in ministry? What happens when one person refuses to use the gift God gave them?** (The ministry doesn't happen. Someone else has to do their job. They miss out on the blessing of doing God's work.)

☞ Bible Activity for Older Children: Generosity!
○ FUN-SIZE CANDY BARS WRAPPED IN A GIFT BOX

Put enough fun-size candy bars in a gift box so that there will be enough for every child later in the activity. Inside the box include a note that says, *Directions: As you have received this gift, be generous in using your gift for others.* Wrap the box, complete with ribbon and bow, so that it looks like a very special gift.

In front of all the, now attentive children, give the gift box to one of the children. Instruct the child to open the box. If they don't notice the note at first, point it out and encourage them to read it aloud. Hopefully, the person opening the gift will understand the message and share the candy with the others.

The children will look up the memory verse, 1 Peter 4:10, in their Bibles. Read it aloud together. **Does this verse sound like anything you've heard recently? What does the verse mean to you? How can you connect the gift box of candy to the Scripture?**

Let's think about our gift box of candy bars. The note first said that it was "directions." Our directions for living are given in the Bible. The note also said to be "generous in using it for others." Even though the gift belonged to one person, they were supposed to use that gift to help everyone. First Peter 4:10 tells us that God has given each of us a gift that He wants us to use to minister to others. He tells us to be good stewards of our gift. What does that mean? As followers of Christ, it is our responsibility to use the gift God gave us to bring God glory.

Enrichment Activity for Younger Children: Giving to God
○ SOME SIMPLE PUZZLES
(Remove three pieces from each puzzle.)

Arrange the children in small groups and give each group a puzzle to work. When they report that they are missing pieces, ask them if they can tell how many pieces are missing. Each group will realize they are missing three pieces from their puzzles.

Some people come to church. They sit and listen to the pastor speak. They sing the songs, but there is something missing. They are not giving of themselves. The Bible teaches us to be good stewards—to take care of and use what God has given us for His work. That means we must use what we have wisely. We have talents that God wants us to use. That is one of the missing pieces in some people's stewardship. They are not using the talents God has given them. Give one piece back to each group and let them add it to their puzzles. We all have 24 hours in each day and God wants us to use our time in serving Him. For some people, giving time to knowing God and doing His work is a missing piece of their stewardship puzzle. Give a second piece back to each group for their placement. We have jobs and make money to buy the things we need and enjoy. God wants us to use our money to serve Him. There are people who hold tightly to their money and don't understand they need to give to God's work. Using our money is the last missing piece from the stewardship puzzle. Return the last pieces of each group's puzzles. We need to follow Christ and be good stewards—good managers—of what we have been given.

What three things did we talk about that we need to use for God? *(talents, time, and money)*

Enrichment Activity for Older Children: What Is a "Tenth"?
○ 11 CHECKERS

All the students will want to try this, so you may want to get 11 checkers for each child. (You can use any item that is in the shape of a disk.) Place 10 checkers in a nice straight pile. Place the eleventh checker back from the pile a few inches. Pull a finger up under your thumb and flick the loose checker, aiming at the base of the pile. The checker you are flicking should hit the bottom checker, knocking it from under the pile. At the same time, the checker being flicked will replace the checker that had been the base checker.

God asks each of us to give a tenth of the gifts He has given us. We had 10 checkers in the pile. How many is a tenth of 10? Let's think of the stack of checkers as everything God has given you. The checker that left the pile is the tenth that you gave back to Him in good stewardship. The checker that replaced it at the base is the blessing God gives to replace what we have given.

To understand the coins in a scientific way ... when the checkers are standing in their stack, they are said to be at rest, which is what we call inertia. When the bottom checker was hit, it was forced to move, but the others on top of it were not hit and had no reason to move.

Memory Verse: 1 Peter 4:10a (ICB)

"Each of you received a spiritual gift. God has shown you his grace in giving you different gifts. And you are like servants who are responsible for using God's gifts."

Alternate Version: 1 Peter 4:10 (NKJV)
"As each one has received a gift, minister it to one another, as good stewards of the manifold grace of God."

Stewardship

By Pat Verbal

> **Scripture:** 1 Peter 4:10
>
> **Lesson Aim:** The children will realize that each believer has been given the responsibility of using the gift God gave them.
>
> **Memory Verse:** 1 Peter 4:10

Carly Patterson was born with talent, but she didn't know how much until she attended a friend's birthday party at a local gym. The owner watched Carly playing on the balance beam and asked her mother if she took gymnastics. When her mom told him she didn't, he said, "She should!"

From her first day of gymnastics' class Carly, age 6, dreamed of going to the Olympics. Maybe you watched television the summer of 2004 and saw Carly Patterson perform in Athens, Greece where her dream came true ten years later. She earned three Olympic medals including the Gold Medal in the Women's All-Around Championship. Only one other American woman ever held that title.

How did Carly get from being a curious child to a World Champion? Do you think Carly was a good steward of her time and talents? Let's make a list of the things Carly had to do (or sacrifice) on her journey to Gold.

Use a white board to list responses. Or for older children, turn the activity into a game. Give them 2.5 minutes to write down as many things as they can before you call time. The one with the most items is the winner. Ask him or her to read the list.

In the New Testament, Christians are called "stewards." A steward takes care of something for another person. Christians take care of the Gospel (the Good News about Christ) by wisely using their time and their gifts. Stewards often have mentors who help them identify their gift and learn time management skills. The Apostle Paul and his young friend, Timothy, are good examples.

Paul met Timothy when he visited Lystra. When Timothy heard Paul preach and watched him heal the sick, he was converted (became a believer in Jesus). On Paul's second missionary journey to Lystra, he asked Timothy to join his team. Timothy left his home and followed Paul. Later, he became a pastor in Ephesus. Paul continued to train Timothy by writing him two letters about how to lead the church—1 and 2 Timothy.

You can learn to be a good steward, too, by setting goals that help you grow as a Christian. If you waste time, ask God to help you make better decisions. If you don't think you have any talents, ask your friends and family to help identify them. Pray for God to guide you and He will.

Carly's hard work, dedication, and love for gymnastics paid off in Athens. As a result, she has many opportunities to talk to others about her faith.

Song Suggestions

"He Paid a Debt" (Traditional)
Nothing But the Blood Songsheets published by CEF Press, P.O. Box 348, Warrenton, MO 63383
"Love with the Love" by Mary Rice Hopkins from *Miracle Mud* (Big Steps U, 1998)
"Before We Say Goodbye" by Jana Alayra from *Believin' On* (Montjoy Music, 2002)

Craft for Younger Children: Verse Puzzle

Make a memory verse jigsaw puzzle to teach children the key verse: 1 Peter 4:10a: "Each one should use whatever gift he has received to serve others."

Cut out a large clock face from poster board and write the memory verse on it. Draw faint lines around and through the words to suggest jigsaw pieces. Cut these out. Give each child a piece of the puzzle and challenge them to see if they can put the clock together as they say the verse.

Craft for Older Children: Clock Our Time!

Challenge each child to make a clock face with "pie shaped" dividers to designate the many things he or she does all day.

As children identify how they use their day, their talents will emerge: music, sports, reading, art, etc. They may also discover the time they waste.

Help children strive for a healthy balance that includes rest, exercise, service, study, prayer, and social activities.

Ask: **Would you be proud to show this clock to Jesus? Why or why not?**

Children's Ministry Sourcebook

Snack: Clock Cakes

O CUPCAKES   O ICING   O SMALL CANDIES   O LICORICE WHIPS

Show children how to make a clock on their cupcakes using the small candies for the time and the licorice whips for the hands.

Say: **Every day we look at our watches or clocks several times, don't we? When we do, we should think about what we are doing and how much time we spend doing things for ourselves and for God. Can you spend more time doing things for God? What can you do for God?** *(Share your answers.)*

Memory Verse: 1 Peter 4:10 (ICB)

"Each of you received a spiritual gift. God has shown you his grace in giving you different gifts. And you are like servants who are responsible for using God's gifts. So be good servants and use your gifts to serve each other."

Alternate Version: 1 Peter 4:10 (NKJV)
"As each one has received a gift, minister it to one another, as good stewards of the manifold grace of God."

Memory Verse Activity

O 15 CUPS   O MARKER

Write one long word or two short words on each cup with marker. Let kids stack them pyramid style as they say the words. Knock the cups down and stack them again!

Prayer Focus

Dear God, thank You for all You do for us! Please help us to learn to give to You, to give You our time and our money to help people know more about You. Amen.

Love

By Tina Houser

> **Scripture:** 1 Corinthians 13:4-7
>
> **Lesson Aim:** The children will enjoy learning that love is at its best when given away.
>
> **Memory Verse:** 1 Corinthians 13:6

☞ Bible Activity for Younger Children: Love and balloons
○ BALLOONS

Hold up a balloon that has no air in it. Try to bat it around like you would a balloon that has air in it. Complain about it not being fun this way! What would change this balloon? How can we make this balloon be something really special?

Give each child a balloon. Think of one certain person in your family or at your school. With only that one person in your mind, share ways that you can show love to that person. Each time one of the children shares a way they can show love, everyone should put a puff of air in their balloons. When the balloons get full, stop the sharing. You've put a lot of love into these balloons. They sure are different now! They're completely different. Help the children tie their balloons so they can keep all their "love air" inside.

The air that we put in the balloons changed our flat, lifeless balloons into something real fun. **Do you think your love can change the person you were thinking about? How does showing our love to other people change them?**

☞ Bible Activity for Older Children: Measuring Our Love
○ RECIPE CARDS ○ VARIETY OF MEASURING SPOONS AND CUPS
○ SEVERAL VERSIONS OF THE BIBLE

Display the various measuring spoons and cups that you have brought in. The children will place them in order according to size. On the board, write the abbreviations for teaspoon (t. or tsp.), tablespoon (T. or Tbsp.), and cup (c.), matching each one to the proper measuring utensil.

Provide several versions of the Bible for the children. They will read 1 Corinthians 13:4–7. Think about what the verse says that is included in love. **What makes up love?** There is truth, patience, trust, kindness, purity, hope, and endurance. Checking out several different versions will give you a wider variety of words (or ingredients).

Give each child a recipe card so they can make up their own special recipe for love. The things they think are more important should be included in larger quantities.

A few examples of things that may be included are:
>   1 c. kindness
>   3 T. trust
>   A pinch of laughter

Enrichment Activity for Younger Children: Marshmallow Heart Monitors
○ MINIATURE MARSHMALLOWS   ○ TOOTHPICKS

What organ in our bodies do we use as a symbol of love? (the heart) **What is the heart's job?** (to pump the blood through our bodies) Let's do a little experiment to find out if our hearts are really doing something right now.

The children will work in pairs. Stick a toothpick into a miniature marshmallow, but not all the way through. If the toothpick is too long to stand without falling over, break part of it off so it's shorter. One child will lay one arm on the table with the palm facing the ceiling. Feel around your wrist until you can locate your pulse. Place the marshmallow/toothpick directly on that spot. Stay completely still and watch what happens to the toothpick. You should be able to see the toothpick move slightly each time your heart beats and pushes the blood through your veins. Try counting how many times your heart beats in 15 seconds.

If our hearts are doing what they are supposed to, then we should be able to feel our pulse and see the toothpick moving to prove it. **If we are loving the way God wants us to love one another, what kind of proof should other people see in us? What things will we be doing and not doing if we are truly being a loving person?** These are the things that prove that God's love is alive and well inside us!

Enrichment Activity for Older Children: Valentine Spoon?
○ WOODEN SPOONS   ○ PERMANENT MARKERS   ○ RIBBON

Miss Esther Howland is said to be the first person to send a Valentine card in the United States. Now, the day is celebrated by huge numbers of cards being sent, along with chocolates, flowers, and stuffed animals. These are just a few ways that we use to express our love to someone dear to us.

Here are some other ways people have used to celebrate Valentine's Day. During the Middle Ages, each young man would draw a piece of paper out of a bowl. On the paper would be the name of a young woman. He would wear her name on his sleeve for one week. There is a saying that people use today, "wearing your heart on your sleeve" which means that it's easy for people around you to see how you are feeling.

Messages haven't always been sent in the form of a card. In Wales they used to carve their Valentine message in a spoon and give it as a gift on Valentine's Day. The most popular things to carve were hearts and keys. **Why do you think keys were carved into the spoon?**

Memory Verse: 1 Corinthians 13:6 (ICB)

"Love is not happy with evil, but is happy with the truth."

Alternate Version: 1 Corinthians 13:6 (NKJV)
"[love] does not rejoice in iniquity, but rejoices in the truth."

Love

By Ivy Beckwith

Scripture: 1 Corinthians 13: 4–7

Lesson Aim: Children will be able to identify several biblical characteristics of love.

Memory Verse: 1 Corinthians 13:6

Preparation:

Gather several Valentine cards, for adults or children. Write the words *patient, not rude, not self-seeking, keeps no record of wrongs,* and *always protects, always trusts* on large strips of paper or poster board. Decorate them with hearts or Valentine stickers.

Ask: **What holiday is coming up this week?** (Wait for the "Valentine's Day" responses.) **What do we celebrate on Valentine's Day?** (Wait for responses.) Sometimes we give the people we love gifts on Valentine's Day. **Who are you giving a Valentine to on Valentine's Day?** (Wait for responses.) **What kinds of gifts do we give?** (Wait for responses.) I have some Valentine cards here. Show the cards. Say: **Let's read what some of these cards say.** Read the cards to the children. These cards talk a lot about love. **Who can tell me what love is?** (Wait for several responses.) In the Bible, God talks a lot about love, too. In the New Testament, the Apostle Paul wrote a letter that helped to describe what true love looks like. Let's look at some of the things Paul said about love in the letter of 1 Corinthians.

Paul tells us love is patient. (Show the "patient" card.) **Who can tell me what patient means?** (Wait for several responses.) When we love someone we're willing to wait for that person even when we're in a hurry. When we love someone we don't care if that person is slower than we are. Being patient is showing love. Paul tells us love is not rude. (Show the "not rude" card.) **Who can tell me what not being rude means?** (Wait for several responses.) It means being kind with words and actions. It means that we show love to others when we treat them with respect and with courtesy. Paul tells us love is not self-seeking. (Show the "not self-seeking" sign.) **What does it mean to be self-seeking?** (Wait for several responses.) When you are self-seeking it means you always put yourself before others. It means you are a selfish person. You are not showing love when you are being selfish. Showing love to others means you share with them and you put their needs and wants before your own. Paul tells us in the Bible that love keeps no records of wrongs. (Show the "keeps no records of wrongs" card.) **What do you think this tells about how a loving person should act?** (Wait for several responses.) When you love someone you don't hold grudges. When you love someone you forgive that person for the things he or she has done to hurt you or inconvenience you. The last thing Paul says about love that we want to talk about this morning is love always protects and always trusts. (Show the "always protects, always trusts" card.) **What do you think these words tell us about what love looks like?** (Wait for several responses.) When we love others we show it by always looking out for their best, by not hurting them, and by trusting them to do the same thing for us.

We talk a lot about love this time of the year. We give the people we love cards, boxes of candy, flowers, and other kinds of gifts to show them we love them. But sometimes our actions don't always line up with what we say about love. Showing people we love them by our actions toward them is more important than any card or gift we give them on Valentine's Day.

Song Suggestions

"You Are the Rock" by Mary Rice Hopkins from *Come on Home* (Big Steps 4 U, 2002)
"Generation Filled with Righteousness" by Cindy Rethmeier from *I Want 2 Be Like Jesus* (Mercy Vineyard Publishing, 1995)
Go! Songsheets published by CEF Press, P.O. Box 348, Warrenton, MO 63383
The Wise Man Built His House Upon the Rock (Traditional)

Craft for Younger Children: Valentines

○ CONSTRUCTION PAPER CUT INTO HEARTS   ○ PAPER DOILIES
○ OTHER ASSORTED DECORATIONS, GLUE AND GLITTER

Lead children in designing their own Valentines. Say: **Valentines are one way to show people how much you love them. Can you think of other ways?** Let children answer.

Craft for Older Children: Valentine Spoon!

○ WOODEN SPOONS   ○ MARKERS   ○ RIBBON

Give each student a wooden spoon to decorate and write a Valentine message on. Provide markers and ribbon to transform the spoon into a very special Valentine.

Snack: Heart Snacks

○ HEART SHAPED CHEESE AND CRACKERS
(These can be purchased ready made or you can cut with a heart shaped cookie cutter.)

Ask: **What does this mean?** (love!) **Why do you think it means love?** Let the children brainstorm the reasons. The Bible says that God is love because God loves so much!

Memory Verse: 1 Corinthians 13:6 (ICB)

"Love is not happy with evil, but is happy with the truth."

Alternate Version: 1 Corinthians 13:6 (NKJV)
"[love] does not rejoice in iniquity, but rejoices in the truth."

Memory Verse Activity: Love Verses
   ○ ONE LARGE POSTER BOARD CUT INTO A HEART SHAPE

Write the verse on the poster board and then cut into a puzzle shape. Let the children work the puzzle as they say the verse.

Prayer Focus

Dear God, thank You for loving us so much. Help us to love others!

Materialism

By Tina Houser

Scripture: Matthew 6:24

Lesson Aim: The children will become aware of materialism and that it has no place in God's plan.

Memory Verse: Matthew 6:24

☞ **Bible Activity for Younger Children:** God's Love Is Permanent!
○ SEVERAL WORN OUT ITEMS (shoes, sweater, lamp, chipped plate, etc.)
○ A PERMANENT BLACK MARKER   ○ DRY ERASE BLACK MARKER   ○ DRY ERASE BOARD

Before the children come into the room, write across the top of the dry erase board, *Our Mighty God* with a permanent marker.

Show the items that you have brought in and complain about how you spent good money on these things and they just wore out. Now you're going to have to save up more money so you can replace them. Ask the children to name items that can be purchased that wear out. Each time they mention something, write it on the board with a dry erase marker. Fill the board with their ideas. Praise them on their good ideas, but then say that even the writing on the board won't last. Pick up the eraser and clean the board. Everything will come off except where you have written "our mighty God" with the permanent marker. **What could this mean?** Accept their interpretations.

All the things of this world will someday be gone. It doesn't matter what brand they are, how much you paid for them, or where you got them. Each and every thing will wear out or rot away. The only thing we can count on is that there is a mighty God and that He wants us to know and love Him. God's love will never wear out or rot away!

(Don't panic ... the permanent marker will come off with dry erase board cleaner OR alternative method—write exactly on top of the permanent marker with a dry erase marker and then erase as usual—it will come right off!)

☞ Bible Activity for Older Children: God's Way or in the Way?

Assign one child these three things to do. Write the instructions where they are visible for the entire class.

> Write your name on the piece of paper on the table (somewhere away from the teacher, but still in the room).
> Get a piece of tape (in a totally different part of the room).
> Tape the paper to the wall (indicate where you want it put, away from the other tasks).

As the leader, your job is to get in the way of the student completing the task. Walk in front of the student as he or she goes to the table. As the child begins to write his or her name, ask for the pencil back or snatch it. Hand him or her an old crayon instead. When the person reaches for the tape, move it to another location. Stand between the student and the wall as he or she starts to tape the paper where you instructed.

What made completing the tasks difficult? (You kept getting in the way!) Some people let the things they own and the money they have get in the way of following Jesus. Think about this example. Stacy is in a Sunday school class that is putting together a gift box for the child of a missionary. All the children in her class were asked to bring one toy to include in the box. That week Stacy's grandmother came to visit. She took Stacy to a huge toy store and gave her $20 to spend on anything she wanted. It was difficult to decide, but Stacy spent every last penny on a game she had been wanting for a long time. The next Sunday when Stacy showed up at Sunday school empty-handed, the teacher asked what she had brought to put in the box. Stacy said that she didn't bring anything, because she didn't have any money.

What got in the way of Stacy doing what God wanted her to do? The things she had were much more important than God wanted them to be. God wanted Stacy to help make a little girl on the other side of the world happy. Even though God had provided a way for Stacy to do that, she had chosen to use the money for herself.

Enrichment Activity for Younger Children
○ DIGITAL CAMERA   ○ VARIOUS PROPS
(play money, jewelry, video games, you can even get as elaborate as a pedal car)

Explore what materialism means with the children. Our Memory Verse today is pretty much a definition of materialism. It's when we get things out of order. We give money and the things it can buy the most important place in our lives. **Who's supposed to have the most important place?** When our minds stay on the things that we want to buy, then those things take charge of our lives. That's not in God's plan.

What does materialism look like? Be thoughtful about the props you choose to bring in, so that they will fuel the imaginations of the children. Using these props and anything else the children find that would enhance their thoughts, encourage them to pose for digital pictures that portray the meaning of materialism. (If you do not have a digital camera, enlist one of the many people who do have one to be your photographer for this one session.) The children will be able to immediately view their poses and make changes if they're not satisfied. Conclude by taking a few pictures of what putting God first looks like.

Enrichment Activity for Older Children
○ COINS

This is a fun experiment for the kids to do. First, find a place where there is some open space and nothing to accidentally break. Bend your arm up and balance three coins on your right elbow. (If you are left-handed, you'll want to balance them on your left elbow.) Keep your hand open, palm toward the ceiling. Quickly jerk your arm down, so that you can catch the coins as they come off of your elbow. As soon as you feel the coins touch your palm, close your hand. It's really not as difficult as it sounds. Don't let those coins get away!

There is a reason this works. The coins are moving slowly coming off your arm. But, your arm is moving very fast. It just takes a split second for your hand to catch up with the slow-moving coins.

Some people are very attached to their money. They don't want to let it go. They might hear about someone in need, and start to share some of their money to help, but because they treasure it so much, they either end up keeping it all together, or giving just a little away.

Memory Verse Matthew 6:24 (ICB)

"No one can be a slave to two masters. He will hate one master and love the other. Or he will follow one master and refuse to follow the other. So you cannot serve God and money at the same time."

Alternate Version: Matthew 6:24 (NKJV)
"No one can serve two masters; for either he will hate the one and love the other, or else he will be loyal to the one and despise the other. You cannot serve God and mammon."

Children's Ministry Sourcebook

Materialism

By Pat Verbal

> **Scripture:** Matthew 6:19-25, Hebrews 13:5, Proverbs 11:4
>
> **Lesson Aim:** To help children trust God for their needs and overcome greed.
>
> **Memory Verse:** Matthew 6:24

Do you like to play Monopoly™? What do you enjoy the most—collecting $200 every time you pass GO or charging a fellow player who lands on your high priced property? Why do you think Monopoly™ is such a popular game? Could it be that we all love pretending we're rich even if we're not?

Playing games with "funny money" is OK, but beware of playing loose with the real thing. The love for money (and things) can make you a very unhappy kid. The trap comes when no matter how many toys, clothes, shoes and electronics you have—you always want more.

In Jesus' first sermon He preached to people sitting on a hillside who didn't have a lot of money or possessions. Jesus taught them that true happiness doesn't come from those things, but from doing what is right. He told them not to worry because God knew about their needs. Read Jesus' words in Matthew 6:19–25.

> **Do you worry about not having enough money?**
>
> **What is the difference between something you need and something you want?**

Today's media has a tremendous influence on how families decide their needs and wants. Television commercials are a part of daily life. Commercials are created to sell us things we don't need such as expensive name brands. Marketers play on our emotions with celebrities who tell us we'll be happier, prettier, stronger, smarter and enjoy life more if we buy their product. They even make us feel like "losers" if we don't have it. So, we work harder or nag our parents until they buy it for us.

Jesus taught us a different way to live. He came to show us that when we follow God's will, we are "rich!" God blesses us with true joy and peace. If you are anxious about money or tempted to want more things, ask God to show you true happiness. Read Hebrews 13:5 and decide that, with God's help, you will be content. Praise Him for His promise to supply your needs and to never leave you.

 **Song Suggestions**

"Believin' On" by Jana Alayra from *Believin' On* (Montjoy Music, 2002)
"Little Is Much" by Mary Rice Hopkins from *15 Singable Songs* (Big Steps 4 U, 1988)
"Faith Will Do" by Dean-O from *You Got It All* (FKO Music, Inc., 1997)
God's Power Songsheets published by CEF Press, P.O. Box 348, Warrenton, MO 63383

Craft for Younger Children: Gimme Monster!
○ PAPER   ○ CRAYONS

Say: **What do you want that you don't have?** Draw a picture of all the things that you want. Now, turn the paper over and draw a picture of all the things that you need.

What is the difference between the things that you want and the things that you need? Lead children in discussion.

Craft for Older Children
○ MAGAZINE ADS   ○ PAPER   ○ MARKERS

Show children print ads from newspapers and magazines. Discuss advertising tricks.

Lead children to write their own advertisement; choose a product, make up an ad and draw the ad. Challenge children to create a commercial advertising True Joy!

Snack: Money food!
○ ROUND FOODS SUCH AS ROUND CRACKERS, CHEESE PIECES, COOKIES, ETC.

Challenge the children to decide which food would be worth the most money—such as a round cracker is worth 25 cents, a cucumber slice 10 cents, etc. Divide the "money" and eat!

Memory Verse: Matthew 6:24 (ICB)

"No one can be a slave to two masters. He will hate one master and love the other. Or he will follow one master and refuse to follow the other. So you cannot serve God and money at the same time."

Alternate Version: Matthew 6:24 (NKJV)
"No one can serve two masters; for either he will hate the one and love the other, or else he will be loyal to the one and despise the other. You cannot serve God and mammon."

Children's Ministry Sourcebook

Memory Verse Activity

○ WHITE BOARD ○ MARKERS

Write the verse on the board. Lead the children in saying the verse. Erase one word of the verse, then say the verse again. Continue saying the verse and erasing more and more words until the verse is memorized.

Prayer Focus

Dear God thank You that You are our Master. Help us to serve You only!

Poverty

By Tina Houser

> **Scripture:** 1 John 1:9
>
> **Lesson Aim:** The children will understand that God's forgiveness brings us back to a right relationship with Him.
>
> **Memory Verse:** 1 John 1:9

☞ Bible Activity for Younger Children: Ping Pong Forgiveness
○ PING-PONG BALLS

What does forgiveness mean? Why is it difficult to ask for forgiveness? (You have to admit that you did something wrong.) The Bible tells us that when we decide to ask God for forgiveness, He is ready and willing at just that moment to forgive us. Not everyone is happy about this, though. **Who doesn't want us to be forgiven?** (Satan) Satan tries his hardest to keep us from asking for forgiveness. He tries to make us believe that what we've done is too big for God to forgive. Or, he wants us to think that God really doesn't care about us. Another one of Satan's tricks is to try to get us to put off asking for forgiveness to another time. Unfortunately, sometimes Satan convinces some people not to talk to God and ask for forgiveness for the things they have done that displease God. But, other times people don't listen to what Satan is trying to tell them; they ask for forgiveness and they start a wonderful relationship with God.

Let's play a game that will help us understand how Satan doesn't like it when we ask God to forgive us. Place a ping-pong ball on a table. The ping-pong ball is the sin in your life. The table represents your life. Player one wants the sin out of his or her life, so that player wants to get the ping-pong ball off the table. Player two will represent Satan and will try to get the ping-pong ball to stay on the table. Satan doesn't want the sin out of your life; he doesn't want you to be forgiven. Here's the fun part: the only way you can move the ping-pong ball is by blowing on it. Anytime the ping-pong ball leaves the table, Player one yells, "I'm forgiven!" (Hint: the bigger the table, the more fun this is.)

☞ Bible Activity for Older Children: Tangles of Lies

○ SHOESTRING   ○ SOME ITEMS THAT HAVE TANGLES IN THEM

Can you tell me what all these things have in common: hair, fishing line, Christmas tree lights, kite string, a necklace chain, a shoestring? All these things get tangled easily! **Can you name any other things that get tangled?** Give the children a couple of samples that you have made up ahead of time, so they can try to untangle the mess that has been made.

Have you ever told a lie? Allow time for the children to share about a lie they have told. Put one knot in the shoestring for that lie. Then, someone asked you about what you said in that first lie, so you told another lie to cover it up. Put another knot in the shoestring for the second lie. Someone else asks you the same thing about the lie and you repeat the second lie you told. Add another knot to the shoestring. Someone else gets in trouble because of the lie you told. Put another knot in the string. **Do you see how you can get yourself all tangled with things that displease God?**

The only way we can get our lives untangled is to ask God for forgiveness and then ask others to forgive us. He is the only one who can take the mess we've made and straighten it out. When we try to straighten things out ourselves we get frustrated and sometimes make an even bigger mess. But, God forgives us of all the tangles and gives us a fresh start with a brand new UN-tangled life.

Enrichment Activity for Younger Children: Blindfolded by Guilt

○ STRIPS OF OLD SHEETING   ○ PAPER CUPS

Blindfold a student. The object is to see how many paper cups they can use to build a wall in only one minute. Quietly, scatter the cups within arm's length of the student, but do not show them where the cups are before they are blindfolded. Repeat the same exercise only without the blindfold this time. Several students can do this at one time in order to let as many as possible get the experience.

When we live without Jesus we are blindfolded by our guilt. We are carrying around our unforgiven sin and it keeps us from living life the way God wants us to live it. When we ask God to forgive us of all the things that we have done that have made Him unhappy with us, then we can see our lives more clearly and we can live free of our guilt. When we took our blindfolds off, building the wall was a lot easier. We can live lives that are full of the good things of God when we ask for His forgiveness.

Enrichment Activity for Older Children: Eclipsing Candy

○ SOME HARD, ROUND CANDIES (LIKE BUTTERSCOTCH OR PEPPERMINT)

Do you know what a solar eclipse is? A solar eclipse is when our small Moon moves in front of the large Sun so that people on Earth cannot see the Sun. It doesn't happen very often and it usually lasts only a few minutes, but it seems strange how something that is a lot smaller than the Sun can keep us from seeing it.

Give each student a piece of hard candy. Hold the candy in front of your face. **Can you "eclipse" something in the room? Can you block something out so it can't be seen?** Move the candy closer to your face and further away. **How does that change what is eclipsed? Isn't it amazing the way a little candy can keep you from seeing something much larger?**

When we do things that displease God we call that sin. Our sin blocks us from seeing God totally. It keeps us from experiencing all that God has for us. Our sin eclipses God from our view. We have a way, though, to clear our view; that way is called forgiveness. When we confess our sin, God is faithful to forgive us of our sin. Then, God removes our sin so they won't eclipse our view of Him anymore!

Memory Verse: 1 John 1:9 (ICB)

"But if we confess our sins, he will forgive our sins. We can trust God. He does what is right. He will make us clean from all the wrongs we have done."

Alternate Version: 1 John 1:9 (NKJV)

"If we confess our sins, He is faithful and just to forgive us our sins and to cleanse us from all unrighteousness."

Children's Ministry Sourcebook

Poverty

By Ivy Beckwith

Scripture: 1 John 1:9

Lesson Aim: The children will understand that God's forgiveness brings us back to a right relationship with Him

Memory Verse: 1 John 1:9

Preparation

Prepare a little bowl of ashes. The ashes stick better if they are prepared with a few drops of olive oil.

For a very long time the church through history and around the world has had a tradition of preparing for the celebration of Easter—the resurrection of Jesus—during a season called Lent. During Lent many people don't eat certain kinds of foods or do certain activities in order to help them focus on the life of Jesus and His death on the cross. Also, during this season, some people give money to the poor or volunteer to help people who don't have as much as they do. During Lent they ask God to help them be better Christians.

The season of Lent begins with a day called Ash Wednesday. On Ash Wednesday many Christians around the world go to special services at their churches where their ministers put ashes on their foreheads in the sign of a cross. (Show the bowl of ashes. Demonstrate the ash sign of the cross on one of the children or, if this is not acceptable in your tradition, demonstrate it on a piece of white paper.) When the minister rubs the ashes on the person's forehead he says something like: "From dust you came and to dust you shall return, turn away from your sin and receive the good news." **Why do you think the minister says those words?** (Wait for several responses.) He's telling people they need to ask God's forgiveness for their sins, for the things they've done that have made God sad and unhappy with them. And he's telling the people to accept the good news that Jesus came to offer forgiveness and a right, good relationship with God and others.

Today, our Bible verse tells us that if we are willing to ask forgiveness for our sin God will always forgive us and make our relationship with him brand new—just like it would be if we had never done anything wrong. (Read 1 John 1:9.) We can practice (can we use a different word here?) asking forgiveness from God on Ash Wednesday and all during the season of Lent.

One of the ways we celebrate the wonderful gift of forgiveness God's given us is by forgiving other people. So for many people entering the season of Lent, Ash Wednesday means it's time for them to forgive others for things done to them or for them to ask forgiveness from other people to whom they might have done hurtful things. Think for a minute of someone you need to forgive or someone you need to apologize to for something you've done. (Wait just a couple of seconds as children think about this in silence.) Now let's take a little time and talk to God. Let's first ask God for forgiveness for the things we've done to make God sad or unhappy. Then, we'll ask God to help us forgive others and ask others to forgive us. (Say a prayer asking forgiveness or say some simple lines of a prayer that the children can repeat after you.)

God wants us to live in a right, good, and loving relationship with Him. And God wants people who love Him and follow Jesus to live in right, good, and loving relationships with each other. Both of these things require forgiveness. Ash Wednesday and the season of Lent remind us how important forgiving each other is.

When we know that God has forgiven us, we know our relationship with God is in good shape. When we live in forgiven relationships with others, then we know all of our relationships are in good shape and pleasing to God.

Song Suggestions

Children All Around the World Songsheets published by CEF Press, P.O. Box 348, Warrenton, MO 63383

"God's Way Right" by Dean-O from *You Got It All* (FKO Music, Inc. 1997)

Let the Lord Have His Way Songsheets published by CEF Press, P.O. Box 348, Warrenton, MO 63383

"Open the Eyes of My Heart" by Norm Hewitt from *Fired Up* (Revelation Generation, 2002)

Craft for Younger Children: Cross Necklace
O CROSSES CUT FROM CRAFT FOAM   O CORD   O DECORATIONS   O BEADS

Show children how to put cord through the cross to form a necklace. Add beads and decorate as desired. Say: **This cross necklace will help you remember that Jesus died for us on a cross.**

Craft for Older Children: Cross Necklace

○ 3-INCH NAILS AND 2-INCH NAILS   ○ CORD   ○ THIN WIRE

Show children how to place a 2-inch nail on the 3-inch nail and attach it with wire to form a cross. String the cord through the cross.

Discuss the significance of the cross with the children and what it means to our Christian faith.

Snack: Cross Food

○ RECTANGULAR CRACKERS OR COOKIES
○ SMALL AMOUNT OF ICING OR CHEESE SPREAD

Show children how to make a cross with their food. Say: **The cross is a symbol that we use to remember Jesus. Why do you think that it helps us remember Him?**

Memory Verse: 1 John 1:9 (ICB)

"But if we confess our sins, he will forgive our sins. We can trust God. He does what is right. He will make us clean from all the wrongs we have done."

Alternate Version: 1 John 1:9 (NKJV)

"If we confess our sins, He is faithful and just to forgive us our sins and to cleanse us from all unrighteousness."

Memory Verse Activity: Clothesline relay

○ ONE CLOTHESLINE HUNG ACROSS THE ROOM
○ TWO SETS THE VERSE PRINTED ON PAPER—ONE WORD PER SHEET
○ CLOTHESPINS

Line children up with a word paper, run across the room in turn and hang up their words of the verse until the verse is complete.

Say: **When we wash clothes we make them clean, don't we? How can we clean ourselves?** (Take a bath!) **How can we clean our sins?** We can start over when we tell God what we have done. That is called "confessing." When we confess our sin, He forgives them!

Cults

By Tina Houser

Scripture: Galatians 1:6–9

Lesson Aim: The children will realize the Bible is the only tool to use when they are questioning the truth of any belief.

Memory Verse: Galatians 1:7

☞ Bible Activity for Younger Children: What Is True?

○ GARBAGE CAN LID   ○ LARGE PIECES OF PAPER

Before class, write one belief that is not true on each of the pieces of paper. Suggestions are listed at the end of this activity's instructions. The garbage can lid is going to act as a shield. It needs to be labeled in large letters where the students can see it easily, *Truth of the Bible*.

Choose one student to hold the shield. Read the first piece of paper. **Is this what the Bible teaches us?** If the answer is no, then give the piece of paper to a student. That person will wad up the paper and throw it at the person holding the shield. The person with the shield will protect him- or herself from being hit by the paper wad by using the "Truth of the Bible" shield. The person throwing the paper wad now becomes the person holding the shield. Continue trading off with the two positions until all the papers have been read.

We will not be tempted to follow wrong teachings if we protect ourselves by knowing what the Bible says. That is a good reason for learning as much as you can about God's teachings. If someone tells you something that does not agree with what the Bible teaches, then you should not listen to them. It isn't the truth.

Statements for the papers:
There is more than one God.
Jesus was a good person, but not the Son of God.
God does not want you talking with anyone about what goes on at church.
If you follow this teaching, God will give you power to rule over anyone you want.
We need lots of guns to protect ourselves.
It's OK to use drugs, because it helps you see God.
You shouldn't talk to anyone from your family ever again.
ALL your money has to go to the church.
Worshiping the Devil is just as good as worshiping God.
There are secret mixtures that have power.

☞ Bible Activity for Older Children: Unlocking the Truth!
○ SEVERAL COMBINATION LOCKS

Depending on how many locks you have, divide the children into groups to share a lock. Of course, the smaller the group, the more experience each child will get. Allow time for each student an opportunity to work the combination and open the lock. **Why did the lock open so easily?** (because we used the right combination) Instruct the children to decide on a new combination for their lock. Change one number in the combination by 5. Write down your new combination so everyone in your group knows what it is. Now, try opening the lock once again. (Remember, in between times of working the lock you will need to spin it several times to clear the settings.) **What happened this time?** (It wouldn't open.) But you only changed one number; the other numbers were the same.

There are other religions that seem to have a lot in common with what the Bible teaches, but there will be one major thing that is not the same. Another religion may believe that we should love our neighbors. **Is that what the Bible teaches?** (yes) They may believe there is a heaven. **Is that what the Bible teaches?** (yes) They also may teach that there is more than one God. **Is that what the Bible teaches?** (no) If the beliefs of a religion do not agree TOTALLY with what the Bible teaches, then it is a false religion and God is not pleased with it. When someone shares their beliefs with you, test them against what the Bible says. Say: **Because all the numbers were right for the combination lock, it would open. If we believe all that the Bible teaches, then God has opened heaven for us.**

Enrichment Activity for Younger Children: Real or Fake?
○ A STRAND OF PEARLS (REAL OR FAKE, BUT KNOW WHICH)

Real pearls are made when a grain of sand gets caught inside a shellfish, like an oyster. The sand scratches the shellfish. To make it stop irritating, the shellfish coats the grain of sand with layer after layer of the soft, gooey substance that is inside its shell. Coating the sand like this makes it stop irritating the little creature. This gooey substance hardens and the shellfish adds another coat. It may take several years before enough of the substance has surrounded the sand so that it becomes a pearl. When the shell is pried open, inside will be the pearl.

There are also fake pearls that look just like the real thing. They have been made, though, by pressing something very tightly into a tiny ball. Some fake pearls are made by pressing cotton into a little ball. It is very difficult to tell the difference between fake pearls and the real pearls. But, it's a good thing to know, because real pearls are worth a lot more money than fake ones.

The main test to tell if pearls are real or fake is to put the pearl in your mouth and rub it against your teeth. If it feels real smooth, then it's fake. It the pearl feels a little gritty, then it's real. Show the children how to drag the strand of pearls across your front teeth to test to see if they are real or fake. Avoid the temptation to allow the children to test for themselves, unless you are able to come up with a fake strand of pearls from the dollar store for each of them. Make sure you thoroughly clean any you use.

People will try to tell you things about God and you will wonder if they are true or false. There is one test for figuring out whether the pearls are real or not, drag them against your teeth, and there is one main test you can always go to that will help you know if what people are telling you is the truth or not. The Bible, God's Holy Word, is that test. If the Bible says that it's true, then you can count on it being true. If the Bible says that it's not true, then you can count on it being wrong.

Enrichment Activity for Older Children: Counterfeit Faith
○ ONE OLDER (BEFORE 1996) PAPER CURRENCY
○ ONE NEWER PAPER CURRENCY OF THE SAME DENOMINATION

Allow the children time to look at both samples of currency. Paper money was changed in 1996 so it would be easier to tell if the money was counterfeit. **Do you know what counterfeit means?** Counterfeit is when something is made to resemble or look like something valuable. Counterfeit money is money that looks just like the real money, but someone has printed it themselves, instead of it being the true money that the government makes. **What changes have been made in the bills that you are looking at?** Hold the newer bill up to a bright light and see what appears. The real bill will have several things that will show up in the light, like a smaller shadowy face of the person on the bill. These are called watermarks. There are also small numbers that will appear, if you look closely.

You can hold a counterfeit bill and a real bill next to one another and not be able to tell which is which. The difference is that one is worth something and the other is absolutely worthless. There are many people in the world who are not teaching the truth about God—who He is and what the Bible teaches. These strange religions look good, just like a counterfeit bill looks like the real thing. Only when we test these beliefs by what God's Holy Scriptures say can we discover something missing, just like the watermarks are missing from counterfeit bills. It's like we are holding these strange beliefs up to God's light to see if they are real. If the belief does not match what the Bible teaches, then you can count on it being a counterfeit, and something you shouldn't believe in.

Memory Verse: Galatians 1:7 (ICB)

"Really, there is no other Good News. But some people are confusing you and want to change the Good News of Christ."

Alternate Version: Galatians 1:7 (NKJV)
"Which is not another; but there are some who trouble you and want to pervert the gospel of Christ."

Cults

By Eric Titus

Scripture: Galatians 1:6–9

Lesson Aim: The children will realize the Bible is the only tool to use when they are questioning the truth of any belief.

Memory Verse: Galatians 1:7

Preparation

○ MIRROR   ○ POSTER BOARD

On the poster board either draw a picture or paste a picture from a magazine of a person. If you do a picture from a magazine, use a picture of a famous "good-looking" celebrity. Cut the poster board out and attach it to the back side of the mirror. For those of you who like to go all out, use a full length mirror, draw a stick body and attach your celebrity head to the top.

Say: **I really need someone that is sure about what they look like. Who really knows what they look like?** (Name the child) **terrific, I could use some help. Would you mind helping me today? I'm going to have (child) look into this mirror, and this mirror is one of the best they make. It shows what a person truly looks like.** Have the child look into the "fake" side of the mirror. You should look to the image as the child and congregation does. **Wow! (child) this mirror gives quite a picture of you. You know, I never saw this side of you before! I mean you look a lot like (name of celebrity). This mirror gives a really good likeness of you, don't you think? Is that really you?**

I think that we can get a better picture of you. Let's turn this thing around. How's that? Is that you? You're sure? How do you know? Oh, because you know how you look. You're familiar with your own face. That's important for today's lesson. Thanks for helping me.

You see, the Apostle Paul was having a bit of trouble. He was preaching what Jesus had told him to preach, the truth about Jesus becoming human, dying for our sin, and then rising from the dead. But other people, even today, say things about Jesus that don't come close to what Jesus and Paul said. Paul said that even if an angel came to us and said things to us about Jesus we knew weren't true that we should not accept it.

But how do we know the truth about Jesus? The very best way is to read our Bibles. It tells us all about the truth of Jesus. It is the best "mirror" we have. **Can anyone think of other things that are "mirrors" for us? What about our creeds?** The Apostle's Creed also tells us about Jesus.

You may learn about that in a class where we learn about the teachings of the Church, and it helps us to understand more about why we believe what we believe. Before we can understand when other people are not telling the truth about Jesus, we have to know the real truth.

Song Suggestions

"G-Mail!" By Dean-O from *Soul Surfin* (FKO Music/ASCAP, 1999)
"God's Holy Book" from *God's Big Picture* (Gospel Light)
The B.I.B.L.E. (Traditional)
"God Wrote Us a Letter" by Mary Rice Hopkins from *Come Meet Jesus* (Big Steps 4 U)
"I Believe the Bible," CEF Press, P.O. Box 348, Warrenton, MO 63383

Craft for Younger Children: Real Bible

○ BLACK CONSTRUCTION PAPER   ○ WHITE PAPER   ○ MARKERS   ○ CRAYONS

Before class, make books for the children using the black paper as the cover and three white sheets in each book. Staple.

Say: **The Bible is the true word of God. Do you remember any stories from the Bible?** Today we are going to make a Bible storybook. Draw the stories that we just talked about, because we know that they are real!

Craft for Older Children: Mirror, Mirror

○ SMALL INEXPENSIVE MIRRORS (1 PER CHILD)   ○ MARKERS
○ CARDBOARD LARGER THAN THE MIRROR

The children will glue the mirror to the cardboard frame. The children will decorate their frames as they wish.

What do you see when you look in a mirror? Yes, you see you! You know that you are real, because you can see yourself.

What things in life are NOT real? (allow children to list) This mirror will remind you to always look for what is real.

🍿 Snack: What's What?

○ CUPCAKE PAN   ○ SUGAR   ○ SALT   ○ CHOCOLATE ○ CANDY BAR SQUARES
○ UNSWEETENED CHOCOLATE   ○ COOKIES, ETC.

Fill cupcake pan with 1/2 c. sugar in one cup, 1/2 cup salt in another, chocolate candy bar squares in one, unsweetened chocolate in another, cookies or another snack in another.

Say: **Which of these do you think is the sugar?** Have children guess and then let someone taste to see if they are right. Do the same for the chocolate.

Say: **Sometimes it is hard to tell what is real and what is not real, isn't it? But we can always know that the Bible is real!**

Serve and eat some real cookies!

✒ Memory Verse: Galatians 1:7 (ICB)

"Really, there is no other Good News. But some people are confusing you and want to change the Good News of Christ."

Alternate Version: Galatians 1:7 (NKJV)
"Which is not another; but there are some who trouble you and want to pervert the gospel of Christ."

📖 Memory Verse Activity

Write verse on the board. Tell children that they will echo you as you say the verse:

> Really there is (really there is)
> No other good news. (no other god news.)
> But some people are (but some people are)
> Confusing you and (confusing you and)
> Want to change (want to change)
> the Good News of Christ! (the Good News of Christ!)

🙏 Prayer Focus

Dear God please help us always know what is real. Thank You for being a very real and present God.

Relationships/Community

By Tina Houser

> **Scripture:** Luke 14:11–14
>
> **Lesson Aim:** The children will explore what it means to be in community.
>
> **Memory Verse:** Luke 14:11

☞ Bible Activity for Younger Children: Community

- ○ BASEBALL ○ BAT ○ BASEBALL GLOVE ○ FOOTBALL ○ BASKETBALL
- ○ SOCCER BALL ○ A WATER BOTTLE ○ WINTER GLOVE ○ SODA CAN
- ○ MILK CARTON ○ COOKIE ○ SNACK BAG OF CHIPS ○ REMOTE CONTROL
- ○ PIECE OF FRUIT ○ A RING

Place all the objects where the children can see them. Ask each child to choose three things that go together and ask them to tell why they put those three things in a special group. They may choose the 3 balls, 3 things to drink, 3 snacks, 3 things associated with watching a football game (football, remote control, and a soda can), 3 things you can put on your hand, or the 3 things that are used in baseball. They may even come up with other associations that didn't come to your mind.

A community is a group of people who take care of one another and look after the needs of each other. There are all kinds of communities. People whom we think we might not have much in common with, somehow become close friends and part of our community. The church is a community. It is made up of all kinds of people. Some people are shy and others love to be up front. Some people are funny, while others are very serious. Some people have only been a Christian for a very short time, and others have known Jesus for 50 years! No matter how different we seem to be, God wants us to be a strong community of believers who have one thing in common: we want to make God happy by the way we live.

☞ Bible Activity for Older Children: Ice Age

- ○ DVD OF THE CARTOON MOVIE "ICE AGE"

Go to scene 14, "A Hot Foot," and watch until the pack of conniving sabertooth tigers are having a meeting. The main characters, Manfred the Mammoth, Sid the Sloth, and Diego the Tiger are trying to take Pinky (the baby) home. The foursome is trying to get away from the ice that is being broken apart by a river of molten lava. As the ice breaks,

Diego is left dangling over the lava, holding feverishly onto a piece of ice lest he fall to his death. Manfred risks his own life to rescue the tiger. The conversation that follows is:

> *Diego:* You could've died trying to save me.
> *Manfred:* That's what you do in a herd. You look out for each other.
> *Diego:* Well, thanks.
> *Sid:* I don't know about you guys, but we're the weirdest herd I've ever seen!

These four cartoon characters were a strange "herd;" they were a community. What kinds of things happen in a community? If our church is the kind of community God wants us to be, what should we be doing for one another? The movie characters were all completely different from one another, and you probably would've never expected them to be traveling together. The church is made up of all kinds of people: rich people and poor people; teachers and doctors; children and adults; moms who work and moms who stay at home; people from America and people from other countries. It seems like a strange "herd" or group of people to come together. Our movie friends made a community, because they had one goal in common and that was to return Pinky to his home. In the church, we have one goal and that is to bring glory to God. When we're all concentrating on that goal, our differences don't seem to matter.

Enrichment Activity for Younger Children: Funky Fruit Basket
○ BASKET(S), AN ASSORTMENT OF FRUIT   ○ PERMANENT MARKERS
○ STICK-ON EYES (CAN BE PURCHASED AT A HOBBY STORE)

Being part of a community means encouraging the people around you and showing them that you appreciate what they do. Sometimes it just means remembering that they are there and telling them that you care about them. Here's a really fun way to make the day of someone in your community.

Make a funky fruit basket. Before class, the fruit should be thoroughly washed and as much of the waxy film removed as possible. Each of the children will work on two pieces of fruit. Apply the stick-on eyes to the fruit. With a permanent marker, give each piece of fruit its own "look" by drawing on a mouth, glasses, ears, hair, etc. If there is still some waxy residue on the fruit, then the markers will periodically stop writing and feel like they are out of ink. Just write on a scrap piece of paper and that will remove the wax from the tip of the marker, so it's ready to go again. You may even want to add a doll's hat to a piece of fruit for a little variety. To keep it in place you will need to use a couple of loops of a strong tape, like duct tape. Fill each basket with your funky-face fruit, arranging it so the faces are easily visible. The baskets can be obtained at yard sales for mere pennies. What an adorable basket this makes!

Take the children to deliver these baskets at a local assisted living complex. Residents who are normally very solemn will find a giggle inside them. Or, take a basket to the local fire department and express your gratitude for helping to keep your community a safe place to live. As much as possible, let the children do the talking when presenting the gift.

Enrichment Activity for Older Children: Ants!

We're going to talk about ants and some things we can learn from them. First of all, let's find out a little about the ant:

An ant can carry 50 times its own weight. **How much do you weigh? How much can you pick up?** If one of the children would not mind being weighed in front of everyone, then do the math and figure out how much he/she would be able to pick up if they were an ant.

Ants move in and out of their ant hill. They go out in search of food and then return as soon as they find some. When they do find food, they go back to the ant hill to tell the other ants. As it runs, it leaves an odor as a trail. Once the other ants have been told, the ants follow the smell back to the food. They do not eat the food where they find it. They carry it back to the ant hill. They get the attention of another ant by tapping their antennae against the other ant.

If the weather is such in your community that you could observe ants outside, then take the children to an area where they will be able to watch some ants move about. **What kinds of things get in the way of the ant? What does the ant do when something gets in his way?** The ants are helping their community get food and nothing seems to be too big of an obstacle.

When something gets in your way of helping your family or friends, do you give up or do you find a way to solve the problem? Share a problem that you were able to solve because you kept at it. (The leader sharing a life experience would inspire the children to share their own.)

Memory Verse: Luke 14:11 (ICB)

"All who make themselves great will be made humble, but those who make themselves humble will be made great."

Alternate Version: Luke 14:11 (NKJV)
"For whoever exalts himself will be humbled,
and he who humbles himself will be exalted."

Relationships and Community

By Pat Verbal

> **Scripture:** Luke 14:11–14
>
> **Lesson Aim:** The children will explore what it means to be in community.
>
> **Memory Verse:** Luke 14:11

Preparation

Give older children a piece of paper and pencil as they arrive. Tell them to make a guest list of children they would invite to a party. Collect the guest lists to use later.

Sarah wanted to invite Emma to her birthday party, but there was a problem. None of her other friends liked Emma. Her hair was curly and sometimes very tangly. She dressed weird and the boys made fun of her. But Emma had lived across the street from Sarah since kindergarten, and they had some great adventures together. It didn't seem right to leave Emma out, but she feared others might not come if they knew Emma would be there.

- **What would you do if Emma were your friend?**
- **What advice would you give Sarah?**

Jesus liked parties. He was often a guest in the home of friends and attended the Jewish feasts. In Luke 14 Jesus talked about good party manners. He taught His followers that it pleased God when they thought of other people before themselves.

We call that being humble. Read Luke 14:7–14. As you read, think about ways you have tried to "honor yourself" or get attention at a party.
- **Have you ever rushed to be first in line for a game?**
- **Have you ever grabbed the biggest piece of cake?**
- **Did you ever play with your best friend and ignore other children?**

Most of us would have to answer yes to these questions. Jesus did not mean we should not enjoy our friends, but He did make us two promises in the passage we just read. He said,

"Be humble and you will be honored."

Invite children, who need a friend, to your party and God will reward you.

Sarah chose not to be rude to her friend, Emma. She not only invited her to the party, but she continued to sit with her at lunch and pick Emma for her team. Other children began to see the good things about Emma and stopped making fun of her. How lucky Emma was to have a humble friend like Sarah.

Song Suggestions

"Play From Your Heart" by Jana Alayra from *Jump into the Light* (Montjoy Music, 1995)
"Good Buddies" by Mary Rice Hopkins from *Good Buddies* (Big Steps 4 U, 1994)
Four Letter Word L-O-V-E Songsheets published by CEF Press, P.O. Box 348, Warrenton, MO 63383
"Change My Heart Oh God" by Eddie Espinosa from *Change My Heart Oh God for Kids* (Mercy/Vineyard Publishing, 1982)

Craft for Younger Children: Party!
○ NAPKINS   ○ PAPER PLATES   ○ COOKIES

Decorate the napkins and plates for a party. Set a party table and have a pretend party. Help children practice good manners such as introducing themselves, using their napkin, passing food to the right, saying "please," "thank you" and "you're welcome." Encourage boys to pull out girls' chairs. Make place cards and encourage children to sit by someone they don't know very well.

Craft for Older Children: Thank Yous
○ CARD STOCK   ○ MARKERS

Show children how to make a thank you card. Decorate as they wish.

Say: **One of the ways to have good manners is to say thank you in a nice way. Thank you cards are one good way to do that! Can you think of someone to give this thank you card to?**

Snack: Party!
○ UNDECORATED PARTY CAKE   ○ DECORATIONS

Let children decorate the cake and eat! Say: **It's fun to have a party. When we go to a party, we need to be polite and nice. What manners do you need to have at a party?**

Let's eat our cake and have good manners at the same time!

Memory Verse: Luke 14:11 (ICB)

"All who make themselves great will be made humble, but those who make themselves humble will be made great."

Alternate Version: Luke 14:11 (NKJV)

"For whoever exalts himself will be humbled, and he who humbles himself will be exalted"

Memory Verse Activity

Write verse on white board where all children can see it.
Chant the verse together several times until the children know the verse.

Prayer Focus

Dear God, Forgive me when I think more about myself than others. Help me love everyone as You love them. Help me to be kind. Forgive me for times when I have called attention to myself. Help me be humble. Amen.

Missing the Mark

By Tina Houser

> Scripture: Romans 3:22b–23
>
> Lesson Aim: The children will recognize consequences for
>   their choices.
>
> Memory Verse: Romans 3:23

☞ **Bible Activity for Younger Children:** What Happened??

In each of the following situations the children will tell you what happened that caused the problem.

- You woke up with gum in your hair. (Went to bed with chewing gum in your mouth.)
- You had a flat tire on your bike. (You ran over some broken glass.)
- Your plant died. (You forgot to water the plant.)
- The dog ate your sandwich. (You left the sandwich on the coffee table where the dog could reach it.)
- You tripped over your baseball bat. (You didn't put your bat away.)
- You spilled your milk. (You left your glass sitting at the edge of the table.)

Name something bad that's happened to you. What was the cause (or the reason)? You made a choice, a bad choice. The choice you made caused something to happen that wasn't good. Go through the above list again and ask what could have been done to keep those things from happening. Note: be careful of some of the things children might list that were not a direct consequence of what they did such as the death of family member or divorce.

The things we have mentioned are mishaps and things that you are learning about by making these mistakes. Sometimes we do things that we know go against what God would have us do. There are consequences to those choices, also.

- What is a consequence of telling a lie?
- What is a consequence of taking something that doesn't belong to you?
- What is a consequence of disobeying your parents?
- What is a consequence of using God's name in a mean way?

The main consequence is that we are separated from God, and God did not make us to be separated from Him.

☞ Bible Activity for Older Children: Consequences
○ SQUIRT GUN   ○ OLD MAID CARDS

Each group of up to six players will need a deck of Old Maid cards and a squirt gun. Place the cards face down in a stack on the floor. The children will sit in a tight circle with the cards in the center where they can easily be reached. The players will take turns drawing a card from the top of the pile. They will show the card to the other players and then put it in a new stack. There is only one rule to this game: if you draw the Old Maid card, the leader will squirt you with the squirt gun. When someone is squirted, put all the cards from both piles together again and shuffle. Start over with a new pile in the center of the circle and the Old Maid hidden somewhere inside. Play long enough that several of the kids get squirted—maybe, even a few times.

Put the cards and the squirt gun away. Let's think about how the Old Maid card is like your sin and the squirt gun is like the consequences. **How did different people react to drawing the Old Maid card?** (tried to talk the leader out of squirting them, tried to avoid the water when it was coming toward them, tried to turn the card over quickly so no one would see that it was the Old Maid, thought it was funny until they got wet, made an excuse why they had to leave the circle) **How is each of these like the way we deal with the consequences of our sins when they come our way?** We try to talk our parents out of punishing us. We talk about something else and avoid the subject of what has been done wrong. We try to cover up what we've done. Some people don't take their sin seriously until they have to live with the consequences. We make excuses for the way we've acted.

Enrichment Activity for Younger Children: Jim Ryun
○ MASKING TAPE

In 1964, there was a high school student in Wichita, Kansas named Jim Ryun who was getting noticed all over the country because of how fast he could run. He became the very first person to be able to run a whole mile in less than four minutes. No one had ever run that fast! In the next several years he set all kinds of records. One of his dreams was to get a gold medal at the Olympics and everyone thought he would be able to do that easily. As a senior in high school he qualified for the Olympic team that would compete in Tokyo, but he was unable to qualify for the finals there. In 1968, he raced in the Mexico City Olympics where he finished second. He qualified for his third Olympics in 1972 being held in Munich, but during his race a fellow competitor accidentally tripped him. Even though he got up and finished the race after falling, he was not able to make up the time that he had lost. Once again he didn't reach his goal of an Olympic gold medal.

We're not going to run races today, but we're going to try a different Olympic event, and that's the long-jump. With masking tape mark a starting line and another line that is the goal for the children to be able to reach in their jump. Make sure the goal is out of their reach. Give each child the opportunity to attempt their best long-jump.

Jim Ryun was a tremendous runner, but he still fell short of the goal he had set for himself to get a Olympic gold medal. We all jumped our best at our long-jump competition, but we all fell short of getting to the goal line that was marked. The Bible tells us that every one of us fall short of who God created us to be. Every time we do something that displeases God, every time we sin, we fall short of what God created us to be. Anytime we try to live our lives on our own power, without God's help and forgiveness, we will always fall short.

Enrichment Activity for Older Children: Water/Ice Drops!

○ A GLASS THAT HAS BEEN DIPPED IN WATER, THEN PUT IN THE FREEZER

Do you see the tiny layer of ice on this glass? Ice on a glass like this means that you're going to have a nice cold drink. But, on an airplane, a thin layer of ice on the wings can mean disaster.

In very cold weather, a plane flies through a cloud and picks up droplets of moisture. Because it's so cold, the droplets turn to ice, and ice is heavy. The ice changes the shape of the wings and weighs down the plane, so it can't fly properly. Doesn't sound like a big problem, but it has caused terrible crashes. Only 30 seconds after take-off from Washington D.C., a plane went down and 87 people were killed. The reason it crashed was that there was ice on the wings. Because the airlines know this is so dangerous, they have some special things they do to planes to keep this from happening, and the planes can still fly safely in very cold weather.

A lie (just like the ice) might seem like a little thing, but it can cause big damage. When we do things that go against the way God wants us to live, they weigh us down and will eventually cause bigger problems.

For a special treat, serve a drink in iced glasses. At the beginning of your time together you can have the children dip their own glasses and place them in the freezer. It only takes a few minutes for the thin layer of ice to form on the glass.

Memory Verse: Romans 3:23 (ICB)

"All people have sinned and are not good enough for God's glory."

Alternate Version: Romans 3:23 (NKJV)

"For all have sinned and fall short of the glory of God."

Missing the Mark

By Rev. Eric Titus

> **Scripture:** Romans 3:22b–23
>
> **Lesson Aim:** The children will recognize consequences for their choices.
>
> **Memory Verse:** Romans 3:23

Preparation

- ○ DART BOARD ○ BALLS OF PAPER ○ BASKET OR WASTE CAN
- ○ SMALL PRIZES (MINTS, PENNIES, KEY CHAIN, ETC.)

Either purchase a dartboard or make one of construction paper. Before the sermon crumple up a large amount of paper balls and place those in the basket or waste can. The dartboard needs to be light enough so you can move it around easily.

How many of you think you can hit this target by throwing a ball of paper at it? How many of you think you can hit the center? How about if I asked you to hit the center every time? I'm going to stand really close to (child's name) and let her/him try to hit the center of the target. (Let the child throw until they hit.) **Now, didn't that seem easy?**

Now, I'm going to let someone else try. (Let another child hit from close range.) And now someone else should try. (Choose a child that has a good disposition and can laugh.) Just as they're about the throw say: **WAIT! This is too easy don't you think?** (Back way up and then tell the child to try again.) **OK, try it now. Oops, the paper ball didn't quite make it! What if I move a bit closer and everyone tries, OK? And, if everyone hits it every time, I'll give everyone a prize—deal? Everyone grab a few paper balls. OK, let me get ready** (back up—not too far) **GO!** (When they start throwing the paper balls, hold the target as far up as you can over your head. It doesn't matter if someone hits and would be good if a couple did.) **That was a little hard wasn't it?**

Does anyone know what sin is? Yes, those are some good and right answers. Sin means missing God's mark. God gives us wonderful rules to live our lives by, but sometimes, every one of us misses the thing that God wants us to do, and that is sin. It's just like missing the center of the target. And no one, not even your mom, dad, or pastor ever hits God's target all the time. The Bible tells us we all "fall short" of God's glory. And that is the bad part.

But there is a great part, and we should never forget the great part! The Bible says that because we all miss God's mark and sin, that God is kind to us and in Jesus we are justified. Justified, now that's a hard word to understand. Let's remember it this way, "Just as if I never sinned." God is kind to us, even when we sin and "miss God's target for our lives". Because of Jesus dying and rising from the dead, God makes it just as if we didn't miss the target at all. It is a gift we get from God, even when we miss the target.

Didn't I promise that if every one hit the target every time I would give you a prize? Well, let's pretend everyone did hit the target every time (give out the prizes).

Song Suggestions

"The Family of God" by Kurt Johnson, a.k.a. MrJ from *Kid Possible* (Kurt Johnson, 1995)
"No One Else I Know" by Mary Rice Hopkins from *15 Singable Songs* (Big Steps 4 U, 1988)
"This Is Love" by Dean-O from *God City* (BibleBeat Music, 2001)
What a Mighty God We Serve Songsheets published by CEF Press, P.O. Box 348, Warrenton, MO 63383

Craft for Younger Children: Hitting the Mark!
  ◯ ONE OATMEAL OR SIMILAR CONTAINER (1 PER CHILD)
  ◯ 3 PLASTIC BALLS FOR EACH CHILD   ◯ MARKERS

Let children decorate the containers that they will use for their very own game. When it is decorated, let the children set the container a few feet away from them and try to toss the balls into the container. Move the container farther and farther as they get better at it.

Ask: **When you first started playing your game, was it hard? Did it become easier?** The Christian life is like that—when you first begin to live a life for God you might mess up, but as you live your life in faith—you get better at it!

Craft for Older Children: Target Practice
  ◯ CARDBOARD CIRCLES (ABOUT 7 IN. ACROSS—CAKE CIRCLES WORK WELL)
  ◯ STICKY HOOK AND LOOPS   ◯ SMALL BALLS (3 PER CHILD)

Let each child make a target with the circles—decorate as they wish. Place the hook side onto the center of the target, put the loop side on the balls and let children try to "hit the mark"

Sometimes we "hit the mark" and sometimes we don't. It is the same in our Christian lives—sometimes we do what God wants us to and other times we don't. But we have a God that always forgives us and lets us begin again!

○ 3 GRADUATING SIZES OF CIRCULAR COOKIE CUTTERS   ○ SLICES OF BREAD
○ BOLOGNA   ○ SLICES OF CHEESE   ○ KETCHUP

Make your own target. The children will use the largest cookie cutter to cut a circle of bread. Use the next largest cookie cutter to cut a circle of bologna. The cheese will be the next size smaller. Then, squirt a dot of ketchup in the center for the bullseye.

Let this target remind you that even when we miss God's target for our lives, through His forgiveness God will make it as if we hadn't missed at all.

Memory Verse: Romans 3:23 (ICB)

"All people have sinned and are not good enough for God's glory."

Alternate Version: Romans 3:23 (NKJV)
"For all have sinned and fall short of the glory of God."

Memory Verse Activity

○ EMPTY WATER BOTTLES   ○ BEANBAGS

Tape a piece of light-colored paper around the center of twelve empty water bottles. On each paper write one word from the memory verse in large print. Place the bottles about six inches apart along a wall and then, determine a "stand-behind" line with a piece of masking tape on the floor. The children will take turns standing behind the masking tape and throwing a beanbag at the water bottles. When a bottle goes down, it is removed from the game, and everyone repeats the verse in its entirety. Continue playing until all the bottles have been removed.

 Prayer Focus

Dear Lord, forgive us when we miss the mark, and give us the strength to live like You want us to. Thank You for Your free gift of kindness in Jesus Christ, who makes it just as if we never sinned. Amen.

Cleansed by the Word

By Tina Houser

Scripture: John 15:3

Lesson Aim: The children will understand that no matter how full their hearts become with unpleasant things, what Jesus did for us can remove it all.

Memory Verse: John 15:3

☞ Bible Activity for Younger Children: Forgiveness
- ○ SHALLOW PAN (LIKE A COOKIE SHEET)   ○ SALT

Give each child a shallow pan that has enough salt in it to cover the bottom. Using only one word, describe something you have done that displeased God. Write that word in the salt with your finger. The leader will then say: When you say you are sorry, God says that you are forgiven." The children will gently shake the pan back and forth. The word they have written will disappear. Repeat this process three times, with the children writing different words each time and the leader responding with the forgiveness statement.

Anytime we ask God to forgive us, He not only forgives us, but He completely forgets it. It's like He throws our sin in the deepest sea where no one can reach it again. It disappears! Our sins written in the salt disappeared when we shook the pan with God's forgiveness.

☞ Bible Activity for Older Children: Pure heart!
- ○ LARGE RED CONSTRUCTION PAPER   ○ CLEAR PLASTIC   ○ TAPE
- ○ WATERED-DOWN BROWN CRAFT PAINT   ○ DISPOSABLE PLATES OR PANS
- ○ PAPER TOWELS

Each child will use the red construction paper to make as large a heart as possible out of that size paper. Place the heart on a surface in front of the student and cover the heart completely with a large rectangular piece of clear plastic. Tape the clear plastic down on the corners so it is securely in place. You should be able to see the heart clearly through the plastic. Place a pan of watered down brown craft paint where each student can reach it easily.

Slowly read the incidents listed. Any of the children who have done something similar should place their hand in the paint and make a hand print on the clear plastic over their hearts. Each time an incident is read, the children will place another handprint on their hearts.

- You didn't tell your parents something you were supposed to tell them.
- You looked on of someone else's paper for help on an assignment or test.
- You made fun of another person by saying mean things.
- You lied about what actually happened.
- You went somewhere you were told not to go.
- You lied about your age to be admitted somewhere.
- You hit someone in anger.
- You were responsible for hurting someone's feelings.

(The children may want to add more of their own statements for consideration.)

Look at the mess you have made on your heart. These are YOUR handprints on YOUR heart. No one else puts sins in your heart. Other people may affect you, but you are the only one who controls what happens in your heart. God provided a way for our hearts to be cleansed. When we admit how filthy we have made our own hearts and ask God for His forgiveness, our hearts are made clean. God can forgive us because Jesus took our punishment. God always does the right thing and the right thing is for evil things to be punished. Jesus did that for us and all we have to do is accept it. Carefully, loosen the tape and pull the paint smeared plastic off of your heart. **What does your heart look like now?** It is clean, because all the things that we talked about have been removed by the power Jesus has to clean hearts.

Enrichment Activity for Younger Children
    ○ MASKING TAPE ○ SMALL POM-POMS (IN ALL SIZES AND COLORS)

Give each child a small handful of the fuzzy pom-poms. Each child will share something they know would cause God to be displeased. Following their statement, the child will toss all the pom-poms he is holding out into the room. Continue doing this until all the children have shared and released their pom-poms. The room is now filthy with a pom-pom mess! Give each child a very long piece of masking tape. They will loop the tape, sticky side out, in their hand to make a sticky ball. Once everyone has a masking tape ball, signal the children to clean the pom-pom mess by picking them up with the sticky ball.

Each time we do something that displeases God we are adding to the sin mess in our lives. The Bible tells us that there is only one way to clean up that mess and that is through God's Son, Jesus Christ. God loves us so much that He sent His Son down to earth from heaven to show us how to live, to help us understand, and to take our punishment so that we could be close to God once again. When we trust in all that God did for us and believe it with all our hearts, then God cleans up our sin mess.

Enrichment Activity for Older Children: Filters
    ○ GLASS ○ TAP WATER ○ MICROSCOPE SLIDE ○ USED WATER FILTER

If you do not know how to use a microscope, ask someone to visit your group and help with this activity. Fill a glass with tap water. Hold the glass up and ask the children if they think this water is clean. Sure, it is; it just came out of the faucet! Place a little water onto the slide and put it in position on the microscope. Give each child an opportunity to view the water through the microscope. A microscope has the power to make very tiny things that we cannot see big enough for us to look at them closely. **Do you see anything strange on the slide? Is the water completely clean?** There are things hiding in the water that no one could easily see.

Some people put a filter on the faucet to catch any extra little things that might still be in the water. **Do any of you have special filters for your water at home?** These filters help make the water cleaner to drink and use. Show a used filter to the children so they can see what has been caught as the water went through it.

When we looked through the microscope we saw that there were mysterious things hiding in our water. **Do we sometimes think we are hiding our sins from other people? How do we hide the wrong things we've done?** (don't talk about it, tell another lie about it, pretend it didn't happen, convince ourselves it wasn't that big of a deal) **Can we hide those things from God?** When we accept the forgiveness that Jesus died for, God will forgive even the tiniest things that we are hiding in our hearts.

Memory Verse: John 15:3 (ICB)

"You are already clean because of the words I have spoken to you."

Alternate Version: John 15:3 (NKJV)
"'You are already clean because of the word which I have spoken to you.'"

Cleansed by the Word

By Tina Houser

> **Scripture:** John 15:3
>
> **Lesson Aim:** The children will understand that no matter how full their hearts become with unpleasant things, what Jesus did for us can remove it all.
>
> **Memory Verse:** John 15:3

Preparation

- A CLEANING LADY COSTUME
- MOP
- COMMERCIAL BUCKET (PREFERABLY ROLLING)
- RAGS
- MIRROR WITH A PIECE OF GUM STUCK TO IT
- WD-40
- BUBBLEGUM
- SOMETHING TO HOLD CLEANING SUPPLIES

(NOTE: THE CLEANING LADY CHARACTER RESEMBLES THE CAROL BURNETT ROLE)

The cleaning lady enters pushing her bucket with the mop handle. She is chewing hard and deliberately on her bubblegum. Occasionally, she blows a bubble. As she enters she picks up some garbage here and there, dusts things off, and straightens up. She starts talking about the many years she's been cleaning this office building. (As she speaks, continue to do a little work here and there, and keep the gum going.)

"Some of the offices I clean are as neat as can be, and all I have to do is flip my feathers around to knock off a little dust. That's the way Mr. Denton is. He likes everything tidy—a place for everything and everything in its place. Oh, but, you take Mr. Hobson down the hall. Completely different office there! I could probably spend the entire evening in his office and not get it spic-and-span. Last night I scrubbed on a spot on his desk for half an hour. I think it was the remains of the burrito he had for lunch! When I go in Mr. Hobson's office I make sure I'm armed with my heavy duty cleaners. (Pull some out to show the children.) There ought to be a warning sign on his door that reads *"Enter at Your Own Risk."*

The cleaning lady sits down to rest for a minute and makes a comment about how she needs to take a few moments during her shift to check her make-up, because it's hard to look beautiful when you're doing all this hard work. When she pulls her mirror out, there's a smashed piece of gum stuck to it and she wonders how in the world that could've gotten there. Her mood changes at this point and she's concerned that she's going to have to throw her mirror away, because there's nothing that can remove bubblegum. As she pulls each cleaning product from her supplies, she reads the label to see if it says it will remove bubblegum. Nothing mentions bubblegum, and she sets each one aside with disappointment.

Then, she picks up the WD-40. She reads the label that says, "This is the only product that will remove really sticky substances, like bubblegum." Quickly, she squirts the WD-40 on the mirror and wipes the bubblegum off with a rag. Her mirror is clean and restored.

Leave the cleaning lady role and speak with the children. **Why was the cleaning lady about to throw her mirror away?** (She thought it was ruined by the bubblegum.) **How many products did she find that could help her get the bubblegum off the mirror?** (only one) **When she found out that the WD-40 would clean her mirror, what did she do?** (She used it right away.) She didn't wait until she got off from work or until she got back to her supply closet. She cleaned the mirror off as soon as she realized she had the product that would help her.

There are people who think their lives are like that mirror with the bubblegum on it. They think they have made so many mistakes that nothing can help them. Surely, no one could forgive all the times they have messed up and dishonored God by the things they have said and done. Then, someone tells them about the One True God who offers His forgiveness to everyone, and who will clean their hearts so they can have a fresh start. When they hear about God's love and forgiveness and His desire to clean their hearts, some people wait to think about it, but hopefully, they will ask God to clean them right that minute. Just like the cleaning lady who only had one product that would clean her mirror of the bubblegum, there is only one true God who can clean our hearts.

If you need to ask for God to forgive you and clean your heart, don't wait; do it right now. We have all done things that have dishonored God, and because God always does what is right, He must punish the things that are against Him. Jesus died to take the punishment for all the things that I have done and for all the things you have done. God can clean our hearts because of what Jesus did.

Song Suggestions

"Say Thank You" by Mary Rice Hopkins *Miracle Mud* (Big Steps 4 U, 1995)
I'm Not Too Little Songsheets published by CEF Press, P.O. Box 348, Warrenton, MO 63383
"Pure Heart" by Norm Hewitt from *Fired Up!* (Generation Ministries, 2002)
"You're in My Heart to Stay" by Jana Alayra from *Dig Down Deep* (Montjoy Music, 1997)

Craft for Younger Children: Clean Heart

○ LAMINATED HEART SHAPES   ○ DRY ERASE MARKERS

Show children how to write on their hearts and then erase what they have written. Say: **What happened to what you wrote?** It disappeared! When God forgives your sin, the same thing happens; it's just as though they disappeared!

Children's Ministry Sourcebook

Craft for Older Children: Clean Heart
○ WOODEN OR CRAFT FOAM HEARTS

The children will write the verse on their heart:
"You are already clean because of the words I have spoken to you."

Say: **God makes us clean no matter what we do. God always cleans our hearts with forgiveness. All we have to do is ask Him.**

Snack: Pure Heart
○ HEART SHAPED COOKIES

Say: **God wants us to have a pure heart. When we do, God loves us very much. The good news is that even when you do something wrong you can have a pure heart again—just ask God to forgive you for what you did wrong and you will be forgiven! You will have a pure heart!**

Memory Verse: John 15:3 (ICB)

"You are already clean because of the words I have spoken to you."

Alternate Version: John 15:3 (NKJV)
"'You are already clean because of the word which I have spoken to you.'"

Memory Verse Activity: Echo Verse

The children will repeat after you:
You are already
Clean
Because of the words
I have spoken
To you!
Repeat until they know the verse.

Prayer Focus

Dear God, thank You for all You do for us! We want to have pure hearts, please help us to follow You. Amen

Who's in Charge?

By Tina Houser

Scripture: 1 Peter 5:5

Lesson Aim: The children will recognize their need to submit to the authority of elders.

Memory Verse: 1 Peter 5:5

☞ **Bible Activity for Younger Children:** Kangaroos, Cows and Elephants!

Divide the group into three sections and label them *kangaroos, cows,* and *elephants.* The sections do not have to sit together. You will be giving instructions to each group, and sometimes to the entire group. They should respond as quickly as possible by doing what you have instructed. Feel free to add to these commands.

Kangaroos, hop 8 times. Elephants, stand up. Elephants, sit down. I want to hear the cows moo. Kangaroos and cows, shake hands. All the animals should touch their toes, then touch their ears and nose. Elephants, spin around. Reach for the sky, cows. Kangaroos, jog in place. Elephants, hold up 3 fingers. Kangaroos, hold up 2 fingers. Everyone pat yourself on the back. Cows, jump over an elephant. Elephants, pat a kangaroo on the head. Kangaroos, do a cartwheel. Elephants, raise your trunks and let me hear an elephant trumpet. Cows, give the teacher a high five.

Why did you do what I told you to do? As the teacher, I am in charge of helping you and teaching you. When you do what I tell you to do, that is called submitting. Someone has authority and you follow them. Name some people you submit to because they have authority. **Who are the people you obey and follow because they have authority? Why should we submit to God? Why should we follow Him?** There is no one who has more authority than God. When you submit to God, you can trust Him to lead you where you need to go.

☞ **Bible Activity for Older Children:** My World
○ INDIVIDUAL LAP DRY ERASE BOARDS AND DRY ERASE MARKERS (OR USE PAPER & PENCIL)

Give each child an individual lap dry erase board and dry erase marker. Children who have grown tired of writing on paper will suddenly be attracted to writing when using a dry erase board. In the center of the board each child will make a circle and write their name in the circle. From that circle draw 6 lines going out. At the end of each of those lines draw another circle. There should now be 6 circles connected to the center circle (the one with the child's name in it).

In each of the attached circles write the name of an adult from whom you have learned something. It can be a value, like learning to have compassion, information about a certain place or event, or it can be a skill, like learning to bowl. Try to identify people who have had various influences on your life. It would be easy to list your mother, father, grandmother, grandfather, aunt, and uncle, but try not to limit yourself to one sphere of influence, like your family. Identify one thing that you have learned from each person. Once everyone has completed their web, break into groups of no more than six. Each person will share about one name on their web. Continue this process as long as time allows.

The person you are has been greatly influenced by these six special people in your life (and many more). God has given you influential people who have the responsibility of teaching younger people, and He has given you the assignment of taking to heart with a humble spirit all they say. Many things are learned from experience and years of living. Be aware that as a young person you have not had the opportunity to have those experiences, and God is reminding you in Scripture that it is wise to respect the knowledge older people can pass on.

Enrichment Activity for Younger and Older Children: Listen Up!

This will take a little advance preparation, but it's guaranteed to be something everyone involved will remember for years to come. In 1 Peter 5:5, it says that younger men should listen and learn from older men. There is so much to learn from the mistakes and experiences of someone older. That verse also reminds us to be cautious about how sure we are of ourselves and how highly we think of ourselves. Name something you have learned from someone older than you. To begin this discussion, the leader should share such an experience from their personal history.

Bring in an older person to share a skill or experience with the children (or you can bring in several older adults and divide the children according to interest or size of manageable group). This person could:
- help the children make a simple tool box
- teach the children how to polish silver
- explain how to read a recipe and bake some cookies
- demonstrate how to care for roses
- make a page for a scrapbook
- teach the children how to peel a potato
- teach the children how to sew on a button

This short list should only start you thinking of the possibilities you have with the older adults you know. The project and the knowledge that is shared does not have to be something huge, so don't overlook the simple things that people need to learn, like how to sew on a button. During the activity take pictures of the interaction between the children and adults. These pictures would make a nice bulletin board with today's memory verse as the caption.

Make sure you take some time to talk with the children about this experience. Allow them time to share what they learned, how it changed their relationship with the guest, and if they would like to do something like this again.

Memory Verse: 1 Peter 5:5 (ICB)

"In the same way, younger men should be willing to be under older men. And all of you should be very humble with each other. 'God is against the proud, but he gives grace to the humble.' "

Alternate Version: 1 Peter 5:5 (NKJV)

"Likewise you younger people, submit yourselves to your elders. Yes, all of you be submissive to one another, and be clothed with humility, for 'God resists the proud, but gives grace to the humble.'"

Who's in Charge?

By Vicki Wiley

> **Scripture:** 1 Peter 5:5
>
> **Lesson Aim:** The children will recognize their need to submit to the authority of elders.
>
> **Memory Verse:** 1 Peter 5:5

Preparation

- ○ ONE DOG COLLAR AND LEASH   ○ ONE PACK OF CHALK
- ○ ASSORTED HATS (FIREMAN, POLICEMAN, ETC.)

Show dog collar and leash. Say: **What is this for?** (let children respond) Ask: **What would happen to your dog if you didn't use these things?**

Show hats, one at a time and say: **What kind of hat is this? Who wears it? If a policeman (fireman, etc.) tells you what to do should you do what he says? Why?**

Show chalk. Say: **Who uses this?** Yes, your teacher! **Should you do what your teacher says? Why?**

You should do what each of these people say because they are "in charge." A fireman that is fighting a fire needs everyone to listen to him so that he can get the fire out very quickly. You need to listen to your teacher so that everyone in your class can learn. You make your dog wear a collar and leash so he won't run in the street and get hit by a car.

Who else is in charge? Yes! Your parents! Your parents tell you what to eat, when to go to bed and many other things. They do this because it keeps you safe and healthy.

But do you know who ELSE is in charge? Yes, God is. God wants us to listen to Him all the time. God also tells us to listen to everyone in the church that is older and wiser than we are. **Can you think of anyone like that?** (Allow them to respond, but point out the pastor, elders and any other wise people that they would know.)

These people are a very special gift from God. God gave them to you so that you could learn from them and treasure them. When someone that is older than you asks you to do something you will know that it is for your own good and that they are also trying to help you become wise and safe.

 Song Suggestions

"Turn It Over" by Dean-O from *God City* (BibleBeat Music, 2001)
Faith Is Just Believing Songsheets published by CEF Press, P.O. Box 348, Warrenton, MO 63383
"It's Gonna Rock!" by Dean-O from *God City* (BibleBeat Music, 2001)
"Little Is Much" by Mary Rice Hopkins from *15 Singable Songs* (Big Steps 4 U, 1988)
"Less of Me" by Mister Bill from *When I Grow Up* (Mister Bill Music, 1997)

Craft for All Children: White Boards
○ A SHEET OF WHITE BOARD (4-IN X 8-IN)

You may purchase boards at your local building supply store. Cut into small lap-size boards with a table saw to make wonderful dry erase boards. There is no sanding necessary—just wipe the dust off and they are ready to use. (This is not a craft for the kids—nothing for them to do.)

Give out individual white boards to each child along with markers. Use for activity in midweek lesson and for Bible verse activity.

Snack: All the People
○ PEOPLE OR ELF-SHAPED COOKIES   ○ DECORATIONS AND ROUND COOKIES

Allow children to decorate cookies to look like their faces. Say: **We all look differently, don't we? God made us the way we are and God loves us all!**

Memory Verse: 1 Peter 5:5 (ICB)

"In the same way, younger men should be willing to be under older men. And all of you should be very humble with each other. 'God is against the proud, but he gives grace to the humble.'"

Alternate Version: 1 Peter 5:5 (NKJV)
"Likewise you younger people, submit yourselves to your elders. Yes, all of you be submissive to one another, and be clothed with humility, for 'God resists the proud, but gives grace to the humble.'"

Memory Verse Activity:
○ WHITE BOARDS MADE IN CRAFT ACTIVITY

Write the verse on a large white board so that all children can see it and copy it onto their own whiteboards. Say the verse together.

Dear God, please help us to always do what You want us to do. We love You!

Salvation

By Tina Houser

Scripture: Luke 19:28–40

Lesson Aim: The children will get a glimpse of how exciting it was for Jesus to be entering Jerusalem.

Memory Verse: Luke 19:40

☞ Bible Activity for Younger Children: Coming to Jerusalem!
○ LOTS OF SHEETS OR BEACH TOWELS ○ MASKING TAPE

Before class, mark off a path through an open room, using the masking tape to make two parallel lines. The path does not have to be straight, but can curve through the room.

Read Luke 19:40 to the children. **What does that verse say to you?** Jesus was coming into Jerusalem and the people were cheering for Him. But, the Scripture says that if they hadn't cheered for Him, then the rocks would've done it for them. Let's pretend that the people didn't cheer. **What kinds of things do you think the rocks would've cried out to Jesus?**

Choose one child to pretend to be Jesus coming down the road into Jerusalem, which has been created with masking tape. Give each of the other children a sheet or large towel to drape over them as they squat down. They will pretend to be the rocks along the side of the road. As the child who is playing Jesus walks down the road, the children who are rocks will yell out the things they had previously suggested as what the rocks would say. Switch roles so several children have the opportunity to play the role of Jesus.

☞ Bible Activity for Older Children: Welcome to Jerusalem!

As Jesus entered Jerusalem, people welcomed Him by yelling wonderful things to Him. **If Jesus were riding down the street in a parade, what would you want to yell so that He would hear you?** Write the children's suggestions on the board.

Children and adults alike love worshiping in this unique way. Give each child two rocks, big enough that each one fills the palm of their hands. Decide on a simple rhythm that you can tap as a group by hitting the rocks together. With enthusiasm, say the first suggestion you have written on the board. Follow that by tapping the rhythm you came up with as a group. Say the next phrase from the board, and repeat the rhythm. Continue doing this until all of the suggestions have been said in praise to the Lord Jesus. End your rockin' praise time with a wild applause using only the rocks!

The Bible tells us that if we do not praise the Lord, then the rocks will do it for us. Let's use our voices and these rocks to give God our praise.

Enrichment for Younger Children: Palm Trees
O BOX OF DATES   O 20-POUND BAG OF POTATOES   O RULER

The people celebrated Jesus' arrival to Jerusalem by laying their cloaks on the road to make a path. In Matthew 21:8, it tells us that they also cut palm branches and placed them on the road.

There are many kinds of palm trees, but more than likely the kind that were there by the road to Jerusalem were date palms. They are a fruit tree, and the fruit that comes from it is a date. The dates are about one-inch long and very sweet. Offer a date to the children who would like to taste this rich, sweet delight. Measure the date to see if it is about one inch long. (Dates can be purchased in the produce section of your grocery in different size boxes.) The dates come from the trees in clusters, much like grapes do from a vine, but the clusters are much bigger. Each cluster will have about 200 dates on it and weigh around 25 pounds. Bring in a 20-pound bag of potatoes for the children to lift, and point out that the clusters would probably weigh even more than this. Once a date palm tree is planted, it will take about ten years before any fruit grows on it. The date palm farmer has to be patient!

The tree itself will grow 40 to 100 feet tall. This would be approximately 4 to 10 stories on a building. If you have a tall building the children are familiar with, point out the similarity between their heights. To get the branches from this tree to place in front of Jesus would have meant someone climbing up the tall, straight tree. **Do you like to climb trees?**

Everything that scientists know about the date palm tells us that it was the very first tree that people intentionally grew for food. These interesting trees grow all over the area where Jesus lived.

Enrichment for Older Children: Popcorn Pressure!
O ENVELOPE OF POPCORN   O MICROWAVE   O NAPKINS

When Columbus met the Indians, he was introduced to popcorn. They not only ate popcorn, but they also wore it as jewelry. It was during the first Thanksgiving feast that the colonists tasted their first popcorn when an Iroquois Indian brought a pouch full of popped corn as a gift.

Can you imagine what it would have been like to be there when those first kernels of corn got too close to the fire and exploded! Right before their eyes, that little hard kernel became a soft, puffy, delicious food. **What makes the kernel change so when it gets hot?**

Popcorn is made up of a lot of water. The hard coating of the kernel (called the pericarp) holds the moisture inside. When the kernel is heated the moisture inside turns into steam. The pressure builds up so strong that finally the pericarp can't hold it any longer and it breaks. The starch that is also inside the kernel turns into jellylike bubbles when the corn explodes, and then those bubbles quickly dry to become the fluffy solid that we love to eat.

The steam built up inside the kernel until it couldn't keep it inside any longer. The Bible tells us that our joy at being with Jesus should constantly come out of us. The verse that we are looking at today says that if we don't show our praise for God, then the rocks will just explode with their own praise—kind of like our popcorn!

Memory Verse: Luke 19:40 (ICB)

"But Jesus answered, 'I tell you, if my followers don't say these things, then the stones will cry out.'"

Alternate Version: Luke 19:40 (NKJV)
"But He answered and said to them, 'I tell you that if these should keep silent, the stones would immediately cry out.'"

Salvation

By Vicki Wiley

> **Scripture:** Luke 19:28–40
>
> **Lesson Aim:** The children will get a glimpse of how exciting it was for Jesus to be entering Jerusalem
>
> **Memory Verse:** Luke 19:40

Prepare

○ PICTURES OR MEMORABILIA OF PARADES OR OTHER SORTS OF HONORS (TROPHY, NEWSPAPER ARTICLES, ETC.)

Have you ever been to a parade? What kind of parade have you been to? (Let the children discuss as you try to get them to mention a parade that honors someone.)

What else do people do to honor someone? (They clap for them. They give them presents.)

We have many ways to honor people, but one of the most special ways to honor someone is to let them lead a parade. At the Rose Parade on New Year's Day this person is called the Grand Marshall. He is the person honored for something important that he or she has done in life. When the Grand Marshall goes down the parade route, people cheer!

When Jesus came into Jerusalem, the people were crazy about Him! They wanted to shout to Him, honor Him and welcome Him! They did something that we don't really do today; they waved palm branches at Him and put their coats down for Him to walk across.

Today, we can't see Jesus in a parade, but Jesus is always there for us. We can honor Him just like the children did back in Bible times. Jesus came to give us a gift—a gift of salvation which means that we can go to heaven! We can get this gift of salvation by telling Jesus that we love Him, we want Him to be our Savior and we will follow Him always.

Instead of being Grand Marshal of a parade, we can ask Jesus to be the King of our hearts! That's better than a parade, isn't it?

Jesus is very special. **What can you do to honor Him today? What can you do to show Him that you are crazy about Him?**

Song Suggestions

"Walking and Singing" by Mary Rice Hopkins from *Miracle Mud* (Big Steps 4 U)
"Faith Will Do" by Dean-O from *You Got It All* (FKO Music, Inc., 1997)
Walking and Leaping Traditional
"Jump Into the Light" by Jana Alayra from *Jump into the Light* (Montjoy Music 1997)

Craft for Younger Children: Palm Sunday Palms!

○ PAPER TUBES   ○ GREEN PAPER CUT INTO PALM SHAPES (3 PER CHILD)

Show children how to put the palm branches into the tubes to form a palm branch. Let children wave them as you talk about Jesus' entry to Jerusalem.

Craft for Older Children: Rocks Cry Out!

○ SMOOTH ROCK FOR EACH CHILD   ○ MARKERS OR PAINTS

Allow children to decorate rocks, leaving room for writing. Say: **The Bible tells us that even the rocks could cry out and praise God! What do you think that means? What words would you use if you were to praise God? Let's write that word on our rocks!**

Snack: Pretzel Palms

○ LARGE STICK PRETZELS   ○ CUCUMBER SLICES

Show children how to put cucumber slices onto end of pretzel stick to form a palm branch.

Say: **This is a silly palm branch isn't it? Can you wave it?** The children waved palm branches when they saw Jesus walk by.

Memory Verse: Luke 19:40 (ICB)

"But Jesus answered, 'I tell you, if my followers don't say these things, then the stones will cry out.'"

Alternate Version: Luke 19:40 (NKJV)

"But He answered and said to them, 'I tell you that if these should keep silent, the stones would immediately cry out.'"

Children's Ministry Sourcebook

Have children repeat after you:
But Jesus answered (But Jesus answered)
I tell you, (I tell you)
if my followers don't say these things, (if my followers don't say these things)
then the stones will cry out. (then the stones will cry out!)

Repeat until the verse is memorized!

🙏 Prayer Focus

Dear God, thank You for Your Son who loves us so much. Help us praise Him more. Amen.

Sink or Float?

By Tina Houser

Scripture: John 20:1–18

Lesson Aim: The children will focus on the significance of the empty tomb.

Memory Verse: John 20:18

☞ **Bible Activity for Younger Children:** What's Inside?

Before class you will need to fill a product box (from toothpaste, cough syrup, graham crackers) with penny candy or little prizes. Glue (not tape) the box closed securely, so that it looks like it has not been tampered with. Choose one of the children to open the box. Everyone will be watching closely to see what is inside. Pass the box around so that everyone sees what is inside and can take a piece.

- **How did you feel when you saw what was inside?**
- **Why were you surprised?** (It wasn't what we were expecting!)

When the women went to the tomb where Jesus had been placed after His death and found it empty, they were surprised. When Peter and John came to the tomb and saw that Jesus was not there, they were surprised. It wasn't what they expected at all!

☞ **Bible Activity for Older Children:** Devil Destruction
  ○ EMPTY WATER BOTTLES   ○ CLIP ART PICTURE OF A DEVIL   ○ DUCT TAPE "ROCKS"
  ○ MASKING TAPE

Before class, you will need to collect some water bottles. Make enough copies of the picture of the devil to tape one to each water bottle. Make some fake rocks by wadding up a full piece of newspaper. Completely cover the paper wad with duct tape. Mark a line on the floor with masking tape about 8 to 10 feet back from the bottles. (Depending on the amount of time, your children can make most of these things.)

When the stone that covered the entrance to the tomb was rolled away, it meant that Satan had been beaten! Hallelujah! **Can everyone say "Hallelujah!" with me?** Jesus was no longer dead. Satan thought he had beaten Jesus when they crucified Him, but Jesus did not stay dead. Boy was Satan wrong! Let's play a game where we beat Satan.

One student will stand behind the line and toss the rock at the Devil bottles. Line the bottles against the wall, about three inches apart. If you knock one down, yell, "Jesus lives!" or the children may want to come up with something (like "Hasta la vista, Satan!") Keep tossing until all the Devil bottles have been knocked down.

Enrichment Activity for Younger Children: It's Hard to Believe!

There is an interesting book called *The Guiness Book of World Records* that comes out each year. In it are all kinds of records that have been set. Some of them are hard to believe. You may want to get the book from the library to show the children. Here are a few of the things listed in the book.
- A man hiccupped for 69 years without stopping.
- A man pulled two railroad cars with his teeth.
- Roger Hickey went 78 miles per hour on a skateboard in 1990.
- Blue whales are noisy. They can be heard 530 miles away.
- The largest pumpkin ever grown weighed 827 pounds.

It is hard for us to believe these things really happened. It would be easier to believe if we could see them. It was hard for the disciples to believe that Jesus was alive after they had seen Him die on the cross. They had seen the tomb where He was buried. They knew His body had been laid there, and yet, all that was left was the cloth that covered Him. Even today, it is difficult for people to believe it. But Jesus IS alive!

Enrichment Activity for Older Children: Bread Crown
◯ CANNED BREADSTICKS   ◯ PLASTIC KNIVES   ◯ WAXED PAPER   ◯ TOOTHPICKS
◯ COOKIE SHEET   ◯ OVEN

Today, we're going to talk about the crown that was placed on Jesus' head. **Normally when you think of wearing a crown, what kind of people do you think of?** (kings, queens, important people, winners in an event) In the time of Jesus, crowns were a symbol of honor, power, and authority. The person wearing the crown had power over a certain group of people. **Why do you think the people put a crown on Jesus' head?** It was a way to make fun of Him. **What was different about the crown that Jesus wore?** (It had thorns.) It took a special kind of love and a lot of patience for Jesus to go through the cruel things that were done to Him.

Let's make a special bread that will remind us of the crown of thorns. Give each child a piece of waxed paper and one strip of breadstick dough from a can. Using a plastic knife cut the breadstick into three long strips. Very gently, stretch the strips a little longer. Take the ends of all three strips and press them together onto the waxed paper. Now braid the strips together. When the braiding is finished bring the ends around to make a circle and press the dough together. Bake according to the directions on the can. After the braided bread ring is baked, break toothpicks in half and stick them into the bread to make the thorns.

If you were the only person in the world, Jesus would have come to take your punishment. Think of the things that you have done that have displeased God—ways that you failed to show Him your love. Look at the toothpick thorns that are in your bread, and think of each one as representing one of those times. Hopefully, you have accepted God's love and have asked Him to forgive you. That's why Jesus did all this—just for you! The children may eat their crown or take it home to share the lesson with their families.

Memory Verse: John 20:18 (ICB)

"Mary Magdalene went and said to the followers, 'I saw the Lord!' And she told them what Jesus had said to her."

Alternate Version: John 20:18 (NKJV)
"Mary Magdalene came and told the disciples that she had seen the Lord, and that He had spoken these things to her."

Sink or Float?

By Vicki Wiley

> **Scripture:** John 20:1–18
>
> **Lesson Aim:** The children will focus on the significance of the empty tomb.
>
> **Memory Verse:** John 20:18

Preparation

○ SEVERAL ITEMS THAT WILL EITHER SINK OR FLOAT (ERASER, NAIL, CORK, MARKER, ETC.)
○ DISHPAN OF WATER

Say: **Jesus is Risen! What does that mean to you?** (gather responses from the children) **What does "risen" mean?** Let's try this experiment.

Which of these items do you think will float and which will sink? (Try each item as the children guess.) **When something sinks, can it float afterwards? When something floats can you make it sink?** No, you can't! Some things are meant to float and you cannot make them sink!

Jesus died on the cross. When Jesus died, it was the saddest day in all the earth. His friends were sad; His mother was sad. His followers were sad, too. But God had a plan for Jesus and, just like this cork, Jesus didn't stay down! No, after He died, He was taken away and put into a tomb. His friends thought they would never see Him again. The tomb was sealed with a huge stone that could not be moved.

When His friends came back to where He was buried, the tomb was open! The stone WAS moved! The tomb WAS empty! Jesus was alive again. He was not dead any longer!

Nothing could keep Jesus down—not death, not angry people, not Satan. Jesus was alive and the tomb was empty. Today we celebrate Easter, because we know that Jesus is alive!

Song Suggestions

"He Is Really God!" by Dean-O from *You Got It All* (FKO Music, Inc., 1997)
Did You Ever Talk to God Above Songsheets published by CEF Press, P.O. Box 348, Warrenton, MO 63383
"Purest of Gold" by Kurt Johnson, a.k.a. Mr. J from *Pure Gold* (Mr. J Music, 1995)
"Believe His Promises" by Dean-O from *Soul Surfin'* (FKO Music, Inc., 1999)

✄ Craft for Younger Children: Cross Necklace

- ○ BEADS ○ CORD
- ○ CROSSES CUT FROM CRAFT FOAM WITH HOLE IN THE TOP FOR STRINGING

Show the children how to string everything on the cord to make a necklace. Say: **Many people wear a cross on a necklace so that they can remember Jesus. Today, we will make a necklace that will help you remember Jesus, too!**

✄ Craft for Older Children: Tissue Paper Cross

- ○ MANY DIFFERENT COLORS OF TISSUE PAPER TORN INTO SMALL PIECES
- ○ LIQUID STARCH ○ CROSS SHAPE CUT FROM BLACK CONSTRUCTION PAPER

(WHEN YOU CUT THE CROSS SHAPE, CUT THE CENTER OF THE SHAPE OUT SO THAT IT IS A "CROSS FRAME")

Show children how to put the pieces of tissue paper into starch and then stick onto the cross frame. Continue until the whole cross is covered with tissue papers. Let it dry.

Say: **When this is dry you will have a beautiful cross to hang up in a window—it will almost look like stained glass! This will help you remember that Jesus died on a cross, but He didn't stay dead! Jesus is alive!**

🍿 Snack: Cross Snacks

- ○ RECTANGLE CRACKERS ○ SMALL AMOUNT OF CHEESE SPREAD

Show the children how to make a cross by placing the crackers in the shape of a cross on top of each other and adhering with cheese spread.

Even our snack today can remind us of Jesus! **What do you think of when you see the cross?** When we see the cross we can remember Jesus!

✒ Memory Verse: John 20:18 (ICB)

"Mary Magdalene went and said to the followers, 'I saw the Lord!' And she told them what Jesus had said to her."

Alternate Version: John 20:18 (NKJV)

"Mary Magdalene came and told the disciples that she had seen the Lord, and that He had spoken these things to her."

✑ Memory Verse Activity

Write the verse on a white board so all the children can see it. Divide the children into three different groups.

Instruct the children that their group will make motions to this verse as follows:
   Group 1: Act it out in play form.
   Group 2: Act it out using fingers only.
   Group 3: Act it out by singing it.

🙏 Prayer Focus

Dear God, thank You for sending Jesus to die on the cross and for raising Him again! Help us to remember Your gift to us each time we see a cross.

Shout for Joy!

By Tina Houser

Scripture: Psalm 100

Lesson Aim: The children will experience different ways
                to worship God.

Memory Verse: Psalm 100:2

☞ **Bible Activity for Younger Children:** Praise Shakers
○ FILM CANISTERS ○ STICKERS ○ DRIED BEANS ○ SPOON

Obtain enough film canisters, preferably the black ones, from a photo developer. Local discount stores and drugstores collect these until they have so many they throw them out. They are happy to give them away. The children will place one spoonful of dried beans in their film canister and snap it shut. The leader may want to check that they are secure, but once snapped, they will endure vigorous shaking. Allow the children to decorate the outside of the canisters with some stickers. Keep these in your room for use when you worship through music in the future.

Can you name some sad sounds? (crying, yelling, your stomach growling, a fire alarm, a balloon popping, strange sound a car makes when it needs repair) **Now, can you name some happy sounds?** (laughter, jack-in-the-box, school bell at the end of the day, squeals on an amusement park ride, toaster popping up with your breakfast, people singing)

There are happy sounds and sad sounds. The sound of children making joyful noises with shakers is definitely a happy sound and surely brings a smile to God's face. When we make God happy, that is worship. Sing a song of praise or thanksgiving, and encourage the children to shake along with the music.

☞ **Bible Activity for Older Children:** Being Thankful
○ A JACK-IN-THE-BOX

What does it mean to be thankful? Telling God how thankful we are for what He has done for us should spring from our hearts. It should be impossible to keep it from happening. We serve God—we thank Him—we worship Him, because we can't keep from doing it!

Pass around the jack-in-the-box. Each child will crank the handle around three times. If the lid does not pop open, then pass the toy onto the next person. If the clown pops out of the box, then that child will tell something they just can't keep from thanking God for. Once the child has shared, push the clown back into the box and start over. Continue doing this until most of the children have had a chance to share or you just can't stand the music any longer!

Enrichment for Younger Children: Solving Problems

Ask the children to recall four people from the Bible who God helped solve their problem. Write these on the board. Now, ask the group to name four people they personally know whom God has helped solve a problem. Prompt them by suggesting they think about people who have made it through a time without a job, those who have recovered from an illness, someone who has lost a loved one, a friend whose parents have gone through divorce, etc. Write these four on the board, also, trying to include a variety of situations that God has provided a way through.

The leader will say, "God helped _____." Insert the first name on your list. If it was Daniel, then say, "God helped Daniel out of the lion's den." The children will say, "We serve a great big God!!" Encourage the children to respond enthusiastically—with two exclamation marks!! Continue down the list which the group has put on the board. Each time the children will respond with the phrase, "We serve a great big God!!"

Enrichment for Older Children: Little Notes
O FLOWER-SHAPED STATIONERY   O PENCILS

Before class, write two notes. One note should read, "Thank you." The other note should say, "It was so nice that you took time out of your day to come help me pull the weeds from my garden. You are such a good friend. Now, every time I look out my window and see the beautiful flowers peering at me, I think of you and that makes me smile."

Show the two notes to the children. Comment that they both look alike on the outside. They aren't the same on the inside, though. Read the cards to the children. **Which one do you think meant the most to me?** I'm not even sure what I was being thanked for in the first note. The second note, though, seemed to speak from the heart of the person and I will probably keep this note for a long time so that I can read it over and over.

I imagine that God likes to hear more from us than a simple thank you. He wants to hear our hearts speak—that's worship. Give each child one of the flower cut-outs or a piece of the flower stationery. They are to write a note to God that says more about what their hearts are feeling than they might normally do. Make a "Message for God" garden on a hallway wall, so that passersby can read what the children have written.

"Serve the Lord with joy. Come before him with singing."

Alternate Version: Psalm 100:2 (NKJV)
"Serve the Lord with gladness;
Come before His presence with singing."

Shout for Joy

By Ivy Beckwith

> **Scripture:** Psalm 100:1–3
>
> **Lesson Aim:** Children will discover how worshiping God is an important part of the life of a person of faith.
>
> **Memory Verse:** Psalm 100:2

Preparation

Gather together your church's bulletin for this Sunday's worship service and several rhythm instruments. Prepare a praise song or chorus the children will know. If you're nervous about singing in front of the congregation prepare the song with a tape or CD.

Gather the children together and show them the bulletin for today's worship service. Ask: **Who can tell me what this is?** That's right. This is our church bulletin. **Do you know what this is for?** The bulletin helps us know what the different parts of the worship service are and when they are going to happen. **Who can tell me what some of the parts of our worship service are? Why do we do these things in a worship service? Who can tell me what a worship service is for?** That's right. Our worship is a time to praise God, thank God, be with God, and learn about God. Today, we're going to look at some Bible verses to help us learn more about ways of worshiping God.

Read Psalm 100:1–3. The first line I read tells us one way we can worship God. **Who can tell me what that is?** The person who wrote the psalm said one way we worship God is by shouting with joy. Let's try that now. I want you to shout "Praise God" as loud as you can. (Do this a couple of times, if you like or turn to the congregation and invite them to shout this phrase as loud as they can.) (Read verse 2.) **What's another way we can worship God?** The person who wrote the psalm said we worship God when we serve God with gladness or when we serve God joyfully, without complaining. **How do we serve God in a worship service?** The people who help make the worship service happen like the ushers, the ministers, and the choirs are serving God with gladness. But, just by being here you are serving God. There are lots of other things to do on a Sunday morning, so when you and your families choose to come to the church building and worship God, you are serving God.

(Read the last phrase of verse 2.) **This psalm tells us one more way we can worship God, what is it?** The psalmist tells us we can worship God by singing joyful songs. We've already sung some joyful songs in our worship service this morning, but let's see if we can do it one more time. (Introduce the song you've prepared. Lead the children with the rhythm instruments in singing the song. Turn to the congregation and ask them to sing the song, too.)

Wow, we've worshiped God in three ways already this morning. We've shouted joyfully to God. We've come here this morning to worship God as a way of serving God, and we've praised God with a joyful song.

♪ Song Suggestions

Faith Is Just Believing Songsheets published by CEF Press, P.O. Box 348, Warrenton, MO 63383
"It's Gonna Rock!" by Dean-O from *God City* (BibleBeat Music 2001)
"Little Is Much" by Mary Rice Hopkins from *15 Singable Songs* (Big Steps 4 U, 1988)
"Less of Me" by Mister Bill from *When I Grow Up* (Mister Bill Music, 1997)

Craft for Younger Children: Praise Shakers!
    ○ FILM CANISTERS   ○ STICKERS   ○ DRIED BEANS   ○ SPOON
    ○ WHITE PAPER CUT TO THE SHAPE OF THE FILM CANISTERS   ○ MARKERS
(If you did the activity in the midweek lesson, you already have these items collected.)

Let children decorate the white paper. Cover the film canisters with the paper. Say: **One way to praise is to sing songs about how much you love God and shake something like this at the same time.**

Think of a song that all the children know and lead them in singing it adding the shakers!

Craft for Older Children: Finger Cymbals
    ○ 2 BABY FOOD JAR LIDS OR TWO LIDS OF THE SAME SIZE
    ○ 1/2-INCH WIDE ELASTIC   ○ HAMMER   ○ NAIL

Cut two 4-inch pieces of elastic. Let an adult use the hammer and nail to punch a hole in the center of each baby food jar lid. Push both ends of a piece of elastic through each hole. Tie the ends of the elastic into a knot. Now you can slip your finger cymbals onto your thumb and pointer finger and make music!

Snack: He Is Risen!
    ○ SMALL SNACKS SUCH AS PRETZELS, FISH CRACKERS, SMALL CANDIES, ETC.
    ○ SNACK SIZE BAGS (2 PER CHILD)

Let the children fill their bags with the snacks. Instruct them to give one to a friend saying "He is risen!"

Say: **This is a good way to tell someone that Jesus is risen, a way to share a snack and share your faith at the same time!**

Memory Verse: Psalm 100:2 (ICB)

"Serve the Lord with joy. Come before him with singing."

Alternate Version: Psalm 100:2 (NKJV)
"Serve the Lord with gladness;
Come before His presence with singing."

Memory Verse Activity

Let the children make up a song using the verse. Sing the song several times until the verse is memorized.

Say: **The best way to memorize a verse is to put it to music. Many of the psalms were actually songs, like this one was.**

Prayer Focus

Dear God, we love You. Help us to serve You with gladness and to sing about You. Amen.

Freedom

By Tina Houser

Scripture: John 8:31–32

Lesson Aim: The children will understand that Jesus is the truth that sets us free from being held tight by sin.

Memory Verse: John 8:31–32

☞ **Bible Activity for Younger Children:** Sin Holds
- ○ OLD SHEETS CUT INTO 4-INCH WIDE LONG STRIPS ○ BREAD ○ SOFT MARGARINE
- ○ JELLY ○ DESSERT PAPER PLATES ○ PLASTIC KNIVES

Using the long pieces of sheeting, tie the children together in groups of four. Tie one ankle from each of two children together and one wrist of two other children. Continue tying the kids together in a confusing mess; avoid keeping them in a straight line. The wrist and ankle of one child should not be tied to the wrist and ankle of another child. Experiment with making one of the children cross their legs and another hold at least one hand behind his or her back. This becomes quite a tangle. To make things even worse, ask each group to make one sandwich from a piece of bread spread with margarine and topped with some jelly. Now, untie the children and listen for their statements in reaction to being released.

How is this exercise we just did like our lives when we let Satan hold us in sin? Sin confuses our lives and causes us to live with a lot of guilt. **What have you done that makes you feel guilty?** Everything the Bible tells us is truth. It tells us that because of Jesus we don't have to be held tight by our sin. We can be free from the sin that is holding onto us when we put our faith in who Jesus is. Review their comments when they were released and relate them to how we feel when we put our faith in Jesus and are released from our sin.

☞ **Bible Activity for Older Children:** Truth Tag

This game is played a lot like Freeze Tag. Hopefully, this time of year, you will be able to go outside and enjoy a nice day. If not, you will need a large open area inside. Wherever you play, you will need to indicate clear boundaries.

The person who is "It" will be called "Lies" in this game. As the game starts, everyone is running around, trying to stay away from "Lies." If "Lies" tags someone, he or she yells, "Gotcha!" and the person tagged must freeze in position. The person who is frozen can be released to freedom and running once again by any of the other players when they tag the frozen player and yell, "The truth sets you free!"

When the game is over, the children will sit for a short time of discussion about the meaning behind the game.

Explain that Satan convinces us with his lies that we should not believe the truth of the Bible. Each time we believe one of his lies, we are no longer free to live the life God has planned for us. We are "frozen." The only way we can be set free from the sin that we have in our lives, because we believed Satan's lies, is to believe in the truth. **What is the truth?** The truth is that the only way we can get rid of our sin and the guilt that goes along with it is to believe in Jesus Christ, His death, and His resurrection. I can ask you "What is the truth?" but I can also ask you "Who is the truth?" Jesus is the only way to be released (or unfrozen) from our sin.

Enrichment Activity for Younger Children: Crazy Fireworks!
○ BUBBLE WRAP   ○ MICROPHONE

When our country celebrates its freedom on the Fourth of July, what do we use to help in that celebration to make it special? (fireworks) We want to celebrate the freedom Jesus gives us from our sin, because He is the truth, with our own unique fireworks. We're going to have some crazy fireworks without lighting a match, and without using a firecracker.

This activity is going to get loud—so be prepared! Give half of the children the celebration statement, "Jesus is the truth!" and the other half the celebration statement, "The truth sets you free!" Lay pieces of bubble wrap all over the floor. Instruct the children to stand around the edges. The leader will need to hold a live microphone down close to the bubble wrap. At the leader's signal, the first half of the children will start jumping on the bubble wrap and yell, "Jesus is the truth!" Then, signal the second half to jump and yell, "The truth will set you free!" Keep going back and forth, back and forth, giving each half of the children opportunities to celebrate with their bubble wrap fireworks. Each time a child makes the bubble wrap pop, they will yell out their celebration statement. The microphone will increase the volume of the popping and make it sound like fireworks. What a great way to celebrate Jesus as our truth!

Enrichment Activity for Older Children: Slavery
○ VIDEO OR DVD OF THE MOVIE "ROOTS"   ○ GLOBE

Show the clip near the beginning of the movie, "Roots," where Kunta Kinte is taken captive as a slave. After viewing the clip, ask the children to relate their feelings. How far away were the slave traders going to take Kunta Kinte? Look at a globe to show the distance between Africa and America. Kunta Kinte was being taken far away from his home. The slave traders went to a lot of trouble to capture the slaves; they went great distances. Was Kunta Kinte fighting harder than some of the other young men captured? Why do you think he did that? What do you think would have been the worst part about being taken captive as a slave? Why would anyone struggle if they were being bound with chains? Kunta Kinte was unable to break free by himself.

Do you have any ideas of how the slave traders and Kunta Kinte are like Satan and the way he tries to get hold of us? The enemy and slave trader that we deal with every day is even stronger and more vicious than the slave traders in this movie. Satan wants us to be under his power and chained by our sin. He doesn't care what he has to do to get us there. Once he has us, he will hold on tightly, and he will take us as far away from the Lord as he possibly can. Satan will go to a lot of trouble to make us his prisoner.

Memory Verse: John 8:31-32 (ICB)

"So Jesus said to the Jews who believed in him,
'If you continue to obey my teaching, you are truly my followers. Then you will know the truth. And the truth will make you free.'"

Alternate Version: John 8:31-32 (NKJV)

"Then Jesus said to those Jews who believed him,
'If you abide in My word, you are My disciples indeed. And you shall know the truth, and the truth shall make you free.'"

Freedom

By Vicki Wiley

Scripture: John 8:31–32

Lesson Aim: The children will understand that Jesus is the truth that sets us free from being held tight by sin.

Memory Verse: John 8:31–32

Preparation

○ ONE WILLING CHILD VOLUNTEER   ○ ONE ROLL OF TOILET PAPER

(Tell the child that they will be totally wrapped up for a few minutes.)

Ask: **What are some of the things that kids do that are "sinful"? What kind of things do kids do wrong?**

As the children talk about the things that kids can do wrong, wrap the volunteer in the toilet paper until the whole roll is wrapped around him or her.

When we do things like lie, cheat on a test, make fun of someone, hit someone, say mean things or don't do what our parents ask us to do, it is called sin. **How do you feel when you sin?** (let children discuss)

Would you say that sinning makes you feel like you are all "bound" up, like he or she feels right now! Ask child: **Can you move? Can you jump? Can you walk?** (the answer should be no) No! When you are all tied up you can't do anything that you need to do to live! You can't even eat!

Ask children: **How should we get our volunteer out of this mess? Can you "break free"?** Let the child try to get out of the mess on his or her own and then help as you say: **It's hard to stop doing wrong all by ourselves. We need help! Jesus tells us that the "truth will set us free."** Telling the truth and knowing the truth about Jesus Christ is sort of like being set free from this tangle of paper this volunteer is in. When you are all tangled up it is hard to do anything, just like when you tell lies or cheat. But when this paper is taken off it is just like being set free because you know the truth! Now you can do whatever you want to do and feel great!

Boys and girls, this was a silly way to show what it is like to be "bound up in sin" because it isn't that hard to get out of it. But sometimes in your lives, you will find that it is hard to stop doing bad things. If this happens, remember that Jesus Christ can help you; Jesus can set you free!

Song Suggestions

"Change My Heart Oh God" by Eddie Espinosa from *Change My Heart Oh God for Kids* (Mercy/Vineyard Publishing, 1982)

"Pure Heart" by Norm Hewitt from *Fired Up!* (Generation Ministries, 2002)

"You're in My Heart to Stay" by Jana Alayra from *Dig Down Deep* (Montjoy Music, 1997)

Craft for Younger Children: Fireworks!

- ○ ONE PAPER TUBE PER CHILD   ○ MARKERS   ○ STICKER STARS
- ○ CHENILLE CRAFT STEMS

Show children how to make a "firework" by coloring the tube different colors. Bend the chenille stems in half. Stick the sticker stars onto the ends of the chenille stems and poke the folded end into the side of the tube forming the "fireworks" on the tube.

Say: **When do we use fireworks?** Yes, on the 4th of July we use fireworks to celebrate our freedom. Freedom is very important to us as a country, but freedom in Christ is also very important to us!

Craft for Older Children: Freedom Poster

- ○ PICTURES OF CHILDREN, TOYS, FOOD FROM MAGAZINES
- ○ CONSTRUCTION PAPER

Explain that there are many things in life that keep us from following God. These things can take away our "freedom." Sometimes these things can be good, like food or toys, but if we do too much of them they become bad. **How can a fun toy become "bad" for us?** (if we play with it too much, if it is all we think about) **How can food become bad?** (if we eat too much, if we only eat junk food)

Let's make a poster about freedom. Draw a picture of Jesus in the center of your paper. Put pictures of other things that you like all around Jesus. Always remember that Jesus is first in your life and is in the center of your life!

Snack: Freedom Crackers

- ○ SNACK CRACKERS   ○ CHEESE SLICES IN STAR SHAPES

(If you cannot find the already shaped star pieces, cut with a cookie cutter.)

The children will form a cracker sandwich with the cheese inside.

Say: **This snack will remind us of celebrating freedom, just like the stars on our flag remind us of the freedom that we have!**

Children's Ministry Sourcebook

Memory Verse: John 8:31–32 (ICB)

"So Jesus said to the Jews who believed in him,
'If you continue to obey my teaching, you are truly my followers. Then you will know
the truth. And the truth will make you free.'"

Alternate Version: John 8:31–32 (NKJV)
"Then Jesus said to those Jews who believed him,
'If you abide in My word, you are My disciples indeed. And you shall
know the truth, and the truth shall make you free.

Memory Verse Activity

Write the verse for all children to see and let the children say the verse together. Break
up the verse into phrases and assign one phrase to each group of children. Go around
the room saying the phrases, putting the whole verse together.

Prayer Focus

Dear God, thank You for our freedom. Help us to obey Your teaching so that we will
know Your truth. Amen

From Bad to Good

By Tina Houser

Scripture: 2 Corinthians 4:8, Genesis 45:5–8; 50:15–20

Lesson Aim: The children will understand that God can help you get past your disappointments.

Memory Verse: 2 Corinthians 4:8

☞ Bible Activity for Younger Children: Walking the Plank
  ○ 2 X 4 LONG PIECE OF WOOD   ○ 2 CONCRETE BLOCKS   ○ NEWSPAPER
  ○ MASKING TAPE

Sometimes we have a difficult time reaching our goal, because unexpected things happen. Maybe you really want to do well on next week's math test, but this entire week you have had a terrible cold and not felt like doing the extra studying. It's disappointing when you don't do as well on the test as you had hoped you would. Name some of your disappointing situations.

We're going to do a little exercise that will help us understand how God wants us to face our disappointments. Lay the two concrete blocks down on their side about six feet apart. Position the two-by-four plank on top of the blocks to make a balance beam. It should only be six to eight inches off the floor. Give each child several pieces of newspaper to make paper wads. Mark two lines on the floor parallel to the balance beam with masking tape. They should be back about six feet from the balance beam. One child is chosen to walk from one end of the beam to the other. The other children take their paper wads and sit behind the masking tape line. As the child walks down the plank, the others will throw the paper wads at him or her, trying to distract the person on the plank from the goal of reaching the end of the beam. Once the paper wads are thrown, the children cannot retrieve them for this player, unless paper wads land behind their masking tape line. Once the child reaches the end, pick up the paper wads and distribute them evenly while another child prepares to walk the plank.

Recite 2 Corinthians 4:8 aloud together. **How does our walking the plank activity remind you of this verse?** The paper wads were our troubles, and we didn't let them keep us from moving forward. Even though disappointing things happen to us, we can't spend a lot of time thinking about how disappointed we are, because that keeps us from experiencing the really great things God has waiting for us.

☞ Bible Activity for Older Children: Life's Obstacle Course
○ PAPER ○ TAPE

Even though we are only kids, we have some pretty big disappointments sometimes. **Can you name a disappointment you have had?** (moving away from my friends and school, a storm on the day we were supposed to go to the amusement park, getting a poor grade on something I had worked hard on) Write a caption for each one of these disappointments on individual pieces of paper for use in the obstacle course later. **What did you learn each time you had a disappointment?** These lessons aren't fun to learn, but they do make us stronger and help build our character.

The children will design their own obstacle course out of chairs, tables, garbage cans, stools, brooms, or whatever is available to you in your area. On each of the obstacles hang one of the signs depicting a disappointment the children mentioned previously. The children will go through the obstacle course one at a time. Each time they pass one of the obstacles, they will say the first part of the memory verse, "We have troubles all around us, but we are not defeated!"

Enrichment Activity for Younger Children: Knots and Strings
○ A PIECE OF EMBROIDERY, NEEDLEPOINT, OR CROSS-STITCH

Show the children the underside of a piece of embroidery or other needlework where the knots are showing and threads are crossing one another. **Is this a pretty picture? Do you think I would put this in a frame and hang it on my wall?** Now, turn the piece of needlework over to reveal the top side and the pretty design. **Do you think I would put this in a frame and hang it on my wall if I was showing this side of it?**

Were the knots and strings on the back necessary? Sure they were. The parts that are ugly on the back actually help to make the front prettier. Sometimes we go through things that are ugly in our lives and disappoint us greatly. If we trust in God, though, He can make something wonderful out of those disappointments.

Enrichment Activity for Older Children: Derek Redmond

In 1992 at the Olympic Games in Barcelona, Spain, there was a young British runner who will always be remembered because of a huge disappointment he endured in front of the entire watching world. The runner was Derek Redmond and he was expected to get a medal in the 400-meter race. He had trained for this very moment, for this very race, for many years.

Right before he got to the finish line he pulled his hamstring and he fell to the ground on the track. He was in terrible pain. He could've laid there on the track in his disappointment, but Derek decided to put his disappointment aside and do something about it. He got up and hobbled toward the finish line. All the other runners had zipped past Derek, but his determination was stronger than his disappointment.

Derek's father was sitting in the stands, watching his son limp toward his lifetime goal. His heart was breaking as he watched his son in pain. No longer able to sit in the stands, Derek's father jumped onto the track and put his arm around his son. Together they slowly made their way toward the finish line.

Derek Redmond became famous for his decision to overlook his disappointment and keep moving toward his goal. He is also famous because he had someone who loved him right there by his side during his most disappointing moment.

Can you name someone who has been there when you have been disappointed? What did they do that helped you through that time? Do you know someone who is facing a disappointing situation right now? What can you do to support them and help them move forward?

Memory Verse: 2 Corinthians 4:8 (ICB)

"We have troubles all around us, but we are not defeated. We do not know what to do, but we do not give up."

Alternate Version: 2 Corinthians 4:8 (NKJV)
"We are hard pressed on every side, yet not crushed;
we are perplexed, but not in despair."

From Bad to Good

By Vicki Wiley

Scripture: 2 Corinthians 4:8, Genesis 45:5–8; 50:15–20

Lesson Aim: The children will understand that God can help you get past your disappointments.

Memory Verse: 2 Corinthians 4:8

Preparation

○ A STRIPED TOWEL WITH SEVERAL COLORS ON IT ○ A SILLY PUTTY EGG

Do you know what this towel reminds me of? What do you remember about the story of Joseph?

Joseph had some things happen to him that weren't fair at all. Have you ever had things happen to you that weren't fair? The Bible tells us that one day Joseph's brothers threw him into a pit in the ground. Then they sold him to some people looking for slaves to take to a distant land and then the brothers pretended that he was dead. He was thrown into a pit and then became a slave. This was bad enough, but it wasn't all!

Next, Joseph was falsely accused of doing something wrong, and put into jail even when he was innocent! He was in jail for a long time, but God never forgot about Joseph. Because Joseph believed in God, trusted His plan and did what was right, God took the bad things that happened and turned them all into good things. Because Joseph ended up in Egypt and was put in charge of all the food in Egypt, he was able to save his family and an entire nation from starvation. Joseph never wanted to end up in Egypt, but God's plan was perfect. God used the fact that Joseph was in the right place at the right time to save the whole nation of Israel!

God does the same thing in our lives today. When we go through bad times, make bad decisions or are affected by unfortunate events—God is always there, and He wants us to trust Him to turn the bad into something good.

Show your group the silly putty. **This is play putty. Right now it fits very nicely inside this egg, doesn't it?** (Show how the silly putty is perfectly formed to the reshape of the egg.) But we can also stretch it out. **When we stretch it out, or re-shape the putty, it doesn't fit perfectly inside the egg anymore, does it?** (Show how the silly putty has to be bended and folded and crammed back into the egg.) But it is still play putty, and if we mold it again and take our time to smooth all the edges, it will go back into the egg. (Demonstrate the smoothing-out of the silly putty with both hands to reshape the silly putty into its original shape.) It isn't quite the same as it was when we started, but it goes back in. (Place the silly putty back into the egg and completely close the egg.) And now, the silly putty not only fits in the egg again, but it has more character to it, such as the stripes and grooves and designs on it.

When bad things happen, we have to be stretched. We might not feel the same for a while (like the silly putty felt when it was bent out of shape) but we really are the same. The difference is that after we are stretched by God, if we let Him reshape us into how He created us, we will become stronger and more able to take on the challenges and hard times that life can bring us. Life isn't always fair, but God is always perfect!

Song Suggestions

"Free Inside" by Dean-O from *Soul Surfin'* (FKO Music, Inc., 1999)
"Turn It Over" by Dean-O from *God City* (BibleBeat Music, 2001)
"Walk Like Jesus" by Mary Rice Hopkins from *15 Singable Songs* (Big Steps 4 U, 1988)
I Believe the Bible Songsheets published by CEF Press, P.O. Box 348, Warrenton, MO 63383

Craft for Younger Children: Egyptian Jewelry

○ PAPER TOWEL TUBES ○ GOLD SPRAY PAINT ○ GLUE ○ SEQUINS OR OTHER FAKE JEWELS

Cut tubes into 3-inch sections and cut down one side (so that if flattened out it will be a rectangle).

The Egyptians wore lots of jewelry. Some of the jewelry was made of gold. Today we are going to make some jewelry that looks like gold. Joseph lived in Egypt and wore and saw jewelry like this.

Show children how to glue sequins onto the gold painted tubes. When finished, the children can wear them on their arms or ankles.

Craft for Older Children: Bad to Good Note Board

○ FOAM BOARD FOR EACH CHILD APPROX 10x14 INCHES ○ MARKERS
○ STICKY NOTES ○ OTHER DECORATIONS SUCH AS STICKERS

Give each child a foam board and markers, stickers. Lead children to draw a line down the center of the board and write *Bad* on one side and *Good* on the other. Allow them to decorate the rest of the board as they wish.

God does not promise that everything that happens to you will be good. **What are some of the bad things that have happened in your life? What are some of the difficult things that are happening in your life right now?** Let children tell about the things that are happening (my mom is sick, my cat got hit by a car).

The children will write bad things that are happening in their lives on sticky notes and put them into the "bad" column.

All of these bad things will have an ending to them. When God answers your prayer, I want you to write on the sticky note how God answered your prayer and then move that note to the "good" column!

 ## Snack: Stretchy Fruit

○ ONE FRUIT ROLL SNACK PER EACH PAIR OF CHILDREN

Each pair of children will have one fruit roll snack. Each child will hold an end and stretch it until it breaks. Ask: **Did this break in half?** (No. The children can compare and show their pieces.)

If each of you had the part that you got when it broke, would that be fair? (No, because he got more!) **If we divided it equally, would that be more fair?**

When God "stretches" us, it might not seem fair or good. But God always turns the bad stuff into good things. When life seems unfair, remember that the Bible teaches us that God is always fair. We may not always get what we want when we want it, but God will always do what is good for us. We have to trust that God knows best!

The children will "re-divide" the fruit roll into more even portions and eat them!

Memory Verse: 2 Corinthians 4:8 (ICB)

"We have troubles all around us, but we are not defeated. We do not know what to do, but we do not give up."

Alternate Version: 2 Corinthians 4:8 (NKJV)
"We are hard pressed on every side, yet not crushed;
we are perplexed, but not in despair."

Memory Verse Activity

This is a great verse to "chant" together. Decide upon a cadence or "beat" and teach the verse section by section to the children.

Prayer Focus

Dear God, thank You that we are never defeated but always victorious. We praise You for what You do in our lives to bring us close to You. Amen

God's Word to Parents

By Tina Houser

> **Scripture:** Luke 2:52
>
> **Lesson Aim:** The children will recognize the four areas of growth: spiritually, physically, socially, and intellectually.
>
> **Memory Verse:** Luke 2:52

☞ **Bible Activity for Younger Children:** Lots of Ways to Grow!
○ 4 SIGNS ○ BIBLE ○ TAPE MEASURE ○ PICTURE OF FRIENDS
○ A TEXTBOOK OR DICTIONARY

Before class, make four signs that say: *Physically, Spiritually, Intellectually,* and *Socially.*

The Bible tells us that Jesus grew in four different ways. Each of us grow in the same ways. The adults in our lives, our parents, teachers, and leaders are supposed to help us grow in all four of these ways. We grow physically. That means that our bodies change as we get older. We grow intellectually, which means we learn new things all the time to help us know about ourselves and the world we live in. The third way we grow is socially. We learn how to get along with others and how to be a good friend. We grow spiritually and that has to do with the way we grow to know more about God and make Him part of our lives.

Hold up the Bible and ask: **Which of these four areas does the Bible remind you of?** (growing spiritually) **Which does the textbook remind you of?** (growing intellectually) **Which does the tape measure remind you of?** (growing physically) **Which does the picture of friends remind you of?** (growing socially) Place each of the four objects, along with the signs that you have prepared, in different corners of your room.

The children will stand in the center of the room as the activity begins. The leader will name a way that you know you are growing in one of these four areas. Each child has to decide which area that falls under and go to that corner. Use the suggestions below, but add more of your own.

You pray with someone who is ill. (spiritually)
You are two inches taller than you were at the beginning of last year. (physically)
You check on a friend who was absent from school. (socially)
You read your Bible regularly. (spiritually)
You study hard for an upcoming test. (intellectually)
You walk away from a bully. (socially)
You complete a project for school without help. (intellectually)

You need new shoes, because yours are too tight. (physically)
You wait your turn. (socially)

☞ Bible Activity for Older Children: 4 Ways to Grow
○ 2 BROOMS   ○ INDEX CARDS

The Bible tells us that Jesus grew in four different ways. Those are the four ways that you grow, also. Parents are responsible for helping us grow in all four ways—not just one or two. We grow physically. That means that our bodies change as we get older. We grow intellectually, which means we learn new things all the time to help us know about ourselves and the world we live in. The third way we grow is socially. We learn how to get along with others and how to be a good friend. We grow spiritually and that has to do with the way we grow to know more about God and make Him part of our lives.

Let's play a game to help us understand ways we grow in each of these areas. Make two sets of identical index cards. Each set should have three cards that say *Physically*, three cards that say *Intellectually*, three cards that say *Socially*, and three cards that say *Spiritually*. Lay both sets of cards face-down on the ground about 20 feet away, if possible. Divide the children into two groups. Since moms clean up after us a lot, when the leader says "Grow!" one person from each group will take the broom to the set of index cards. They will choose one without seeing what is written on it and sweep it back to his or her group. The first person to return the card will look at it and tell one way we can help ourselves grow in that area. (Example: a card that says "physically" may get a response from the child of "get lots of exercise.") Take the cards out of the game and go to the next two sweepers. As the game progresses try not to repeat answers.

Enrichment Activity for Younger Children: Tea-rrific!
○ SMALL-PRINT WALLPAPER SCRAPS   ○ CONSTRUCTION PAPER   ○ TEA BAGS

Before class, you will need to make a sturdy pattern of a teacup. The children will trace around the teacup pattern onto the back of a piece of wallpaper. Cut out the teacup. Fold the construction paper in half to make a large card. Glue around the edges of the wallpaper cup, but not across the top or in the center. Place the teacup on the outside of the construction paper card. Inside the children will write, "Mom, you are tea-rrific!" Once the teacup has dried, push a teabag down into the cup, with the paper tag hanging out.

The children will enjoy giving their mothers these special one-of-a-kind cards.

Enrichment Activity for Older Children: Total Growth
○ LARGE PIECES OF WHITE PAPER

Divide the paper into four squares. Each square represents one of the four areas you grow: physically, spiritually, intellectually, and socially. God wants you to grow strong in each of these areas. Think about your future and how you will grow in each area. **What do you want to be like spiritually years from now? What do you want to look like physically? What kind of job will you be devoted to? Will you enjoy being by yourself, or will you be surrounded by friends and family?** Draw a picture to depict each of these in one of the squares on your paper. God wants to be part of your total growth—in all four areas!

Memory Verse: Luke 2:52 (ICB)

"Jesus continued to learn more and more and to grow physically. People liked him, and he pleased God."

Alternate Version: Luke 2:52 (NKJV)
"And Jesus increased in wisdom and stature, and in favor with God and men."

God's Word to Parents

By Tina Houser

Scripture: Luke 2:52

Lesson Aim: The children will recognize the four areas of growth: spiritually, physically, socially, and intellectually.

Memory Verse: Luke 2:52

Preparation

○ CARD TABLE   ○ SIGNS   ○ TAPE

Before class, make a sign for the top of the card table that says "Growing Up!" Then, make four signs on long thin strips of paper that say, *Physically, Intellectually, Socially,* and *Spiritually.*

Walk in with the card table, so the audience can read the sign across the tabletop that reads "Growing Up!" I thought I'd bring along my card table to help me talk with you about the way you grow up. Lay the card table top against the floor and legs where they can be unfolded upward. I see that some of you have gotten taller since the last time I've seen you. Show me a muscle if you think you've grown in the last couple of weeks. Marvel at how the children are changing. Pull up one of the legs of the card table so that it's sticking up in the air. Part of growing up is to grow physically. We can tell we're growing because we can reach things that we couldn't before, our shoes get too small, and the sleeves on our shirts have a difficult time making it past the elbow! God made us to grow PHYSICALLY. (Place the sign for physically on the leg of the card table.)

Another way we grow is intellectually. That means our minds are taking in more information and we're learning about the world around us. **How can you tell you're growing intellectually?** You use bigger words; you read harder books; you talk about new subjects with people older than you; you help students younger than you learn. Ask a couple of the children to name something they have learned this school year. God plans for us to grow INTELLECTUALLY. (Pull up another leg of the card table and put the appropriate sign on it.)

Are you ready for the third way we grow? We grow socially. That's when you learn how to get along with people and feel comfortable talking with new friends. **How can you tell that you are growing socially?** You can politely tell people how you feel; you use good manners; you respect the property of others; you wait your turn; you enjoy having friends! Isn't it great that God wants us to grow SOCIALLY, too? (Pull up a third leg of the card table and add the "socially" sign.)

I think you're growing into a pretty neat person if you've grown physically, intellectually, and socially. Turn the card table over and try to get it to stand steady. Of course, it won't on three legs. I thought you were growing just fine. **What's wrong with my table?** (There's still a leg stuck under the table.) There must be another way God wants us to grow. Let's check the Scriptures to see how Jesus grew and maybe that will give us a clue. Read Luke 2:52. "Jesus continued to learn more and more;" we've got that, because we said that we grow intellectually and that's learning. "And to grow physically;" we've got that. I see here that we've got a leg labeled "physically." "People liked him;" that sounds like He grew socially and was learning to get along with people. "And he pleased God." Oops! I think that must be where we're missing something. Our fourth leg of growing should be growing SPIRITUALLY. (Pull out the fourth leg of the card table and label it "spiritually.") **How do you know you are growing spiritually?** It becomes important to you to please God; you read your Bible regularly; you think about how Jesus would act in situations; you want to be around people who believe in God so you can worship with them; when something bothers you, you pray about it.

Set the card table up now. See how strong the table stands now that we have all four legs extended. We grow strong when we grow in all four areas that God planned for us. Each one is important, and God doesn't want us to neglect any of them. God gives us parents and other adults to help us along the way as we grow in all four ways. You're not on your own—God gave adults the responsibility of helping you grow physically, intellectually, socially, and spiritually.

Song Suggestions

"Gramma's House" by Mary Rice Hopkins from *15 Singable Songs* (Big Steps 4 U, 1988) *STOP! Songsheets* published by CEF Press, P.O. Box 348, Warrenton, MO 63383
"I am the Apple" by Cindy Rethmeier from *I Want 2 Be Like Jesus* (Mercy/Vineyard Publishing, 1995)
"Watch It Grow" by Mary Rice Hopkins from *Good Buddies* (Big Steps 4 U, 1994)
Children All Around the World Songsheets published by CEF Press, P.O. Box 348, Warrenton, MO 63383

Craft for Younger Children: Growth Chart
○ STRIPS OF BROWN CONSTRUCTION PAPER   ○ YELLOW PAPER SUNFLOWERS

Cut paper into strips that are 3 inches wide—cut as long as possible and tape together to make 4 foot strips—one for each child.

Show children how to glue the flower to top of brown paper strip to make growth chart. Mark their height on the strips.

When you were very little, you were about THIS (point to growth chart) big but now you have grown to THIS size. You are growing in height and getting taller and you are also growing in your Christian life and becoming closer to God!

Craft for Older Children: Measuring Our Faith Bible Marker
○ PAINT STIRRERS ○ MARKERS (OR CHRISTIAN SYMBOL STICKERS)

When we grow physically, we see ourselves getting taller. We outgrow our clothes too! When we grow intellectually we promote in school. When we grow socially we make new friends. **How do we know when we have grown spiritually?**

Let's make a measuring stick so that we can measure our growth! It's hard to really measure spiritual growth, but we can try! The children should draw symbols on the paint stirrer such as a Bible, a dove, praying hands, a fish, cross, etc.

Keep these markers in your Bibles. **When you see it, what will it remind you to do?** Yes! It will remind you to work on your spiritual life; read the Bible, pray, go to church, etc. When you do those things your spiritual life will grow!

Snack: Praying Pretzels
○ LARGE SOFT PRETZELS

This pretzel will not only taste good but will remind you of prayer. It looks like arms crossed in prayer. Praying is one of the best ways to grow in your spiritual life!

Memory Verse: Luke 2:52 (ICB)

"Jesus continued to learn more and more and to grow physically.
People liked him, and he pleased God."

Alternate Version: Luke 2:52 (NKJV)
"And Jesus increased in wisdom and stature, and favor with God and men."

Memory Verse Activity

Write the verse on a white board where all children can see it. Break the verse up and instruct children to repeat it after you as you say it:

Jesus continued (Jesus continued)
To learn more and more (To learn more and more)
And to grow (and to grow)
Physically (physically)
People liked him (people liked him)
And he pleased God (and he pleased God)
Yeah!!!

All Business Is God's Business

By Tina Houser

Scripture: Matthew 28:19–20; Proverbs 10:16; Acts 20:24

Lesson Aim: To help children understand that work is honorable and can bring glory to God.

Memory Verse: Jeremiah 29:11

☞ **Bible Activity for Younger Children:** Hit the Target
  ○ A PAPER TARGET ○ A SOFT FLEXIBLE BALL ○ A BLANK WALL

Take the children to an area where there is a blank wall. Instruct them to throw the ball at the wall—anywhere on the wall. They will be confused, but that's exactly how they are supposed to react. Now, take them to an area where you have a target hanging on the wall. They will throw the ball once again, but this time at the target.

God has a plan for your life, but He's not going to just throw it in your lap. God puts a desire in your heart and gives you special talents that He wants you to develop and use for His kingdom. Even now, as young as you are, God wants you to think about the plan He has for your life and He wants you to set goals for learning more about that plan. You need target to aim for. When there was no target on the wall, you were confused about what you were supposed to be doing. When there was a target, you knew where you were headed and what you were trying to do.

Does God have a plan for you at school? How do you see God using you at school? Does God have a plan for you at home? How do you see God using you at home? On your team? In your quiet time? As you get older, God will show you His plan for your job and your family. Aim at God's target—aim at God's plan for your life!

☞ **Bible Activity for Older Children:** Newspaper Hockey
  ○ PAINT STIR STICKS ○ NEWSPAPER ○ BRIGHT MARKERS ○ DUCT TAPE
  ○ COFFEE CAN

Give each participant a half-sheet of newspaper. In big letters across the middle of the paper, each child will write with a bright marker "God's plan for _____'s life." They will put their names in the blank. This paper represents God's plan for your life. Wad the paper up and wrap it with a couple of pieces of duct tape (just enough that it will hold the shape of a ball).

Each child will move an object, such as a chair or garbage can, around the room to make some clutter. On one side of the room place the coffee can on its side. The duct tape balls will be on the other side of the room with the clutter scattered in between the two. The object is to get the duct-taped balls into the coffee can. Half the children will place their duct-taped ball on the floor. Using a paint stir stick, they are going to try to take the balls through the clutter. At the same time the other half of the students will be trying to get in the way. They will not be allowed to kick or knock the ball away, but just cause another obstacle for the person to have to move their balls around. When everyone in this group gets their newspaper balls into the coffee can, switch roles.

Is it always easy to stay with God's plan for your life? What kinds of things get in your way? Sometimes we think we know what God has planned for our lives, and something happens and changes the plan. **What could possibly happen that would change where we thought God was taking us?** (your illness, a parent's illness, moving, changing schools, not being as good at something as you had hoped, finding out about something you'd never heard of before and it really touching your heart, divorce, unexpected bills) **Whose plan was it that was written on our newspapers before we made the balls?** God has a plan for us that may take us around, over, under, through some strange places, but it's still God's plan, and that means it's a good one—the best one!

Enrichment Activity for Younger Children: Special Guest

God has a plan for each one of us. When we are young it is difficult to see so far into the future. Part of God's plan is happening right now. He wants you to serve Him now; He is preparing you for what you will do with the rest of your life.

Invite someone to join your group for the evening, to share his or her experiences in God's plan for his or her life. You will want him or her to share what God's plan has been for his or her family, job, and place to live. If God has worked things out for them in mysterious ways, ask him or her to share those experiences. You will want them to make a special point of sharing how God used childhood as part of His plan for his or her life and to talk about how God now uses his or her occupation. It is important to leave time for the children to ask questions.

Enrichment Activity for Older Children: Going on Safari

Break into groups of two or three children. Give each group paper and pencils. Pretend you are going on a safari in Kenya, Africa. You need to come up with a plan, so you will be ready for this dangerous trip. **What kind of questions will you need to ask yourselves?** Make sure you plan so you will have a safe trip, so you will have plenty of ways to remember the trip, so you will have food and a place to stay once you get there.

Once they have completed their plans, allow time for each group to share a little about what they decided upon.

Did you know that God has a plan for your entire life? The Bible tells us that it is a good plan that will give you a good future. It's not only a good plan—it's the best plan for you! He cares about you enough that He made a plan just for YOU. Your plan is different than anyone else's. **Can you name something that God has already shown you that He planned for you?** Name two things you think God may have in your future plan. We'll have to wait and see, won't we?

Memory Verse: Jeremiah 29:11 (ICB)

" 'I say this because I know what I have planned for you.' says the Lord.
'I have good plans for you. I don't plan to hurt you. I plan to give you hope and a good future.' "

Alternate Version: Jeremiah 29:11 (NKJV)
"For I know the thoughts that I think toward you, says the Lord, thoughts of peace and not of evil, to give you a future and a hope."

All Business Is God's Business

By Pat Verbal

Scripture: Matthew 28:19-20; Proverbs 10:16; Acts 20:24

Lesson Aim: To help children understand that work is honorable and can bring glory to God.

Memory Verse: Jeremiah 29:11

Have you ever wondered why Jesus chose such a varied group of men for His disciples? Among the Twelve (as they are called) we find uneducated fishermen, a wine dresser, a patriot, and a tax collector. Some grew up in cities, while others lived by the sea. Jesus Himself worked as a carpenter in the family business, before becoming a teacher and preacher. The disciples were a jumble of occupations and temperaments with one thing in common. Can you guess what it was?

They all said, yes to Jesus' call. It was not an easy answer. It involved self-denial and fierce loyalty. This motley crew changed their world, because they shared a common mission to spread the Good News of the Gospel.

Now, think about the people in your church. Do they come from different backgrounds? When they leave for work each morning do they drive to hospitals, law offices, schools, stores, diners, factories, farms, businesses, churches and airports?

(Allow time for the children to write peoples' names and occupations on the board.)

Which of these occupations do you think is the more important to God? The answer is that all business is God's business. The Bible tells us that the work (or labor) of the righteous leads to life (Proverbs 10:16). God planned for people to work and support their families. All work is honorable when done with a Christian character, but it isn't jobs that unite believers. It is our mission—the same Great Commission that the Twelve carried on so long ago when Jesus said, "Go therefore and make disciples of all the nations, baptizing them in the name of the Father and of the Son and of the Holy Spirit" (Matthew 28:19). This commission gives the church power to serve as brothers and sisters in a lost world.

Our mission is a privilege and a great responsibility. **Have you said yes to Jesus? Are you prepared to take up this life-long work?** If so, you can begin today. If your job is being a first-baseman or goalie, you can play fair and share Jesus with your teammates. At school, you can pray for classmates. You can invite neighbors to church activities and watch for opportunities to serve them without expecting anything in return. Some children your age even go on mission trips to share their faith with children in other countries.

People have been passing this mission on for over two thousand years, but God has an exciting life map just for you. The most important job you could ever have is to find and complete your mission. **Who does God want you to share your faith with today?**

Song Suggestions

"He Is God" by Jana Alayra from *Believin' On* (Montjoy Music, 2002)
"Little Is Much" by Mary Rice Hopkins from *15 Singable Songs* (Big Steps 4 U, 1988)
"Faith Will Do" by Dean-O from *You Got It All* (FKO Music, Inc., 1997)
God's Power Songsheets published by CEF Press, P.O. Box 348, Warrenton, MO 63383

Craft for Younger Children: I Said Yes!

○ PAPER PLATES (WITH *YES* WRITTEN ON THEM)   ○ ASSORTED DRIED BEANS
○ GLUE

Show children how to put glue on the letters and then put beans on the glue forming the word *Yes.*

God wants us to say Yes! to serving Him. **What do you want to be when you grow up?** Whatever you do, you can still say yes to God and serve Him!

Craft for Older Children: Life Mapping

Guide children in creating a life map. Using shelf paper, roll out a long poster, six inches for each year of their lives; i.e. a ten-year-old will have a five-foot strip. Children can draw or cut out pictures to create their life stories including as many dates as they can for special events in their lives and families. For example: birthday, family moves, sibling birthdates, dates they joined the church or became a Christian, baptism, schools, vacations, special events.

On the other side of the paper, ask children to create a life map for the next five years with goals and dreams. Include Bible promises and a life verse. This might include how they will live out the Great Commission in the coming year.

Snack: Say Yes!

○ RICE CAKES   ○ SQUEEZE PEANUT BUTTER OR CHEESE

Write the word *Yes* out on each snack. **When you say yes to God, what does that mean?** It means that you will follow Him always! This snack will help us remember to do just that!

Memory Verse: Jeremiah 29:11 (ICB)

" 'I say this because I know what I have planned for you.' says the Lord.
'I have good plans for you. I don't plan to hurt you. I plan to give you hope and a good future.' "

Alternate Version: Jeremiah 29:11 (NKJV)
"For I know the thoughts that I think toward you, says the Lord, thoughts of peace and not of evil, to give you a future and a hope."

Memory Verse Activity

Have the kids repeat after you:
"I say this
because I know
what I have planned for you."
says the Lord.
"I have good plans for you.
I don't plan to hurt you.
I plan to give you hope
and a good future."
YES!!!

Prayer Focus

Dear God, thank You for all the desires for fun work that You have given us. As we prepare for our lives, please help us to always remember to say yes to You first. Amen

Let Justice Roll!

By Tina Houser

Scripture: Matthew 25:31–46

Lesson Aim: The children will realize that God judges our love for Him by how we show love to others.

Memory Verse: Matthew 25:32

☞ Bible Activity for Younger Children: Sheep and Goats

○ M&M'S AND SKITTLES   ○ BOWL

Before class, combine the M&Ms® and Skittles®; then, separate them by color, putting all the yellow candies in a pile, the red candies in a pile, etc.

The Bible tells us that one day God will gather all the people of the world. Name a country in the world. God will call all the people of that country. Let's say they are the yellow candies. Place all the yellow candies in a bowl. Name another country. God will call all the people of that country also. Let's say they are the orange candies. Place all the orange candies in the bowl with the yellow candies. Continue doing this until all the candies have been added to the bowl. God has called all the people of the world together.

The Bible also tells us that God will separate the people who have followed Him from the people who refused to follow Him. It also tells us that God will separate them like you separate sheep and goats. Sheep and goats look a lot alike, but they are very different. The M&Ms® and the Skittles® that we have placed in this bowl look a lot alike, but they are very different. Some people from the countries we named will be followers of Jesus; others will not. Let's say the M&Ms® are followers of Jesus and the Skittles® are not. Separate the candies so that we have those who follow Jesus (M&Ms®) and those who did not (Skittles®). There are some yellow candies in both piles. There are green candies in both piles. In every country of the world there are people who follow Jesus and people who do not.

God will punish those who do not follow Him and He will reward those who did follow Him. The people who follow Jesus will get to be in God's presence forever.

☞ Bible Activity for Older Children: God's Triangle
○ A SANDWICH   ○ A BOTTLE OF WATER   ○ A BLANKET   ○ A SWEATER
○ COUGH MEDICINE   ○ A GREETING CARD

How can we use these objects as gifts to God? Does He want us to send Him a card or buy Him a present? Read Matthew 25:34–36 and decide how each item could be used as a gift to God. Some items may be able to be used in several different ways. When we serve the people who have special needs we are showing them our love. We are also showing them God's love, and we are showing God how much we love Him.

Draw a triangle. On one corner write *Me.* On another corner write *Others.* And on the third corner write *God.* On each of the lines of the triangle write *Love.* Follow the lines of the triangle from "Me" to "Others," then to "God" as you say: **When I show love to others, I am showing love to God.** Now, follow the lines the other direction and say: **When I love God, I do that by showing love to others.**

Enrichment Activity for Younger Children: Cheer!
○ HERSHEY'S CHOCOLATE BARS   ○ PIECES OF WHITE PAPER   ○ MARKERS   ○ TAPE

There are children in the hospital and some of them have to stay for weeks and weeks, because they are very sick. **How would you feel if you had to stay in the hospital for a whole month?** You couldn't see your friends or go to school or practice with your team. Any little thing would brighten your day. We're going to make a special candy bar to take to some children in the hospital.

Give each child a piece of paper that has already been cut to the size that will wrap around a Hershey's chocolate bar. Draw pictures and write an encouraging message on the piece of paper. Wrap it around the candy bar and fasten with a piece of tape.

There are several possibilities for delivering these. If you have a children's hospital near-by and are able to take your group of children to hand-deliver the candy bars, that would be the ultimate experience. If there is no special hospital close, or time or transportation prohibits you from taking the children, then assure the children that you will make certain the candy bars get to the children's wing of the local hospital this week. At your next meeting, share with the children about your experience of delivering the gifts.

Enrichment Activity for Older Children: Baaaaa!
○ PICTURE OF A GOAT AND A SHEEP   ○ INDEX CARDS

Before class, on the index cards write these words or phrases: *recognizes the caretaker's voice, strong-minded, goes off in own direction, responds obediently, devious, unpredictable, never content, good followers, bad followers, has faith in the leader, independent nature, likes being in the group.*

Post the pictures of the goat and sheep on the wall. The children will try to determine which characteristics belong to the goat and which ones to the sheep. Place the appropriate cards under each picture. Characteristics that go with the goat are: *strong-minded, goes off in own direction, devious, unpredictable, never content, bad followers, independent nature.* The characteristics of the sheep are: *recognizes the caretaker's voice, responds obediently, good followers, has faith in the leader, likes being in the group.*

Why would Jesus think the characteristics of the goat were worth being punished? Why would Jesus think the characteristics of the sheep were worth being rewarded?

Memory Verse: Matthew 25:32 (ICB)

"All the people of the world will be gathered before him. Then he will separate them into two groups as a shepherd separates the sheep from the goats."

Alternate Version: Matthew 25:32 (NKJV)
"All the nations will be gathered before Him, and He will separate them one from another, as a shepherd divides his sheep from the goats."

Let Justice Roll

By Ivy Beckwith

Scripture: Matthew 25:31–46

Lesson Aim: The children will understand that being a follower of Jesus means taking care of others who have less than they do.

Memory Verse: Matthew 25:32

Preparation

Collect pictures of people living in poor countries or poorer people living in the United States. You might also collect pictures of older people, prisoners, or people who are ill or disabled. Also, find a picture of a king.

One day Jesus told His followers a story about a king. (Show the picture of the king.) This king had two groups of people before him. First, the king looked at the people who were seated on his right side and he said to them, "You are a specially blessed people. You will be given my entire kingdom." The people wanted to know why the king would want to give them his kingdom. He answered them, "When I was hungry you gave me food to eat, when I was thirsty you gave me water to drink, when I was a stranger you invited me into your home, when I had no clothes to wear you gave me clothes, when I was sick you helped me get well, and when I was in prison you came to visit me." Still, the people on the king's right didn't understand what the king was talking about. "But, king," the people asked, "When did we see you hungry or thirsty? When did we invite you into our homes? When did we give you clothes and when did we visit you in prison?" The king looked at the people and said, "Whatever you did for one of the least of your brothers and sisters, you did for me."

Then the king looked at the second group of people, the ones who were seated on his left. To these people he said, "Go away. You are cursed I want nothing to do with you. For when I was hungry you gave me nothing to eat, when I was thirsty you gave me nothing to drink, when I was a stranger you didn't invite me in and when I was sick and in prison you did not take care of me." Like the other group, these people didn't understand what the king was saying about their actions. "Lord," they asked, "When did we see you hungry, or thirsty, or without clothes, or in prison and did not help you?" The king answered them. "Whatever you did not do for one of the least of your brothers and sisters, you did not do for me." The people on the left were sent away from the king and the riches of the king's kingdom.

Why do you think Jesus told His followers this story? What do you think Jesus wanted His followers to learn? (Wait for several responses.) Jesus wanted His followers to know how important it was for people who followed Him to care about and take care of other people, especially those people who don't have enough food or water to eat and drink. I'm going to show you some pictures. I want you to look at the pictures and tell me some ways a person who follows Jesus could help these people. (Show children the pictures of people in need. Ask them what they think the people in the pictures need and what people who follow Jesus could do to help them.)

Jesus told this story to His followers because He wanted them to understand how important taking care of others who have less or who are in need is important to God. This means God wants people who follow Jesus to show justice or fairness to all people, including people who are not like us or who have less than we do. This is something that people who follow Jesus do.

 Song Suggestions

Little by Little Songsheets published by CEF Press, P.O. Box 348, Warrenton, MO 63383
"The Family of God" by Kurt Johnson, a.k.a. MrJ from *Kid Possible* (Kurt Johnson, 1995)
"No One Else I Know" by Mary Rice Hopkins from *15 Singable Songs* (Big Steps 4 U, 1988)
"This Is Love" by Dean-O from *God City* (BibleBeat Music, 2001)

Craft for Younger Children: TP Sheep
- ONE TOILET PAPER ROLL PER CHILD ○ COTTONBALLS ○ GLUE
- CHENILLE STEMS

Poke holes into the bottom of the TP roll for chenille stem "legs" to go through. Show the children how to form the legs of sheep and then cover the body with cottonballs. Glue several cotton balls together to form the head of the sheep and glue the head onto the body.

Craft for Older Children: Field of Sheep
- BLUE AND GREEN CONSTRUCTION PAPER ○ COTTON BALLS
- SMALL GOOGLE EYES ○ GLUE ○ MARKERS

The children will design a "field of sheep" by adding cotton ball sheep to the construction paper background.

Jesus loved sheep and talked about them many times. **What is so loveable about sheep?**

Snack: Sheepy Sheep
- ONE WHITE SNOWBALL-TYPE SNACK CAKE ○ SMALL CANDIES FOR EYES

Show children how to push the "eye candies" into the snack cake to form a sheep.

The Bible talks about sheep many, many times. **Why do you think God likes sheep so much?** (let children explore answers)

✒ Memory Verse: Matthew 25:32 (ICB)

"All the people of the world will be gathered before him. Then he will separate them into two groups as a shepherd separates the sheep from the goats."

Alternate Version: Matthew 25:32 (NKJV)

"All the nations will be gathered before Him, and He will separate them one from another, as a shepherd divides his sheep from the goats."

📖 Memory Verse Activity

Divide kids into two groups; sheep and goats. The goats will say part of the verse, repeated by the sheep. Reverse the action until the children know the verse

Group 1	**Group 2**
All the people of the world	All the people of the world
will be gathered before him.	will be gathered before him.
Then he will separate	Then he will separate
them into two groups	them into two groups
as a shepherd separates the	as a shepherd separates the
sheep from the goats	sheep from the goats

🙏 Prayer Focus

Dear God we thank You that we belong to You! Help us to grow closer to You all the time. Amen.

Love in Every Language

By Tina Houser

Scripture: Acts 2:1–4

Lesson Aim: The children will understand that after Jesus resurrected, God sent the Holy Spirit to empower believers.

Memory Verse: Acts 2:4

☞ Bible Activity for Younger Children: A Mighty Wind
○ FAN ○ PINWHEELS

Set up the fan and let the children stand in front of it. **Can you feel the fan push the air across your body? What kind of things can wind do?** (pump water from underground, move a sailboat, blow a garbage can down the street, knock you off balance, blow down a house during a tornado or hurricane) It sounds like wind is pretty powerful! **When the wind is blowing real hard, what does it sound like?** Oh, you can sound like a more powerful wind than that! It's easy to imagine, then, how wind could represent power.

Read Acts 2:1–2. After Jesus went back to heaven His followers were together in a room when they heard a sound. It sounded like there was a very strong wind coming through the room. God sent the Holy Spirit to the believers so they would have power that they had not experienced, to do the work God wanted them to do. It was work that they were not able to do on their own. With the Holy Spirit's power to help them, though, they could accomplish what God wanted them to.

Give each child a pinwheel to blow. Now, hold it in front of the fan. The power of wind can also be used to play with this toy.

☞ Bible Activity for Older Children: What Does That Mean??

After Jesus had gone back to Heaven, God sent the Holy Spirit to believers. **Why do you think God sent the Holy Spirit?** The Holy Spirit was sent to give the believers power to tell others about what Jesus did for each person. Jesus' followers were together in a room when they heard what sounded like a strong wind. Then, they saw what looked like a flame above each head. This was God's way of showing them something power-ful and new was happening. The Bible tells us that after that experience they were able to speak languages they had never learned, so they could go and tell people all over the world about Jesus. **Do any of you know any other languages? Have you ever tried to learn a new language?** We're going to play a game that will help us understand that learning a new language is not an easy thing to do. When the Holy Spirit came the believers were able to do far more than they had ever imagined possible.

Make two sets of identical cards with these languages written on them: *Swahili, German, Spanish, Italian, Hawaiian, Japanese,* and *sign language.* When you go to a place that doesn't speak the language you speak, you definitely will need to know how to say "hello" so you can get someone to help you! Go through each language and ask the children to repeat how to say "hello" in that language. Mix them up and go through them again. Divide the children into two groups. Each group will have a set of the cards placed face-up on the floor at the other end of the room. The leader will say "hello" in another language, then "go." A player from each group runs to their cards and chooses the language they think you have said "hello" in.

> Swahili = Jambo
> German = Guten tag
> Spanish = Hola
> Italian = Buon giorno
> Hawaiian = Aloha
> Japanese = Konichewa
> Sign language = something like a salute, move the hand away from the forehead in a forward and downward motion.

In our world today there are 2,796 different languages and almost 6 billion people. It is important that everyone, no matter what language they speak, learn about Jesus.

Enrichment Activity for Younger Children: Power of the Holy Spirit
- STAPLER   ○ STRIPS OF POSTER BOARD (2 IN. WIDE, 16 IN. LONG)
- MEDIUM-SIZE BOOKS

Give each child a strip of poster board and a book. Instruct them to hold the poster board strip on its edge and place the book on top of it. **Will the poster board support the book?** Of course not. We're going to change the shape of the poster board strip so that it will be able to hold the book. Fold the strip in half, and then fold each half again. Staple the ends together. You should be able to form something that looks close to a square shape. Set this new shape on its side on the table. It should stand up and look something like a horse corral. Now, set the book on top of it. **Does the poster board strip hold the weight of the book?** In order for it to use that power, though, it had to change its shape.

Jesus was God in the form of a man. Jesus told His disciples that God would come in a different form to live with them after He was gone. The Holy Spirit is God in spirit form. In this form, God can live inside us, in our spirits. Jesus couldn't live inside us, because He was in the form of a man. But, the Holy Spirit can. The Holy Spirit gives us power that we never thought possible.

Enrichment Activity for Older Children: Power!

○ LARGE MAGNET   ○ LARGE NAILS   ○ SMALL PAPER CLIPS

Give each child a nail and a paper clip. Try to pick up the paper clip with the nail without running the nail through the center of the paper clip. **By touching the paper clip, will it stick with the nail?** Now, stroke the nail against the magnet. Take long strokes in one direction. Do not rub the nail back and forth, and don't change directions. Make about 20 strokes and then try to pick up the paper clip.

Without the help of the magnet, the nail had no power. When you stroked the nail against the magnet, the magnet gave the nail some power. God sent the Holy Spirit so that we could have God's power living within us. Without the help of the Holy Spirit, we do not have the power God wants to give us. The more we trust God and spend time learning about Him and worshiping Him, the more of God's power we will notice in our lives.

Just for fun, see how many paper clips you can pick up using your new nail magnet.

Memory Verse: Acts 2:4 (ICB)

"They were all filled with the Holy Spirit, and they began to speak different languages. The Holy Spirit was giving them the power to speak these languages."

Alternate Version: Acts 2:4 (NKJV)

"And they were all filled with the Holy Spirit and began to speak with other tongues, as the Spirit gave them utterance."

Love in Every Language

JUNE 4 2006

By Rev. Jim Miller

Scripture: Acts 2:1-4

Lesson Aim: The children will understand that after Jesus resurrected, God sent the Holy Spirit to empower believers.

Memory Verse: Acts 2:4

Preparation

○ TRANSLATION DICTIONARY FROM A FOREIGN LANGUAGE TO ENGLISH

Do any of you know any words from another language? Do you know how to say "hello" in Spanish? It's "Hola!" (pronounced oh'-la). **How about in French?** They say, "Bonjour!" (pronounced bone-shoo-wer'). In Japanese, they say, "Konnichiwa!" (pronounced ko-nee-chee-wa). **Can you imagine what it would be like if I were going to teach a whole lesson to you in another language that you didn't understand? What would that be like? How would you feel listening to it?**

What would it be like if I spoke a different language than you and tried to translate every word of my sermon into your language? Let's try! (Using the dictionary, pretend to look up and say one word at a time, very slowly, such as "Good . . . morning . . . how . . . are . . . you?) **How long do you think this is going to take?**

So here's a tricky question. **After Jesus lived His life here on earth, rose from the dead and went to Heaven, how do you think God would tell the whole world about Jesus, since there are so many different languages? If the people who followed Jesus all spoke the same language, how would they tell everyone else?**

I'll tell you the story of what happened from the Bible. All of Jesus' friends were together in a room. Suddenly, they heard a sound like wind coming out of heaven. They saw something that looked like fire coming down from the sky, but when it touched them, it didn't burn them; it just rested on them. Then they were all suddenly able to speak in different languages. Suddenly, they could talk to people from all over the world that would never have been able to understand them before. And you know what made them able to do that? The HOLY SPIRIT. The Holy Spirit is the part of God that helps us do what God asks us to do. So then they went out and told everyone all over the world about how much Jesus loved them.

We have the Holy Spirit here today, too. We may not see cool things like fire coming down from the sky, and we may not be able to suddenly speak in different languages, but that's because that's not what God needs us to do right now. What God needs for us to do right now is to believe in Him and to love each other. That's what the Holy Spirit is doing here. He is teaching us to believe and helping us to love. Think about what God wants you to do today. Quietly ask God to help you with the Holy Spirit.

Song Suggestions

"Believin'On" by Jana Alayra from *Believin' On* (Montjoy Music, 2002)
"Little Is Much" by Mary Rice Hopkins from *15 Singable Songs* (Big Steps 4 U, 1988)
"Faith Will Do" by Dean-O from *You Got It All* (FKO Music, Inc., 1997)
God's Power Songsheets published by CEF Press, P.O. Box 348, Warrenton, MO 63383

Craft for Younger and Older Children: Pinwheels

- ◯ SQUARES OF CONSTRUCTION PAPER ◯ ONE PUSH PIN
- ◯ ONE PENCIL PER CHILD

Let children decorate one side of the construction paper square. Make four cuts; from the corner almost to the center of the square.

Gather the four points to the center and push the push pin through. Attach to the pencil. Show children how to work the pinwheel by blowing on it.

Say: **We can't see the wind, but we know that it's there because we can see what the wind can do. We can't see God either but we can see what He does!**

Snack: Food from Other Lands

- ◯ TORTILLAS ◯ REFRIED BEANS ◯ CHEESE ◯ MICROWAVE OVEN

Show children how to make a burrito by layering small amount of refried beans and cheese on the tortilla. Microwave for 15 seconds.

Say: **In Mexico, people eat burritos and sometimes we eat them here, too! Many countries have foods that are favorites for us as well.**

Memory Verse: Acts 2:4 (ICB)

"They were all filled with the Holy Spirit, and they began to speak different languages. The Holy Spirit was giving them the power to speak these languages."

Alternate Version: Acts 2:4 (NKJV)
"And they were all filled with the Holy Spirit and began to speak with other tongues, as the Spirit gave them utterance."

Memory Verse Activity

Write a few words on each flame-shaped paper. Mix them up and let the children sort them out to form the verse. Say the verse together.

Prayer Focus

Dear God, we thank You for the power You give us through Your Holy Spirit. Help us to learn to rely on You for this power. Amen.

What Is a Missionary?

By Tina Houser

Scripture: Matthew 28:19

Lesson Aim: The children will realize that God wants ALL people to hear His message.

Memory Verse: Matthew 28:19

☞ **Bible Activity for Younger Children:** Why Be a Missionary?
○ PILLOWCASE   ○ EMPTY PRESCRIPTION BOTTLE   ○ TEXTBOOK   ○ TOOTHBRUSH
○ GARDENING TOOL   ○ HAMMER   ○ GLASSES   ○ COMPUTER DISK

Each one of these items you have collected represents a reason a missionary may go to serve in a foreign country. Children often think that missionaries only go to preach to the people. Missionaries also go to see how they can help the people.

Place all the items in the pillowcase. The children will pull an item out of the bag one at a time. As each item is pulled from the bag, talk about who might use it. Then, ask why that person might want to go to another country to work. Continue until all the items have been drawn from the pillowcase.

There are a variety of people who become missionaries. These people all use the talents they have to help others. They go to foreign countries to make the lives of the people there easier, healthier, and happier. Then, the people are more willing to listen to what the missionaries have to say about God.

☞ **Bible Activity for Older Children:** God Wants Everyone to Follow Him!
○ AN INFLATABLE GLOBE   ○ SOURCE OF MUSIC

The children will spread out in the area you have. Toss the inflated globe into the midst of the children and start the music playing. The children will send the globe throughout the room by batting it into the air, volleyball style. (If your group is large, use several globes at the same time.) When the music stops, the person with the globe in their possession will yell out, "God wants the people of _____ to follow Him!" That player will fill in the blank with the name of a country. If they cannot think of one on their own, the globe is in their hands and they can find the name of a country. There are plenty of countries in the world, so there's no need to repeat any country.

Enrichment Activity for Younger Children: Chinese Yummies
○ CHOPSTICKS   ○ COOKED RICE   ○ MARSHMALLOWS

Missionaries to China have to learn to eat different kinds of food than they are used to. They also have to learn a different way of eating that food. **What do you use to eat soup? What do you use to cut meat into small pieces? What do you use to eat green beans?** In China the people use chopsticks to eat rather than knives, forks, and spoons. They also eat from very low tables. If you have a table that does not adjust in height, then fold the legs under and set the table right against the floor or up on some concrete blocks. The children will enjoy eating in this different environment.

Give each child a set of chopsticks and a small portion of white rice. Allow them a little time to experiment with trying to pick up the rice with the chopsticks. Then, to make it easier, give each child a small cup of miniature marshmallows. These are much easier to handle. If the children cannot pick up the marshmallows correctly, they can always poke the end of the chopstick through the marshmallows.

It is important that missionaries learn as many of the customs of the country they are living in as possible. This helps them understand the people. It also sends a silent message to the people of that country that the missionary really wants to be there.

Enrichment Activity for Older Children: Albert Schweitzer
○ A PICTURE OF ALBERT SCHWEITZER (FROM THE INTERNET)

Show the picture of Albert Schweitzer to the children. **What do you think this man did?** After their guesses, then tell them he was a missionary. **What do you think he did as a missionary?**

Albert Schweitzer was a brilliant man who worked as a missionary in the early 1900s. He could do many things extremely well. He was a magnificent organ player and was paid a lot of money to give concerts. He was a great writer and wrote wonderful books about his belief in God. He was a university lecturer and at one time, was the head of a monastery where men trained for the ministry. But, Albert Schweitzer felt like God was calling him to be a doctor in Africa, so he went back to school and got his degree in medicine. Using the money he made from giving lectures and performing organ concerts, he went to Africa and built a hospital. It became too small and he built an even bigger hospital right next to the first one. Dr. Schweitzer became famous for the wonderful work he did with the sick people of Africa. He continued to do what God called him to do and helped the people who needed him until he died in 1965. Even after his death, the hospital he built is still being used today.

"So go and make followers of all people in the world. Baptize them in the name of the Father and the Son and the Holy Spirit."

Alternate Version: Matthew 28:19 (NKJV)
"Go therefore and make disciples of all the nations,
baptizing them in the name of the Father and of the Son and
of the Holy Spirit."

What Is a Missionary?

By Rev. Jim Miller

> **Scripture:** Matthew 28:19
>
> **Lesson Aim:** The children will realize that God wants ALL people to hear His message.
>
> **Memory Verse:** Matthew 28:19

Preparation

○ A LARGE, CONSTRUCTION PAPER CUT-OUT OF A THREE-LEAF CLOVER (& A REAL ONE) For added effect, wear something bright green.

What do you think of when you see one of these? (Show the children the clover, St. Patrick's Day or Lucky Charms® Cereal.)

Those are all good ideas. I know someone who lived a long time ago who thought of something different when he looked at a three-leaf clover. His name was St. Patrick. We even have a special day to remember him every year when people like to dress up in green, but most people don't know who he was. St. Patrick was a little boy who was made to do hard work in the country of Ireland, a long way from his home. However, when he became an adult, he decided he would help the Irish people by becoming a Christian preacher there. **Do you know what we call someone who goes to another country to be a preacher?** We call them a MISSIONARY.

The three-leaf clover was his favorite thing to use to explain what God is like. He would say, "God is the Father, the Son, and the Spirit, all wrapped into one." But people got a little bit confused by this. They would say, "How can God be three people and one God all at the same time?" And he would say, "Look at this clover! There are three leaves, but it's still one clover, and you can't have one without the other!" Do you know what we call that? That's called the TRINITY, which is just a fancy way of saying 'Three things in one.' God is the Trinity of Father, Son, and Spirit."

So now you know how St. Patrick used the three-leaf clover when he was a missionary. Now here's something interesting to think about. **What do you want to be when you grow up?** (Let them share answers.) I'll bet you'll be good at whatever you choose to do. But here's one that you might not have thought of. You could be a missionary, too, just like St. Patrick. If you wanted to, one day you could go to another country to help people out and to tell them about Jesus. Sometimes missionaries are doctors who help people who are sick, and sometimes they build houses for people who are poor. It's just a way of letting everyone in the world know how much God loves them.

That's what Jesus told us to do at the end of His life. He said, "Go all over the world, baptizing people in the name of the Father, the Son, and the Spirit, and teach them to obey everything I taught you." And we can do that even with our friends right here at home, just like a missionary!

Song Suggestions

Good News Songsheets published by CEF Press, P.O. Box 348, Warrenton, MO 63383
"He's the One" by Dean-O from *Soul Surfin'* (1999 FKO Music, 1999)
Happiness Is the Lord Songsheets by CEF Press, P.O. Box 348, Warrenton, MO 63383
"Faith Will Do" by Dean-O from *You Got It All* (1997 FKO Music, 1997)

Craft for Younger Children: Shamrock Hat
　　○ 3 GREEN PAPER HEARTS PER CHILD　○ STRIPS OF GREEN PAPER
(The strips should be 2 inches wide and long enough to go around the child's head.)

Make the head band for each child by stapling the ends of the strip to fit their heads. The children will make a shamrock by attaching the three hearts together. Attach the shamrock to the headband to form a hat. Say: **This hat will help you remember St. Francis!**

Craft for Older Children: Shamrock Pin
　　○ FLAT WOODEN HEART SHAPES　○ SPARKLE CHENILLE STEMS　○ GLUE
　　○ GREEN PAINT OR MARKERS　○ SAFETY PINS

Paint the wooden heart shapes with the dark green craft paint or green markers. Let dry. Glue 3 hearts together to form a clover. Glue pin on the back.

Say: **When we think of St. Patrick, we think of the clover shape. This will remind us of St. Patrick and how he was a missionary.**

Snack: Shamrocks
　　○ GREEN SNACKS OF ANY KIND

Enjoy!

"So go and make followers of all people in the world. Baptize
them in the name of the Father and the Son and the Holy Spirit."

Alternate Version: Matthew 28:19 (NKJV)
"Go therefore and make disciples of all the nations,
baptizing them in the name of the Father and of the Son and
of the Holy Spirit."

Memory Verse Activity

Cut shamrock shapes from construction paper. Write a few words from the verse on
each one. Make two sets.

Divide children into two teams. When you say "go" children will sort out the verse. The
first team to sort out the verse says the verse together.

Repeat until the children have learned the verse.

Prayer Focus

Dear God, thank You for all that You do for us, especially for giving us the great example of St. Patrick. Thank You for the trinity which You gave us, too!

What Does a Father Want?

By Tina Houser

Scripture: Proverbs 22:6

Lesson Aim: The children will appreciate the responsibil-
                 ity God has given fathers.

Memory Verse: Proverbs 22:6

☞ Bible Activity for Younger Children: Pass It Along
○ CONSTRUCTION PAPER   ○ STAPLER   ○ TAPE   ○ A SMALL BALL OF PLAY DOUGH

Each child needs to make a tube by rolling a piece of construction paper and stapling it together. You will want to secure the mid-section of the roll with some tape. (Paper towel rollers would be even better, if you have enough.) Make a small ball out of some play dough. The first person places the play dough ball in one end of their tube. The object is to roll it through that tube and into the next person's tube. Pass the play dough ball around the room (maybe even several times) by rolling it through the tubes.

The Bible tells us that parents are responsible for passing along God's teachings. They are to train their children in the way that God wants them to live. That's a big job, isn't it? **What kinds of things are parents supposed to teach their children? What have you learned from your parents?**

☞ Bible Activity for Older Children: Cross-Out
○ PAPER   ○ PENCILS   ○ CONTAINER

Ask the children to name things that parents teach their children. Put each one on the board with a number next to it. Try to come up with twelve different ones. Encourage the children to think of values, rather than physical training. (Parents teach their children to use manners, to respect adults, to wait their turn, to take care of their possessions, to be responsible, to know the Bible, to cherish their church family, to be a good friend, to love God.) Each child will choose five of the items that their parents have taught them and write the five corresponding numbers down on their papers. Each child should have a different set of numbers. Do not show these numbers to anyone else. (The numbers might be 4, 7, 9, 2, and 12. There is no special order to them.) The leader writes each number on a separate piece of paper and puts it in a container.

Draw out a number from the container and read it. Read what is written on the board next to that number, emphasizing that this is something a parent trains his or her child to do. Every child who has written that number on their paper can mark it off. Draw another number out and continue this process. The first person to mark all five of their numbers off their paper is the winner.

The Bible tells us that the things our parents teach us when we are children will stay with us the rest of our lives. That is a huge responsibility for parents!

Enrichment Activity for Younger Children: You're the Best, Dad!

- ○ PLAIN NAME TAG STICK-ON LABELS   ○ MARKERS   ○ QUART-SIZE MASON JARS
- ○ CIRCLES OF PLAIN OR PLAID MATERIAL   ○ RUBBER BANDS   ○ RIBBON

Before class, cut circles from the material that will cover the lid of the jar and leave a "skirt" around the edge. The circle needs to be quite a bit larger than the size of the lid. We're going to make a container for your father's favorite snack. (If there is not a father in the family structure, encourage the child to make a jar for one of the influential men in the church or for a coach.) Decorate the large label with markers. Include something like, "Greatest Dad" or "You're the Best!" Stick the label on the side of the jar. Center a circle of the material on the lid and secure it by placing a rubber band around the lid edge. Glue a piece of ribbon to cover the rubber band.

Think about what your dad likes to snack on the most. Is it peanuts? lemon drops? candy corn? chocolate candies? Before you give Dad the jar, fill it with the snack he is sure to love.

Enrichment Activity for Older Children: Celebrating Father's Day

The United States is one of the few countries in the world that sets aside a special day to honor fathers. A woman named Sonora Dodd (in 1909) came up with the idea of a special day for fathers while she was in church listening to a sermon on Mother's Day. Sonora's mother had died when she was giving birth to her sixth child, so Sonora's father was left to raise all six children by himself. When Sonora was grown, she realized that this was no easy task. She was sure that he had given up some of the things he would've liked to have done. All those years he had put his family first, and she wanted to find a way to recognize his sacrifice. In 1910, Sonora organized the first celebration to honor fathers in Spokane, Washington where she lived. It wasn't until President Nixon signed a law in 1972, 63 years later, that there was a special day set aside that would always be known as Father's Day. The law declared the third Sunday in June as the day we recognize our fathers each year.

Memory Verse: Proverbs 22:6 (ICB)

"Train a child how to live the right way.
Then even when he is old, he will still live that way."

Alternate Version: Proverbs 22:6 (NKJV)
"Train up a child in the way he should go,
And when he is old he will not depart from it."

What Does a Father Want?

By Rev. Jim Miller

Scripture: Proverbs 22:6, Galatians 4: 6–7

Lesson Aim: The children will appreciate the responsibility God has given fathers.

Memory Verse: Proverbs 22:6

Preparation

○ 3 POSSIBLE FATHER'S DAY GIFTS   ○ 1 POSSIBLE MOTHER'S DAY GIFT

Bring in at least three gifts that someone might give their father for Father's Day, such as a tie, cologne, or a football. Also bring one gift that would be more appropriate for Mother's Day, like flowers. These should be out of sight in a bag.

Say: **Today is Father's Day, and I can tell because the stores are all trying to get people to buy things for fathers. What kinds of things do people usually buy for Father's Day?** (Take answers.) Yup, you guys go to the same stores I do.

Well, Jesus called God His Father, too. He even has a special name for God, which was Abba. In Jesus' own language, that was the same as calling God "Daddy." Most people would have been surprised to hear Jesus use a name like "Daddy" to talk to God. I guess that just showed how close Jesus and God were.

Some people ask me, "Why do I need to be a Christian to know God? Can't I just be any old religion and believe anything I want to? Aren't they all just the same?" Well, looking at all of the Father's Day gifts in the stores made me think about that. Imagine this. Imagine a little boy named Matt wants to buy a gift for his father on Father's Day, but he can't think of what to get. So he goes and asks a friend, "What should I get?" Well, this friend happens to live with his mom, and he says, "Maybe your dad would like what I always get my mom for Mother's Day—flowers!" (Pull the flowers out of the bag.) Do you think this would make a good Father's Day gift? This time Matt goes to another friend and says, "What should I get my dad for Father's Day?" The second friend knows a little more about fathers and says, "I would get my dad a football!" (Pull out the football.) Is this a good Father's Day gift? It could be, but then Matt remembers that his Father got hurt playing football in college and has a really bad knee. So Matt thinks, "Hmm, that might be a good gift for some fathers, but not mine." Finally, Matt gets the idea of asking his very own sister. He says, "What should I get dad for Father's Day?" His sister remembers, "Dad said he wanted a new tie." (Pull out the tie.) Is that a good gift? It's an especially good gift if that's what Matt's dad asked for! And that's how Matt chose his gift.

Now what does all that have to do with Christianity? Well, if you want to find out how to be close to God, you probably don't want to ask someone who doesn't believe in God, or even someone who believes in a different kind of god. You probably want to ask someone who knows your God personally. And that's Jesus. Because, after all, Jesus is the one who said we could call God "Daddy." Think about what good gift you might give to God on Father's Day.

Song Suggestions

"A Dad Like You" by Mary Rice Hopkins from *Good Buddies* (Big Steps 4 U, 1994)

"*One Step At a Time Songsheets* published by CEF Press, P.O. Box 348, Warrenton, MO 63383

"Praise His Holy Name" by Norm Hewitt from *Ablaze with Praise!* (Revelation Generation Music, 2000)

"He Is God" by Jana Alayra from *Believin On* (Montjoy Music, 2002)

"Little Is Much" by Mary Rice Hopkins from *15 Singable Songs* (Big Steps 4 U, 1988)

Craft for Younger Children: Dad's Business Card Holder

Make the card holder described in the Older Children craft, but pre-glue the sticks and let children just decorate the card holder.

Craft for Older Children: Dad's Business Card Holder
○ CRAFT STICKS

Lay out a piece of wax paper or recycle a plastic bag to protect your work surface. Lay three craft sticks flat next to each other side to side. Glue the three sticks together to make the front section of the card holder. To make the base of the business card holder, lay two craft sticks flat next to each other and glue together as you did for the front section. For the back: lay four craft sticks flat next to each other side to side, and also glue together. For the sides: cut 2 1/2 inches off of four craft sticks (two for each side). Lay two long edges together, side to side and glue together. Repeat with other two ends for the other side of the card holder. Glue the front to the base at a right angle. Glue the back to the base also at a right angle. Glue the right and left sides to the base, front, and back of the card holder. Let dry and decorate as you wish!

Snack: Chips and Dips
○ SOUR CREAM AND DIP MIX   ○ CHIPS OR VEGGIES

Show children how to make the dip by mixing the sour cream and mix. Give each child a little dip and chips or veggies. Say: **This is a great Father's Day snack to make and you can make it for your dad when you get home. Dads often like to eat chips and dip when they watch sports on TV. Does your dad like to do that?**

"Train a child how to live the right way.
Then even when he is old, he will still live that way."

Alternate Version: Proverbs 22:6 (NKJV)
"Train up a child in the way he should go,
And when he is old he will not depart from it."

📖 Memory Verse Activity

Draw a simple train shape on the board, with a few words from the verse in each car. Say the verse together.

Say: **We can remember to "train" a child by looking at this "train", but they are not really the same kind of train are they?** No! This train will help us remember that when our parents tell us to do something they are "training" us.

🙏 Prayer Focus

Dear God, we thank You that You are our wonderful Heavenly Father! We also thank You for our fathers that are here on earth. Amen.

Who Is Your Neighbor?

By Tina Houser

Scripture: 1 John 3:18

Lesson Aim: The children will be able to identify preju-
               dice and recognize it is not part of God's
               plan.

Memory Verse: 1 John 3:18

☞ **Bible Activity for Younger Children:** Many, Many Colors!
○ LARGE PIECE OF PAPER FOR EACH CHILD   ○ CRAYONS

Instruct the children to draw a line down the center of their papers. Draw a picture of a scene (like a seashore, a valley, an orchard) on one side of the paper using only one color of crayon—any color you want. On the other side of the paper draw the same picture only this time you can use as many colors as you like.

When the pictures are completed, ask some debriefing questions. **Which of your two pictures do you like the most? Which side is most interesting? Which was more fun for you to draw? Can you imagine our world if everything was one color?** Choose one color and think about the entire world being in that color. The trees, the ocean, the animals, and all the people would be the same color. How boring! God enjoyed creating us all to be different, so shouldn't we enjoy being with one another?

☞ **Bible Activity for Older Children:** Xs and Os
○ PRETTY DECORATED CUPCAKES   ○ CRACKERS   ○ SLIPS OF PAPER
○ CONTAINER   ○ SCRAP PAPER   ○ PENCILS

Before class, mark enough slips of paper with an *X* for half of the group. Mark enough slips of paper with an *O* for the other half of the group. Fold the slips of paper and place them in a container.

Each child will draw out a slip of paper. If they had an *X* on their paper, then they get a cupcake for their snack. If they had an *O* on their paper, they get one small cracker for their snack. While the children are eating their snacks, they can play tic-tac-toe with a partner, but only a partner who is eating the same kind of snack. (The children who got the crackers will be upset with you, but endure.)

Ask the children who got the crackers how they felt about their snacks. **What was the reason for not getting a cupcake? If you got a cupcake for a snack, how did you feel** when the others had only a cracker? Did it bother you, or were you just glad that you had pulled an X out of the container? What was unfair about the way we played tic-tac-toe?

This was a demonstration of prejudice. **Can someone give me a definition of prejudice?** We show prejudice in many different situations. It was wrong to treat part of the class differently just because they had a slip of paper with an O on it. We do the same thing when we treat others differently because their skin is a different color or because they have an accent when they speak or because they learn slower than we do. When you played tic-tac-toe, you could only play with people who were just like you, because of the piece of paper they chose. There was no good reason that you shouldn't have been able to play tic-tac-toe with anyone here. **How is that like the way we treat people who are different from us?**

Now, before the children who got the crackers want to duct tape you to a chair, give the O kids a cupcake. Thank them for being so patient and for being the object of the lesson on prejudice.

Enrichment Activity for Younger Children: Just Lean Back!

Position all the children in a large circle. With arms outstretched they should just be able to join hands with the person next to them. This is going to make a very large circle. (8-12 participants is an excellent size.) Everyone needs to put their feet together and be determined to keep their feet from moving. Join hands with the people on both sides of you. When the leader gives the signal, everyone leans back very gently and slowly. If done correctly, the participants will be supporting one another and all be leaning back further than they could do alone.

God created all kinds of people. He also created us to get along with one another and to work together to make this world what He created it to be. That takes understanding one another. God wants us to join together. He wants us to depend on one another. He wants us to respect one another and make the world a better place, because we were able to work together. One person letting go or not working with the group would have had an effect on the success of this activity. It's a real cool circle when we all do the right thing. **How does this special circle help you to understand how the many races of the world should relate to one another?**

Enrichment Activity for Older Children: Stretch Yourself
   O LARGE SUPPLY OF RUBBER BANDS

Create groups of three children. Give each group a supply of rubber bands. Instruct them to tie the rubber bands together to make one long rope of rubber bands. You can tie rubber bands together easily by following these simple steps:
   • Lay the end of one rubber band over the end of another rubber band. This should make a little circle where they overlap.

- Take the end of either of the rubber bands and push it through that circle.
- Pull the free ends of both rubber bands to form a knot.

Set a timer and give the groups a certain amount of time to complete their rubber band chains. When the timer goes off, challenge the groups to see how long they can stretch their chains.

When we think about how we can better get along with people who are different from us, there is one important thing we have to keep in mind. We may have to stretch ourselves, a little or a lot. Most of the time conflicts arise, because we don't understand one another. We need to stretch our thinking to help us understand how the other person is thinking. If we refuse to try to understand the other person, it becomes a place for hard feelings to get a start.

Memory Verse: 1 John 3:18 (ICB)

"My children, our love should not be only words and talk. Our love must be true love. And we should show that love by what we do."

Alternate Version: 1 John 3:18 (NKJV)
"My little children, let us not love in word or in tongue, but in deed and in truth."

Who Is Your Neighbor?

By Vicki Wiley

Scripture: 1 John 3:18

Lesson Aim: The children will be able to identify prejudice and recognize it is not part of God's plan.

Memory Verse: 1 John 3:18

Preparation
○ BOTTLE OF OLIVE OIL   ○ BOTTLE OF VINEGAR
○ BANDAGES & OTHER FIRST AID SUPPLIES

Who is your neighbor? Did you know that someone asked Jesus that question once? They did and do you know what He said? He answered by telling a story. I am going to tell you that story now; it's about a man who helped someone. I bet you have already heard this story! It's about a man that we call "the Good Samaritan." **Who knows this story?** (The children can tell what they know.)

Yes! Jesus told a story about a man that was a Samaritan. That meant that he lived in a place called Samaria. The Jewish people did not like the people that lived in Samaria. They did not think of each other as neighbors.

Even though the Jews did not like the Samaritans, this Samaritan man saw a Jewish man who had been beaten. He took his first aid kit out. (Show the oil and vinegar.) Oh, yes! Back in Bible times this was what first aid was like! Oil soothed the injury and vinegar killed the germs. (Let the children smell the vinegar and put small drops of the oil on their hands.)

But there is another part of the story, too. Before the Samaritan man came by, other people came by and those people were Jews. Even though they were Jews and the man that was hurt was a Jew, they didn't help him. Not only were they Jews, but the first person that walked by and didn't help him was a priest, like a pastor! The priest didn't help him. The next person that walked by was a priest's helper, and he didn't help him, either.

Then the Samaritan came by. Well, Samaritans and Jews did not get along very well—they had prejudice and didn't like each other very much, but the Samaritan man didn't care about that. He helped the Jew anyway.

Who was the neighbor—the priest who was a Jew just like the injured man, or the Samaritan who the Jews didn't like? You're right! The Samaritan was the one that acted like a neighbor, just like Jesus wants us to act!

Song Suggestions

"Turn It Over" by Dean-O from *God City* (BibleBeat Music, 2001)
Faith Is Just Believing Songsheets published by CEF Press, P.O. Box 348, Warrenton, MO 63383
"It's Gonna Rock!" by Dean-O from *God City* (BibleBeat Music, 2001)
"Little Is Much" by Mary Rice Hopkins from *15 Singable Songs* (Big Steps 4 U, 1988)
"Less of Me" by Mister Bill from *When I Grow Up* (Mister Bill Music, 1997)

Craft for Younger Children: Mini First Aid Kit
   ○ FILM CONTAINER WITH HOLES IN THE LID   ○ YARN   ○ BANDAGE
   ○ ANTISEPTIC WIPE   ○ SAFETY PIN   ○ RED NAIL POLISH

Put holes in the top of a film container, and attach a long piece of yarn to go around the neck. Feed one end of the yarn through the hole; thread that end through a pony bead; and then push the end of the yarn back through the hole. Tie the yarn into a knot so it is snug against the film container lid. Tie another knot in the yarn so you can wear it around the neck.

Fill the film container with supplies and paint a red cross on the front with the nail polish. Explain how to use each supply.

Craft for Older Children: First Aid Kit
   ○ RED PLASTIC LUNCH BOX OR ANY SHOE BOX WITH RED CROSS ON FRONT
   ○ SUPPLIES

Purchase supplies as your budget permits to put inside such as: a box of assorted sizes of adhesive bandages, package of sterile gauze, sterile non-stick bandages, anti-biotic ointment, elastic bandage wrap, adhesive tape, plastic gloves, emergency phone numbers (doctor, hospital, and poison control).

Show the children how to decorate their containers with a red cross and explain how to use each supply as you distribute them to put in their kits. Say: **It's always good to be prepared for any injury that you might have. The man in our story really helped someone, because he was prepared.**

Snack: Cupcakes
   ○ CUPCAKES FROM BIBLE ACTIVITY
Let children decorate them as they wish.

Memory Verse: 1 John 3:18 (ICB)

"My children, our love should not be only words and talk. Our love must be true love. And we should show that love by what we do."

Alternate Version: 1 John 3:18 (NKJV)
"My little children, let us not love in word or in tongue, but in deed and in truth."

Memory Verse Activity
○ WHITE BOARD   ○ MARKERS

Write the verse on the board. As children say the verse together, erase one or more words. Continue saying the verse until all the words are erased.

Prayer Focus

Dear God, thank You for showing us how to love everyone. Please help me as I try to be a good neighbor. Amen.

What's My Culture?

By Tina Houser

Scripture: Colossians 3:11

Lesson Aim: The children will realize that God's eyes only see the hearts of the people He loves.

Memory Verse: Colossians 3:11

☞ **Bible Activity for Younger Children:** Eggs-actly!

○ A BOWL   ○ A BROWN EGG   ○ A WHITE EGG

How are all people alike? How are people different from one another? Show the children the brown egg and the white egg. Look at them closely and tell me how they are alike and different by just looking at them this way. Break both eggs into the bowl, discard the shells, and then let the children look into the bowl. **Can you tell which egg came from which shell?**

The eggs were different colors on the outside, but on the inside they were the same. We can use either egg to add to our cookie batter and we can use both eggs when we're scrambling up some breakfast. The eggs are the same on the inside and it doesn't matter what they were like on the outside. Our hearts are not different colors and they don't speak in different languages. God hears our hearts speak to Him in His language, and that's the language of love.

☞ **Bible Activity for Older Children:** Pictograph Stories

○ BLACK PERMANENT MARKERS   ○ TERRA COTTA CLAY POT FOR EACH CHILD   ○ PAPER

Each culture offers us ways to learn about ourselves and about the people of that culture. Brainstorm some ways we learn about a different culture. (We learn through their music, their art, their beliefs, their family structure, their crops, their homes.) This unusual activity is going to help us learn more about the Native American Indians. **Does anyone know what a pictograph is?** A pictograph is a set of pictures that tell a story. Native American Indians painted these pictographs on their clay pots to tell a story about something that was happening within the tribe or relay a message/greeting. There are actually pictograph dictionaries, but we're going to design our own pictographs today.

Before you draw your pictograph on your clay pot of something that has happened to you, sketch it out on a piece of paper. That will keep you from making mistakes on the pot. When you are ready with your story, draw it on the sides of the clay pot with a permanent marker. As the children finish they can tell their stories to the others.

Even though the Native Americans may do things differently than you would, the Bible tells us that in God's sight there is no difference between people. God does not see skin color; He does not hear our accents. God doesn't love the rich person more than the poor. He doesn't love the genius more than the person with average intelligence. It makes me feel good to know that God loves me just the same as He loves everyone else. I need to try to love everyone the same, also.

Enrichment Activity for Younger Children: Clothing of India
○ SEVERAL VERY LONG PIECES OF LIGHTWEIGHT MATERIAL   ○ WORLD MAP

Show the children where India is on a world map. One of the ways we know someone is from India is by their very unique clothing. They use very long pieces of material (called a sari) and drape it around their bodies to make their clothes. Depending on the way the material is draped, a woman can make what looks like a long dress or she can make something similar to pants. The men, also, use long scarves to make something to wear on their heads called a turban. The size, shape, and the color of the turban may tell other people how important the man is or what part of the country he is from. **Would you like to wrap your head in a turban?** Give the children time to experiment with making their own turbans from the material you have provided. You may want to take pictures to show parents.

Does God love people who are from India? Does He love them more or less than He loves you and me? God put people in different parts of the world and they have used the creativity God gave them to make a life for themselves in that special place. Some people learn how to live in the desert; others learn to live by the seashore. People who live in the icey northern lands need to wear heavy clothes and keep their hands, feet, and heads covered warmly. Because India is a warm place, the people have designed their clothing so the air will move through it and keep them cool.

In God's eyes we are all His special creation and He loves us all! Jesus came for all of us.

Enrichment Activity for Older Children: Food Clues

Understanding some unique characteristics of the people in the Bible helps us understand why they did certain things and what influenced their decisions. Let's look at some of the foods mentioned in the Bible and see what kind of clues they give us to help us understand more about the Scriptures.

Although some people lived out in the desert, many people lived close to the seas. **What foods would the people probably eat because they were near the seas? What do we know about who made their living getting food for the people from the Sea of Galilee?**

It was the custom for wealthy farmers to leave some grain in the field when they were harvesting, so the poor could come and pick it up (gleaning). **Do you remember a story that talked about a woman who gleaned grain to keep her and her mother-in-law fed?** There were a lot of olive trees in that area, which gave olives to eat, but also something else that is very important. The olives can be squeezed and oil comes out. This oil had many different uses. **Can you think of any Bible stories that mention oil?** The oil could be used to fuel lamps. It could also be used to put on wounds, like the Good Samaritan did for the wounded man, or like the shepherds did for the wounds the sheep might have. When you hear of someone being anointed, it was olive oil that was being used for the anointing.

Foods give us clues about a particular culture. It's just another way God made people so interesting!

Memory Verse: Colossians 3:11 (ICB)

"In the new life there is no difference between Greeks and Jews ... But Christ is in all believers. And Christ is all that is important."

Alternate Version: Colossians 3:11 (NKJV)
"Where there is neither Greek nor Jew . . ., but Christ is all and in all."

What's My Culture?

By Vicki Wiley

> **Scripture:** Colossians 3:11
>
> **Lesson Aim:** The children will realize that God's eyes only see the hearts of the people He loves.
>
> **Memory Verse:** Colossians 3:11

Preparation

O ITEMS FROM DIFFERENT CULTURES (HATS, ROBES OR OTHER CLOTHING, MISC. ITEMS) (whatever you can find that defines another culture besides your own)

Show items one at a time. As you show the items, ask the children to guess what country it might be from. **What do you do with it? How is it different from what we wear (use, cook with, eat, etc.)?**

In Bible times, there were two cultures that were very different; the Jews and the Greeks. The Jews worshiped God and the Greeks worshiped idols. They had different languages and alphabets. They wore different clothes.

When Paul was teaching the people about Jesus, he said that when you become a Christian there is no difference between people. All Christians are alike in God's eyes no matter what culture they are.

Show items again and with each one say: In Mexico the people are called Mexicans. But when they become Christians they are called "Christians"! We call the people in China, Chinese. But when they become Christians we call them _____! (keep showing items and repeating this scenario until all items are brought up again) No matter what culture you are, God loves you and thinks you are special!

Song Suggestions

"Generation Filled with Righteousness" by Cindy Rethmeier from *I Want To Be Like Jesus* (Mercy Vineyard 1995)
"God Bless America" Traditional
"Fingerprints" by Mary Rice Hopkins from *Juggling Mom* (Big Steps 4 U 1999)
"Jesus Loves the Little Children" Traditional

Craft for Younger Children: Culture Collage

○ DIFFERENT COLORS OF CONSTRUCTION PAPER TORN INTO SMALL PIECES
○ ONE LARGE SHEET OF PAPER FOR EACH CHILD   ○ PASTE OR GLUE STICKS

Show children how to make a collage by pasting the different colors of torn paper onto the backing paper. Make collage as they wish.

These colors represent different kinds of people. God loves all kinds of people and we can, too! This collage will help us remember that!

Craft for Older Children: Different Culture Wreath

○ PEOPLE SHAPES CUT FROM MULTI-ETHNIC CONSTRUCTION PAPER COLORS
○ WREATH SHAPES CUT FROM PAPER PLATES   ○ MULTI-NATIONAL FLAGS
○ STICKERS OR OTHER ITEMS THAT REPRESENT OTHER CULTURES

Cut circles from the center of the paper plates and discarding them. Show the children how to paste people shapes onto the wreath. The children will then decorate the people by adding fabrics for clothes, drawing hair and faces. Add other details as you wish to show different cultures with the wreath.

God loves everyone—God loves you no matter what your culture is! Everyone is special in God's sight!

Snack: What's the Difference?

○ GINGERBREAD MAN COOKIE CUTTER   ○ WHEAT AND WHITE BREAD
○ BROWN AND WHITE SUGAR   ○ CINNAMON   ○ SOFT MARGARINE

Use a gingerbread man cookie cutter to cut into a slice of bread. Spread some soft margarine on the bread man. Sprinkle with white sugar or brown sugar and top with cinnamon.

Ask: **What is the difference between the gingermen we just made?** (some are white, some are brown) People are like that too; some of us have white skin and others are browner. God loves everyone, no matter what color our skin is just like we love all these gingerbread men no matter what color they are!!

Memory Verse: Colossians 3:11 (ICB)

"In the new life there is no difference between Greeks and Jews . . . But Christ is in all believers. And Christ is all that is important."

Alternate Version: Colossians 3:11 (NKJV)
"Where there is neither Greek nor Jew . . ., but Christ is all and in all."

Memory Verse Activity

Divide children into two groups. Write the verse on the board. Tell one group that they are the "Greeks" and the other group that they are the "Jews." The children will decide how they want to say the verse together adding motions or accents. Each group can perform their version of the verse.

Prayer Focus

Dear God, thank You that You love us all so much! Help us to love all people like You do.

Ordinances

By Tina Houser

Scripture: Luke 22:19–20

Lesson Aim: The children will understand that communion is a time when we reflect on what Jesus did for us personally.

Memory Verse: Luke 22:19b

☞ Bible Activity for Younger Children: Show and Tell
○ SOUVENIRS

You will need to contact the children to bring a souvenir that they have from a family vacation or school trip. If they don't have one from their personal experience, encourage them to get one from a grandparent.

Give each child the opportunity to share with the others about the souvenir he or she has brought with them. Tell where it is from, when you went to this place, and what the souvenir reminds you of. You will want to start the sharing time yourself to demonstrate how long the child has to talk or you might get some pretty long stories!

Jesus gave us some things to help us remember our experience in accepting Him as our Savior. Communion is one of those ways He gave us to remember. When we eat the bread it should remind us of Jesus' body and that He died on the cross for us. When we drink the grape juice we should think about the sacrifice that He made for us.

☞ Bible Activity for Older Children: Remembering Challenge
○ 12 THINGS (OR MORE) ASSOCIATED WITH A BIRTHDAY PARTY ○ TRAY
○ PILLOWCASE ○ PAPER ○ PENCILS

Suggested items: invitation, birthday hat, noisemaker, candles, picture at the party, paper plate, crepe paper, balloons, small gift, gift bag, wrapping paper, bow, birthday card, pizza tokens.

Place all the items you have accumulated on a tray and cover it with the pillowcase. Do not tell the children that all of the items have to do with a birthday party. Give them 30 seconds—only 30 seconds—to look at the items. Then, cover the tray once again with the pillowcase. The children will write down as many items as they can remember.

What did all of these things remind you of? A birthday party, of course. When you see all of these things together, you can't help but think of a birthday party. Jesus knew that sometimes we need to be able to see something or to be able to do something so we can better remember an experience we had. Jesus had something very special He wanted His followers to be reminded of all the time and that was the way He died for each one of us. Jesus told His disciples that every time they drank the juice of the grape that they should be reminded that He gave His blood as their sacrifice. He also told them that every time they ate bread to be reminded that it was His body that died for them. The grape juice and the bread serve as our reminder of the wonderful love that Jesus showed us by taking our punishment and being our sacrifice.

Enrichment Activity for Younger Children: Juice from Grapes
○ GRAPES   ○ SOUPS BOWLS   ○ SMALL GLASSES

In Bible times the people used a press to make juice from grapes. The vat where they would put the grapes was like a huge stone bowl. Then, they would roll a large stone around in the vat to crush the grapes. The juice would come out of the grape skins. On the side of the vat toward the bottom would be a hole where the juice could drain out into another container.

Give each child a soup bowl with some grapes in it and a small glass. (You may want to slice the grapes in half to prevent excessive squirting.) Using the bottom of the glass, press down on the grapes until the juice comes out. Keep pressing. In Bible times they would not need to pour the juice from the vat, because of the hole in the side, but we don't want to make a hole in our bowls. Pour the juice out of the bowl and the children can taste the grape juice they made.

Enrichment Activity for Older Children: Candy Bar Mix Up
○ HEAVY WEIGHT PAPER   ○ ASSORTMENT OF ANY SIZE CANDY BARS
(Almond Joy®, Riesens®, Good 'n Plenty®, Reese's Cup®, Mounds®, Hugs®, Mint®, Starbursts®, Smarties®)

When we take communion it should be a time to think about how precious our relationship with the Lord Jesus is. Accepting what Jesus did on the cross and in His resurrection is the most important thing we could possibly do in our lives. Communion is a time to remember how "sweet" that experience was to us and continues to be each and every day.

Lay the candy bars out on the table where the kids can see the different names. Using these "sweet" treats as inspiration, come up with a statement about Jesus' sacrifice. Example: Having Jesus in my life brings me (Almond "JOY"). Where the children insert the word from the candy bar that gave them their inspiration, leave a space where they can tape the candy bar to their paper.

"'This bread is my body that I am giving for you. Do this to remember me.'"

Alternate Version: Luke 22:19b (NKJV)
"'This is My body which is given for you; do this in remembrance of Me.'"

Remembering

By Tina Houser

Scripture: Luke 22:19–20

Lesson Aim: The children will understand that communion is a time when we reflect on what Jesus did for us personally.

Memory Verse: Luke 22:19b

Preparation

- ○ 12 THINGS (OR MORE) ASSOCIATED WITH A BIRTHDAY PARTY ○ TRAY
- ○ PILLOWCASE ○ PAPER ○ PENCILS ○ ITEMS USED IN COMMUNION

Suggested party items: invitation, birthday hat, noisemaker, candles, picture at the party, paper plate, crepe paper, balloons, small gift, gift bag, wrapping paper, bow, birthday card, pizza tokens.

Place all the items you have accumulated on a tray and cover it with the pillowcase. Do not tell the children that all of the items have to do with a birthday party. Give them 30 seconds—only 30 seconds—to look at the items. Then, cover the tray once again with the pillowcase. The children will write down as many items as they can remember.

What did all of these things remind you of? A birthday party, of course. When you see all of these things together, you can't help but think of a birthday party. Jesus knew that sometimes we need to be able to see something or to be able to do something so we can better remember an experience we had. Jesus had that something very special He wanted His followers to be reminded of all the time and that was the way He died for each one of us.

(show communion items) Jesus told His disciples that every time they drank the juice of the grape that they should be reminded that He gave His blood as our sacrifice. He also told them that every time they ate bread to be reminded that it was His body that died for them. The grape juice and the bread serve as our reminder of the wonderful love that Jesus showed us by taking our punishment and being our sacrifice.

"Purest of Gold" by Kurt Johnson, a.k.a. MrJ from *Pure Gold* (Mr. J Music, 1995)

"Believe His Promises" by Dean-O from *Soul Surfin'* (FKO Music, Inc. 1999)

"Do Not Fear" by John J.D. Modica from *Ablaze with Praise* (Revelation Generation Music, 2000)

What a Mighty God We Serve Songsheets published by CEF Press, P.O. Box 348, Warrenton, MO 63383

Craft for Younger Children: Memory Poster

○ POSTER BOARD FOR EACH CHILD (YOU MAY CUT LARGE ONES INTO FOURTHS)

What is the best time you have ever had? The children can share their experiences. Now draw a picture of that very special time. This poster will help you remember that very special time!

Craft for Older Children: Memory Box

○ PAPER MACHE BOX FOR EACH CHILD   ○ MARKERS

Each child will decorate their own memory box. **What will you put inside your memory box? What kinds of things are special enough to go inside?**

You can remember things and people by looking inside your memory box. Everyone wants to be remembered! Jesus wanted to be remembered too and thought of a very special way for us to do that—it's called "communion."

Snack: Memory Foods

○ HOLIDAY FOODS (WHATEVER IS AVAILABLE)

What do these foods remind you of? Yes, there are different foods that remind us of different holidays; turkey for Thanksgiving, birthday cakes for birthdays, etc. The children can discuss their associations with each food.

What do these foods remind you of? As you give out the snack, remind the children that Jesus asked us to remember Him with some foods too; bread and wine (or grape juice).

"'This bread is my body that I am giving for you. Do this to remember me.'"

Alternate Version: Luke 22:19b (NKJV)
"'This is My body which is given for you; do this in remembrance of Me.'"

📖 Memory Verse Activity
O ONE POSTER BOARD WITH VERSE WRITTEN ON IT

Cut apart in puzzle shapes so that there will be one piece for each child. Jesus wanted us to remember Him. One of the ways that we can do that is to remember this verse. Say the verse as each child hands you his piece. Say the verse all together.

🙏 Prayer Focus

Dear God thank You for the special way You gave us to remember Jesus, Your Son. Help us to always remember Him that way. Amen.

Telling Others

By Tina Houser

> **Scripture:** Psalm 119:105
>
> **Lesson Aim:** The children will learn how to share the gospel with other children.
>
> **Memory Verse:** Mark 1:17

☞ **Bible Activity for Younger Children:** Fishers of Men
   ○ DOWEL ROD   ○ CONSTRUCTION PAPER FISH (AT LEAST 3 FOR EACH CHILD)
   ○ PAPER CLIPS   ○ STRING   ○ MAGNET

Before class: Attach a paper clip to each of the construction paper fish. Make a fishing pole with the dowel rod. Tie a string from one end of the dowel rod to a magnet.

Say the memory verse, Mark 1:17, for the children. Jesus was asking Simon Peter and Andrew to follow Him. Jesus also called other men to follow Him and become His disciples. **Were those men the only people Jesus wanted to follow Him? Who else does Jesus want to follow Him?**

Write each child's name on one of the construction paper fish. Then, ask each child to name two of their friends or family members. Write each of those names on a paper fish. Lay the fish on the floor. The children will take turns retrieving a fish with their magnet fishing poles. When they remove the fish from the magnetic fishing line they will say, "Jesus wants _____ to follow Him." Insert the name on the fish in the blank.

Jesus wants all of us to follow Him and become fishers of men. He wants us to help our family and friends to also believe in Him.

☞ **Bible Activity for Older Children:** 15 Times
   ○ BALLOON   ○ CD OF THE SONG "15" BY SCOTT KRIPPAYNE

People do not usually give their hearts to Jesus the first time they hear about His offer of forgiveness. Most people have to hear about Jesus over and over again. You may be one of the people who talks to them along the way.

Listen to the song by Scott Krippayne called "15." This song says that a person may need to hear about Jesus 15 times before they believe in Him. You may be the third person to tell them, or the eleventh person, or you might be the fifteenth person. If you are, you get to celebrate with them when they ask Jesus into their heart. Some people accept Jesus the very first time they are told about Him. For other people, it takes many, many times hearing and watching the believers around him or her.

Draw a face on the balloon. This balloon represents someone who needs to hear about Jesus. Bat the balloon around the room. Each time the balloon is tapped, everyone will count. The person who is the fifteenth person to tap the balloon will grab the balloon and yell, "Another one became a believer!"

Enrichment Activity for Younger Children: Stand out!
○ 2 HALF-CUPS OF SALT   ○ 1 TBSP. WHITE SUGAR   ○ 1 TBSP. COLORED SUGAR
○ 2 bowls

Pour a half-cup of salt into a bowl. The salt represents the people we know and come in contact with each day. Let one of the children add one tablespoon of white sugar to the salt. Mix thoroughly. The sugar represents the person who knows Jesus, but doesn't want to stand out and be different from his friends. **Can you tell where the sugar is in the mixture?** It just blends in to the salt that is around it.

Now, take the other half-cup of salt. Add a tablespoon of colored sugar to this salt. Mix thoroughly. This sugar represents the person who knows Jesus, and acts differently from the people around him. When we believe in Jesus it should show in the way we act and the things we say. **Can you tell where the sugar is in this bowl?** Even though this person is around friends and family who may not believe in Jesus, they can still be different.

Ask the children to name ways that they can "stand out" in the world. **What kinds of things can you say that will help other people know that you are a follower of Jesus Christ? How do you act that is different from the people around you? Do you use the same words others do when they get upset? Do you watch the same movies that other kids watch? Do you deal with bullies the same way others do?**

Enrichment Activity for Older Children: Roots and Seedlings
○ A PICTURE OF AN ASPEN TREE
(look under Aspen Grove, CO or Squaw Valley on the Internet)

Did you know there is a tree that can cover as much as 100 acres? The world's largest living organism is an Aspen Grove in Colorado. Its interconnected roots cover several square miles. The aspen tree is a very interesting tree because of its unusual root system. A little seedling can send its roots out as far as 100 feet in all directions. From these roots grow up other little seedlings. As they grow they look like separate trees, but they're all connected by the same roots. That makes them one tree. One little seedling has enormous potential to become the start of a huge living organism called an aspen tree. The seedling never stops sending out roots, full of potential and possibilities.

What can we learn from the aspen tree? How can we be like the aspen tree when we tell others about Jesus? Just like the aspen seedling never stops sending out roots, we need to keep telling others about Jesus.

There are lots of possibilities of people who will accept Him. The aspen seedling sends out new roots in all directions. We need to tell all the people we come in contact with—in all directions. That would mean people at home, friends and teachers at school, our teammates that we compete with, relatives that come to visit, and people we meet in our community. All the people who follow Jesus are connected and are one large living organism of believers. The aspen tree is an unusual tree and Christians are different, also.

Memory Verse: Mark 1:17 (ICB)

"Jesus said to them, 'Come and follow me. I will make you fishermen for men.' "

Alternate Version: Mark 1:17 (NKJV)

"Then Jesus said to them, 'Come after Me, and I will make you become fishers of men.' "

Telling Others

By Vicki Wiley

Scripture:	Psalm 119:105
Lesson Aim:	The children will learn how to share the gospel with other children.
Memory Verse:	Mark 1:17

Preparation

○ CHENILLE STEMS ○ BEADS: GOLD, BLACK, RED, CLEAR, GREEN

Today we are going to learn the very best part of the Bible, the Salvation message. This bracelet will help you remember what we talk about. When you know this lesson, you can lead other children to Christ! When we lead other children to Christ it is called "Evangelism."

Give out the chenille stems and GOLD beads (one each). Each child will put the gold bead on the chenille stem. **What does this gold remind you of?** (money, jewelry) Those things are very valuable and special. But today the gold is going to represent Heaven. The Bible tells us that in Heaven, the streets are made of gold. God tells us many other things about His home. No one is ever sick there. No one ever dies. There is no night there. Heaven is a very special place. There is one thing that can never be in Heaven. **Does anyone know what that is?** (sin)

Give out the BLACK beads. **Do you know what sin is?** The black bead stands for sin. Sin is anything we think, do or say that is wrong and that does not please God. God cannot live with anything sinful, but it is impossible for us not to sin. Because God wants us to live in Heaven and because we sin, God had to think of another plan for us.

Give out the RED beads. God loved us so much and wanted us to be in Heaven with Him. So God sent His Son, Jesus Christ to the world. Jesus lived on earth just like we do, but Jesus never sinned. The Bible tells us that Jesus died on the cross, because He was being punished, even though He did nothing wrong. Instead of dying for His sin, He died for our sin—all the sin we already did and all the sin we will do in our lives. The red bead stands for the blood of Jesus.

Give out the CLEAR beads. God wants to forgive your sin and make it so they never happened at all. No matter how good you are, you still will sin. There is nothing you can do to take away your sin—nothing except one very special thing. You can "receive" Jesus. **How do you do that?** You tell Jesus that you know that you are a sinner. You tell

Jesus that you believe in Him and that you want Him to be your Savior. That's it. That's all you have to do. Then, when God looks at you, He doesn't see the sin, He only sees the "clear" part of you, that has no sin at all. The clear bead will stand for a pure heart.

Give out the GREEN beads. The color green reminds me of things that are growing, like trees, plants, and grass. When you are a Christian and have received Christ, you begin to grow, too. You learn more and more about Jesus and that means that you are growing in Christ! **Would anyone like to receive Jesus right now?** We are going to pray and when we pray let's all bow our heads. I will tell you what to pray and if you would like to receive Jesus, you can pray along with me, OK?

Dear Jesus:
I know that I am a sinner. But I would like to receive You right now so that You can be the Lord of my life. I love You and I want to follow You. Please forgive me for my sin and come into my life. Thank You, God.
Amen

Let's review what the beads mean and then let's twist the wire to make a bracelet for us to remember this lesson.

Song Suggestions

"G-Mail!" by Dean-O from *Soul Surfin'* (FKO Music, Inc., 1999)
"This Is Love" by Dean-O from *God City* (BibleBeat Music, 2001)
"Walk Like Jesus" by Mary Rice Hopkins *15 Singable Songs* (Big Steps 4 U, 1988)
Children All Around The World Songsheets published by CEF Press, P.O. Box 348, Warrenton, MO 63383

Craft for All Children: Telling Everyone!

Today for the craft, go over the lesson again giving each child a baggie with the materials in it so that they can tell someone else about Jesus. Repeat the lesson so they will remember what to say.

Snack: Fishy Crackers
○ FISH SHAPED CRACKERS   ○ JUICE

Give out the crackers saying to each child:
I will make you a "fishermen" for men! Ask: **Why do you think Jesus called us fishermen? Have you ever been a fisherman for fish? What about people?**

✒ Memory Verse: Mark 1:17 (ICB)

"Jesus said to them, 'Come and follow me. I will make you fishermen for men.' "

Alternate Version: Mark 1:17 (NKJV)

"Then Jesus said to them, 'Come after Me, and I will make you become fishers of men.' "

📖 Memory Verse Activity

O FISH SHAPES FROM CONSTRUCTION PAPER   O WRITE ONE WORD PER FISH
(MAKE TWO SETS; ONE FOR EACH TEAM)

Divide the children into two teams and give them a pile of fish. Let them sort out the verse and learn it.

🙏 Prayer Focus

Dear God, thank You for all You do for us! We thank You for making us "fishermen."

Turn on the Light!

By Tina Houser

Scripture: John 12:35–36

Lesson Aim: The children will understand the relationship between taking in God's truth and being able to share it with others.

Memory Verse: John 12:36a

☞ Bible Activity for Younger Children: Pass the Light
○ EXTRA TALL TAPER CANDLE

Half of the children will be at each end of the room. One child will be given the candle to hold between their head and shoulder, with the instructions they have to carry the candle to the other end and pass it to one of the players at that end without using their hands. Before they pass it off they will say the first part of the memory verse today, "Believe in the light while you still have it." The person receiving the candle will say the last half of the verse, "Then you will become sons of light." No hands can be used when passing the candle. (That's why it is important to get a fairly tall taper candle.) The child now holding the candle will carry it to the other end where he will pass it off to another child, saying the first half of the verse this time. Continue doing this until all the children have had an opportunity to carry the candle.

The light this verse is talking about is Jesus and God's truth. Every opportunity we have to learn more about God's truth is an opportunity to become a stronger light—or a child of light. **How can we take in light right now so we can become children of light? What things help us know God's truth better?** When we worship we are giving ourselves to God and making ourselves available to Him. When we study the Bible we learn how God's truth has helped other people live. When we pray we share our hearts with God and listen to God's heart speak to us. All these things fill us with the light of God's truth, so we can share that truth with others.

☞ Bible Activity for Older Children: Soak It Up
○ DRY SPONGE FOR EACH CHILD ○ TABLESPOONS ○ WATER ○ BOWL ○ BUCKET

When Jesus was talking to His disciples, He told them to take in as much about Him while He was with them, because He would be going away. Then, they would be responsible for sharing God's truth with the world. We do not have Jesus sitting here with us today to learn from, but we have other ways that we can take in the truth of God which the Bible calls light.

Give each child a dry sponge and a tablespoon. A bowl of water should be within reach of each child. Ask everyone to squeeze their dry sponges and see if they can get anything out of them. Encourage the children to name ways they can be filled with God's truth. Each time one of the children names something, everyone will take a tablespoon of water and pour it on their dry sponges. The sponge will soak up the water as it is being fed. When they have had an opportunity to infuse their sponges with water, then ask them to squeeze them once again only this time over a bucket! **Why were you able to get something out of the sponge this time when you weren't the last time you squeezed it?** We can only be lights of God's truth when we have God's light of truth within us. We put all those good ways of taking in God's truth in the sponge and now it is able to give off the same. We take in God's truth and then we can share it with others.

Enrichment Activity for Younger Children: The Refrigerator Light
○ CAMCORDER   ○ REFRIGERATOR

The kids will have a great time with this wacky experiment. **Do you ever wonder about that light in your refrigerator?** When you open the refrigerator door the light is always on. No matter how fast you open the door, the light is already on. **Does it stay on when the door is shut? Well, it's not supposed to, but how do you know?**

Here's the experiment. Turn on your camcorder and record a few seconds before placing it on one of the racks inside the refrigerator. Shut the door. While the door is shut the camcorder will continue to record. Leave it there for about 30 seconds and then open the door again. The kids will be giggling at how ridiculous they think you are! Rewind the camcorder and view the footage that you have taped. **Did the light go off?**

The Bible calls Jesus the Light of the World. The light in the refrigerator goes off when the door is shut, but when you shut the door at night when you go to bed, Jesus is still there. He does not go away when you're not looking. The refrigerator light can fool you, but you can be sure that Jesus is the light that will not go away, as long as you continue to believe in His love.

Enrichment Activity for Older Children: Glow-in-the-Dark Toys
○ GLOW-IN-THE-DARK STARS

Before class, place the stars in a very well lit area for the time suggested on the package. These stars can be found in the toy department of any discount superstore. Keep them in light until time to use. Also, prepare a room that will be able to get completely dark when needed later.

While Jesus walked the earth, He poured Himself into the disciples. He constantly taught them the truth about God the Father. In John 12:36, our memory verse, He told the disciples that while He was with them, they should concentrate on taking in everything He had to teach them. He reminded them that as God became more real to them, they would be able to tell others the truth of God. One of the names the Bible gives Jesus is the Light of the World. Jesus came to pass on that light, so that (like our memory verse says) we would become lights in this world, also.

Give each of the children one of the glow-in-the-dark stars. Turn the lights out and see what happens. You won't be able to see the children very well, but their stars will be lighting up. Walk around the room with your star held over your head. It is a strange sight to see these stars wandering around a dark room.

Why do the stars light up, but the people don't? Everything soaks up light, but some things hold onto it longer than other things. When the light is turned off, the table is not able to hold onto the light that it took in. All of the objects in the room are made out of substances that get rid of their light quickly. The glow-in-the-dark stars, though, are made out of a substance that lets go of the light it has collected very slowly, so it's still glowing when the lights go out.

Jesus is not walking here on earth today, so how do we soak up spiritual light, God's light, today? (through worship, praise, Bible reading, studying with others, prayer) When our light is strong we can be a light in our world. In a world that is dark because of the way people have turned against God, we are to be glow-in-the-dark people to share the Light of the World.

Memory Verse: John 12:36a (ICB)

"So believe in the light while you still have it.
Then you will become sons of light."

Alternate Version: John 12:36a (NKJV)
"While you have the light, believe in the light,
that you may become sons of light."

Turn on the Light!

By Graham Bingham

Scripture: John 12:35–36

Lesson Aim: The children will understand the relationship between taking in God's truth and being able to share it with others.

Memory Verse: John 12:36a

Preparation
○ BIBLE ○ FLASHLIGHT

Boys and girls, I would like you to imagine that you are out in the woods late at night. There is no moon in the sky and the clouds are hiding all the stars. It is so dark you can hardly see a thing! Perhaps your family went camping with some friends and on your way back from the bathroom you wandered off the path and got lost.

You take a few steps forward, but in the darkness it is so hard to see that you stub your toe on something that causes you to trip and fall. Perhaps it was a rock sticking up from the earth, but you couldn't see it in the dark so you took a painful fall to the ground.

You start stumbling forward again hoping you are going in the right direction when suddenly you trip over something else. This time it is a broken branch lying on the ground. You fall really hard hitting your head against a jagged rock and warm blood starts running down your face.

Suddenly, you are afraid! You are hurt and your heart is pumping furiously in your chest. You get up and try walking again, but it seems that you end up spending more time tripping, stumbling, falling, and hurting yourself than you do walking.

You start feeling hungry and thirsty, realizing that you have been wandering in these dark woods a long, long time. You hear strange noises like the rustling of the leaves and twigs cracking. And what was that scary sound? Is it some ferocious animal getting ready to pounce on you? You have no idea, because it is so dark and you cannot see anything!

You start to run, but this only causes more problems as you bump into things like shrubs and trees, low hanging branches and rocks, tree roots and pot-holes. Finally you realize it is hopeless—you are lost and you are going to die all alone in these dark woods. You are never going to find your way home!

Then you remember that your friend at camp gave you a flashlight. Your friend told you that you will need a flashlight in the dark or else you will get lost. You fumble for the flashlight, find the switch, and all of a sudden there is light!

Now, with the flashlight you are able to search till you find the path that leads to camp. The flashlight also enables you to see the rocks and fallen branches lying in your path. Now you can step around them and not trip and fall.

You are so happy because now you have light and you have found the right path—the path that leads to family and friends, food and drink, shelter and life. You are no longer lost! The light from the flashlight has helped you find your way home! From now on, you treasure that flashlight for it was the flashlight that saved your life.

The psalmist said that the flashlight is like the Word of God. "By your words I can see where I am going; they throw a beam of light on my dark path" (Psalm 119:105, *The Message*).

Every time I try to find my own way in this dark world without following the guidance and instruction of God's Word, do you know what happens? I get lost and start stumbling and falling over all the temptations and sins that lie in my path. But when I follow the light of God's Word, I find that it leads me in a safe path—a path that leads to God.

Song Suggestions

"God's Way Right" by Dean-O from *You Got It All* (FKO Music, Inc. 1997)
Let the Lord have His Way Songsheets published by CEF Press, P.O. Box 348, Warrenton, MO 63383
"Open the Eyes of My Heart" by Norm Hewitt from *Fired Up* (Revelation Generation, 2002)

Craft for Younger Children: Candles
  ○ ONE VOLTIVE CANDLE   ○ ONE BABY FOOD JAR FOR EACH CHILD   ○ STICKERS

Show the children how to put the candle into the baby food jar and decorate the jar with stickers.

This will make a beautiful candle! **What kind of light does a candle make? If you were a candle, what kind of light could you make?**

Craft for Older Children: Candles
  ○ SAND   ○ WATER   ○ WAX   ○ WICKS   ○ PLATE FOR EACH CHILD

Be very careful! Supervise the children well for this activity.

1. Put the sand in a LARGE bowl.
2. Pour water over the sand to make it wet.
3. Make a hole in the wet sand as big as you want your candle to be.
4. Have an adult melt the wax
5. Pour the wax in the sand mold while holding the wick up enough to keep it straight.
6. Hold the wick there for about a minute or until the wax has hardened enough for the wick to not fall in it.
7. When it's hard and cold, dig about an inch away from the candle a trench about 6-10 inches deep, depending on how big your candle is, and then GENTLY pull the candle out.
8. Put the candle on the plate.

A candle is a great way to have light!

Snack: Light and Dark

○ SANDWICH COOKIES   ○ BOTH VANILLA AND CHOCOLATE

Each child will get one of each.

What does this vanilla cookie remind you of? What does the chocolate cookie remind you of? Light and dark are very important parts of our lives, aren't they? That's why Jesus uses light and dark to remind us of important things!

Memory Verse: John 12:36a (ICB)

"So believe in the light while you still have it.
Then you will become sons of light."

Alternate Version: John 12:36a (NKJV)
"While you have the light, believe in the light,
that you may become sons of light."

Memory Verse Activity

Write the verse on the board so that all the children can see it. Draw a candle instead of writing the word *light*.

The children can say the verse several times. **What is the "light" that this verse talks about? How can we become "sons of light?"**

Prayer Focus

Dear God, thank You that You gave us light in this world! We love You!

One Body Working Together

By Tina Houser

Scripture: 1 Corinthians 12:27

Lesson Aim: The children will understand that each believer is an important member of the body of Christ, the church.

Memory Verse: 1 Corinthians 12:27

☞ **Bible Activity for Younger Children:** Signs
○ PREPARED SIGNS   ○ CONSTRUCTION PAPER   ○ MARKERS

Before class, you will need to make some signs, all different colors and shapes. They should read: *Keep Out, No Trespassing, Keep Off the Grass, No Parking, No Stopping,* and *Tow Away Zone.*

Ask individual children to hold one of the signs and read it to the group. **Where might you see this sign?** After you have gone through each sign, ask: **How do these signs make you feel?** These signs tell you that you are not wanted—that the grass is more important than you are—don't even stop here—and even your car shouldn't be here!

Name some places that you always feel welcome. The church should be a place where you feel comfortable, loved, and always welcome. **How can we make people who are visiting this church for the very first time feel welcome? How can we make the people who have attended here for years feel welcome?**

Let's make a welcome sign. Encourage the children to decorate their "Welcome" signs with lots of bright colors that will grab the attention of people passing by. Make sure there is a place for the children to post these where they will be easily seen. Seeing the cheerful signs will bring a smile to everyone's face, and definitely make them feel welcome here!

☞ **Bible Activity for Older Children:** Who's Missing?
○ COPY OF A GROUP PHOTO FOR EACH CHILD   ○ ENVELOPES

You will need to take a photo of the group prior to this session. This activity takes a little set-up, but it is well worth the time. Run a five-by-seven-inch copy of the group picture and label an envelope for each child. Cut each picture so that each child's face is on a different piece. Put the pieces to each puzzle in an envelope, but leave out the piece showing the picture of the child who will get that envelope. Save that piece for later in the activity.

Give the envelopes out to the children to whom they are addressed. Ask them to put the puzzles together. They will soon notice that one piece is missing, and then realize it is their picture that is missing.

Each person is important to God and to His church. When one person is missing, then the church is not all God intended it to be. **Why would someone be missing from the church?** People can even be missing when they are actually right here in the pews, because their hearts are not with God. When God's people are not participating in His plan, then they are missing from the puzzle.

Give each child his or her missing piece. Provide a piece of cardstock paper for them to glue the pieces together and complete their photos.

Enrichment Activity for Younger Children: Mix It Up!

○ A SIMPLE RECIPE FOR COOKIES WITH AT LEAST 6 INGREDIENTS   ○ THE INGREDIENTS
○ MIXING BOWL   ○ LARGE SPOON   ○ COOKIE SHEET

Each ingredient should be pre-measured and in a container/bowl of its own. Give each ingredient to a different child. Open your ingredient and tell me what you think you have. Ask each child if they would like to eat their ingredient the way it is. **What will make you want to eat these ingredients?** (Mix them together and bake them.) **Can I decide to leave out one of the ingredients? What would happen if I left out the sugar? the flour?** Place the ingredients in the mixing bowl and combine them. (Children get a little messy when stirring, so encourage them to be gentle, unless you just really want a clean-up project.) Finish the cookies according to the recipe.

God has a list of ingredients for His church. It includes each person. Each person is needed to make the church complete. When we are all together, the Bible says that we are the body of Christ. All the ingredients in our cookie recipe were important, and so are all the people who make up God's church.

Enrichment Activity for Older Children: Good Penmanship

Up to a dozen kids can be in a group. If you have a large group, divide them into groups of twelve, and each group will need a name. In addition, each group will need a captain who will help direct the group when they are called upon. The leader will yell out a group name and a letter in the alphabet. The group will have to work together to form that letter by lying on the floor, head to toe. Arms can be used to complete shapes where needed. Every person must be included in the pattern, even the captain. Once the letter is complete, the leader will call out a different group and a new letter.

How is this activity like the way God designed the church? Everyone needs to be part of it. Each group had their own assignment, just like different churches are involved in different ministries. We need to be flexible so that everyone can have their places in the church.

"All of you together is the body of Christ.
Each one of you is a part of that body."

Alternate Version: 1 Corinthians 12:27 (NKJV)
"Now you are the body of Christ, and members individually."

One Body Working Together

By Ivy Beckwith

Scripture: 1 Corinthians 12:27

Lesson Aim: The children will understand the concept of church as a community that works together toward one purpose.

Memory Verse: 1 Corinthians 12:27

Preparation

Gather as many pictures of different kinds of church buildings as you can find.

Gather the children together and hand out all the pictures of the church buildings to the children. Tell me what you are holding a picture of. (Go around the group and get the "church" response from all the children holding the pictures.) **How do you know it is a picture of a church? Did you know that just because a building looks like a church on the outside—that doesn't mean it's always a church on the inside?**

The Apostle Paul wanted to make sure all the people who wanted to follow Jesus knew what a church really was. And he wanted to make sure the people in the church at Corinth, a Greek city, knew what really made a church. So Paul wrote them a letter to help them understand what a church really is. In that letter, what we call 1 Corinthians, Paul compared a church community to our human bodies. He talked about how all the parts of the human body need each other to work their best. The eye may be able to see where the person is going, but without the feet it would be hard for the person to get there. Our ears may be able to hear what other people are saying but without our mouths we'd never be able to talk back to the people and answer their questions. So, Paul said, the church is just like that. It's a place where all different kinds of people with all different kinds of abilities need to work together in order for the church to do what it was meant to do. And he told the people in the letter just like no part of the body is any better than the other, no member in the church is any better than the other.

Also, Paul explained all the parts of the human body have a special job. Let's talk about some of those jobs. Tell me what our eyes do. Tell me what our hands do. Tell me what our stomachs do. And, tell me what our brains do. All of our body parts have a special job, and our bodies don't work well if one of these parts isn't doing its job. The church is like that, too. Everyone has a special job to do in the church in order for the church to be what God wants it to be. Some people have the job of teaching the Bible to you and your family. Others have the job of making sure the building is in good repair. God wants some people in the church to spend lots of time praying for other people in the church and God wants others to help people who are sick or unhappy. Everyone in the church needs to do their job if the church is to work well.

God gives kids jobs to do in the church, too. Helping the church be a good place where people can learn about Jesus is not just for adults or for the church's ministers. So let's talk about some things you can do to help our church. **What kinds of things can you do?** Let's see—you can pray for people in the church, maybe the ministers or your Sunday school teachers. You can make friends with people in the church you don't know yet. You can help keep the church building clean by throwing your trash in the trash cans. You can give money to the church so the church can use it to help other people.

Being a kid is not an excuse for not doing a job at church. God wants everyone to work together so the church can do everything God wants it to do.

Song Suggestions

One Step At a Time Songsheets published by CEF Press, P.O. Box 348, Warrenton, MO 63383

"Praise His Holy Name" by Norm Hewitt from *Ablaze with Praise!* (Revelation Generation Music, 2000)

"He Is God" by Jana Alayra from *Believin' On* (Montjoy Music, 2002)

"Little Is Much" by Mary Rice Hopkins from *15 Singable Songs* (Big Steps 4 U, 1988)

Craft for Younger Children: Bricks and Mortar
   ○ BRICK SHAPES CUT FROM FUN FOAM   ○ CONSTRUCTION PAPER   ○ MARKERS

The children will form a church building with the brick shapes. Say: **These are really good churches! You did a good job designing them. The church is MORE than bricks and mortar, though. You are part of the church, too!** The children can draw themselves into the picture.

Craft for Older Children: Stained Glass
   ○ TRANSPARENCIES FOR MARKERS   ○ MARKERS

The children will draw a stained glass design on the transparency. Explain that many churches have stained glass. This makes the church beautiful, but do you know what else is beautiful in a church? YOU!

Snack: Trail Mix
   ○ CEREAL   ○ RAISINS   ○ NUTS   ○ PRETZELS   ○ M&M'S   ○ LARGE BOWL

To demonstrate all ingredients coming together to form a "church," give each student an ingredient to add to the mixture in the large bowl. You can add as many ingredients as you'd like—possibilities are endless!

Memory Verse: 1 Corinthians 12:27 (ICB)

"All of you together is the body of Christ.
Each one of you is a part of that body."

Alternate Version: 1 Corinthians 12:27 (NKJV)
"Now you are the body of Christ, and members individually."

Memory Verse Activity

○ BRICKS (EITHER REAL OR CARDBOARD)

Write one or two words on each brick. The children will form the verse by putting the bricks in order. Say the verse together.

Prayer Focus

Dear God, thank You that we are a part of the body of Christ! Thank You for making us a part of Your church.

Transformation

By Tina Houser

Scripture: Romans 12:2

Lesson Aim: The children will understand that they should let God change the way they think.

Memory Verse: Romans 12:2

☞ Bible Activity for Younger Children: What's That Blob?
○ LARGE PIECE OF CONSTRUCTION PAPER   ○ SEVERAL COLORS OF CRAFT PAINT

Give each child a large piece of construction paper. They need to fold the paper in half, making a nice crisp crease. The children will gently squirt a little of the craft paint onto one side of the paper. Use no more than two different colors. Fold the blank side onto the painted side and press down to spread the paint. Now, pull the folded paper apart and lay it flat.

Each child will show their design to the rest of the group and describe what they think the squished paint looks like. The other children will see if they can see something else in the squished paint. Turn the paper different directions to see if that will help you see something new. This is an exercise similar to describing what you see in the clouds. Give every child an opportunity to show his or her picture and to see how many different things can be seen in the paint.

When the Holy Spirit is directing our lives, we look at things differently. The Bible tells us that our minds need to be changed to a new way of thinking. We are not to think like other people think, but to think like God would want us to. Other people may think it's alright to use curse words, but we know that God would not want us to say those things. **Can you name some other ways of thinking that are different?**

☞ Bible Activity for Older Children: Pressed into a Mold
○ PLAY DOUGH   ○ PEOPLE COOKIE CUTTERS   ○ CANDY MOLDS (ANY DESIGN)

Each child will flatten some play dough and use a cookie cutter to make a person. Get rid of the excess play dough, so that you only have the person. Now, take your play dough person and press it into a candy mold. **What happens to your play dough person? Can you tell that it was ever a person? What does it now look like?**

The Bible teaches us that we shouldn't let the world squeeze us into its mold. We shouldn't act and talk like people who do not believe. We should be different because we follow what the Bible teaches. **What would other people have us believe?** (about our language, movies, music, cheating on tests, sneaking into movies) People who are not believers in Jesus Christ would have us think that some things aren't really as bad as you've been told. Your friends may tell you that sneaking into a movie isn't wrong. **How is sneaking into a movie stealing? How is cheating on a test lying and stealing? What are other ways that the world tries to squeeze us into its mold?** Each person has to work at changing the way they think as they follow Jesus.

Enrichment Activity for Younger Children: The Chameleon
○ PICTURE OF A CHAMELEON

A chameleon is a little lizard that is found mainly on the island of Madagascar, off the coast of Africa. Do you know what chameleons are most known for? They are able to change the color of their skin. Some people think they can change to any color they want, but the truth is they can only change to brown, green, blue, yellow, red, black or white. The chameleon changes color to communicate its attitudes. If a chameleon is calm, it will be green. An angry chameleon will turn yellow.

Have you ever "changed color" to be like your friends? Think of a situation when your friends were doing something they shouldn't have been doing, and you were tempted to become part of it, because you didn't want to be different, or you didn't want to be left out. Talk about times when the kids have given in to peer pressure and compromised what they knew to be right.

Enrichment Activity for Older Children: Temperature Rising!
○ THERMOMETER   ○ STEEL WOOL   ○ VINEGAR   ○ JAR WITH A LID

Beforehand, place the thermometer in the jar and fasten the lid. Present the thermometer and the jar to the group. Pull the thermometer out of the jar and read the temperature. Leave the thermometer out of the jar while you soak the steel wool completely in vinegar for at least a minute. Squeeze the vinegar out of the steel wool and wrap it around the bulb of the thermometer. Place it back in the jar and fasten the lid. Leave it in the jar. When 5 minutes has passed pull the thermometer out of the jar and read the temperature again. **What happened to the temperature? Do you have any idea what caused the temperature to rise on the thermometer?**

A chemical reaction is when one substance is chemically changed into a different substance. The vinegar started a chemical reaction with the steel wool and it began to rust. Most chemical reactions give off heat. **Can you tell me now why the temperature rose on the thermometer?**

Read Romans 12:2. This verse talks about changes ... not chemical changes, though. It mentions two different kinds of changes. **What kind of change is it warning us against? What kind of change is it telling us to make?**

Memory Verse: Romans 12:2 (ICB)

"Do not change yourselves to be like the people of this world.
But be changed within by a new way of thinking.
Then you will be able to decide what God wants for you.
And you will be able to know what is good and pleasing to
God and what is perfect."

Alternate Version: Romans 12:2 (NKJV)

"And do not be conformed to this world, but be transformed by the renewing of your mind, that you may prove what is that good and acceptable and perfect will of God."

Transformation

By Vicki Wiley

Scripture: Romans 12:2

Lesson Aim: The children will understand that they should let God change the way they think.

Memory Verse: Romans 12:2

Preparation

○ TRANSFORMER TYPE VEHICLE/ACTION FIGURES   ○ COOKIES AND COOKIE DOUGH
○ PLAY-DOH

Hey everyone! I have some cookies for you today. (Begin to open cookie dough and pass around.) **What? This isn't a cookie? What's wrong with it?** Oh, it isn't cooked yet – it isn't finished! **What needs to happen to this dough so that it becomes a cookie?** It needs to be baked—it needs to be "transformed" from cookie dough to a cookie!

Show a transformer-type vehicle. **Wow, look at this. It is a man now, and if I just change this and this and this—here it is! Now it is a vehicle!** (change words to go with whatever type toy you brought) **This toy "transformed" from a man to a vehicle.**

Show play dough. **What can you do with this?** Yes, you can take this lump of play dough and make anything you want with it! **What are some of the things that you can make?**

Do you know that God transforms us too? God takes us as we are, a child like you or an adult like me. Then God "transforms" us to be people that can have a new way of thinking—we can begin to know what God wants for us. When we know what God wants for us we will also know what God thinks is good and what pleases God.

You have a choice to make—you can choose to think like the world thinks. You can watch lots of TV and play lots of video games. If you do, you will begin to think like that! But instead you can learn to think like God thinks, you can learn what pleases God. To do that you need to go to church, read your Bible, and pray.

Do you want to be transformed into what the world wants or what God wants? You can choose today!

 Song Suggestions

"Little Is Much" by Mary Rice Hopkins from *15 Singable Songs* (Big Steps 4 U, 1988)

"You Got Game" (It's In the Name) by Dean-O from *Game Face* (BibleBeat Music, 2003)

"We Will Shout for Joy" by Cindy Rethmeier from *I Want To Be Like Jesus* (Mercy Vineyard, 1995)

"Take My Heart" by Kurt Johnson, a.k.a. MrJ, from *Kid Possible* (Kurt Johnson Music, 1995)

Craft for Younger Children: Handprint Butterfly
○ CONSTRUCTION PAPER   ○ GLUE

On construction paper, trace each child's handprint. Cut out 6 handprints for each child. Cut out a long oval (about 8 inches long) and a two-inch circle. The oval will be the body of the butterfly and the circle will be the head.

The children will arrange the handprints behind the body forming the wings. Add the head and glue together. Butterflies begin as caterpillars. They 'transform" into beautiful butterflies. **How do we transform?**

Craft for Older Children: Butterfly Puppet
○ 2 PAPER PLATES   ○ SCISSORS   ○ TAPE   ○ MARKERS   ○ CHENILLE STEMS
○ GOOGLE EYES   ○ HOLE PUNCH

Show children how to fold their paper plates in half (so that the back side of the plate is touching itself). Using another plate, cut a strip out of the middle (about 2 inches wide) and discard.

Tape each of the half round pieces to the folded plate. Posotion them so that the eating surfaces are facing each other. (This will form two pockets where you will later put your fingers and control the puppet.)

Draw a butterfly on your puppet. Use chenille stems for antennae and google eyes for eyes if desired.

Snack: Transformation of Butterflies
○ BUTTERFLY SHAPED CRACKERS   ○ GUMMY WORMS   ○ CHEESE PIECES

First, the butterfly looked something like this. (Pass out the worms.) Then the caterpillar "transformed" into a beautiful butterfly like this! (Give out the crackers and cheese.) **What else transforms besides a butterfly?** We transform too! When you love God and become God's child, you transform into a new person!

 ## Memory Verse: Romans 12:2 (ICB)

"Do not change yourselves to be like the people of this world.
But be changed within by a new way of thinking.
Then you will be able to decide what God wants for you.
And you will be able to know what is good and pleasing to
God and what is perfect."

Alternate Version: Romans 12:2 (NKJV)
"And do not be conformed to this world, but be transformed by the renewing of your
mind, that you may prove what is that good and acceptable and perfect will of God."

Memory Verse Activity
     ○ VERSE TYPED OUT ONTO PAPER (ONE FOR EACH CHILD)
     ○ CONSTRUCTION PAPER ○ MARKERS
This is a long verse but well worth learning.

Show children how to attach the verse paper onto the construction paper making a
poster of the verse. Decorate with markers.

Prayer Focus

Dear God, thank You for who You are. Thank You for helping us think the way You want
us to! Thank You for changing us on the inside to be more like You.

Christian Disciplines

By Tina Houser

Scripture: 1 Timothy 4:12–13

Lesson Aim: The children will realize they need to develop spiritual disciplines to make their faith walk stronger.

Memory Verse: 1 Timothy 4:13

☞ **Bible Activity for Younger Children:** Digesting the Word

○ BREAD   ○ A CLOCK WITH A SECOND HAND

Give each child a half-piece of bread. Instruct them to gobble down the bread as fast as they can. Give the signal and see how fast the children can eat the bread. Make it a big deal by timing the event.

Did you enjoy the bread when you ate it so fast? Have you ever swallowed something before you got it chewed up? Ouch, that hurts! **What would have made it a more enjoyable snack? What would you have liked to have had with the bread? Do you think it was good for your stomach to receive the bread eaten this way? What would help your stomach with its job of digesting the bread?**

Eating this bread is a lot like the way we read and study the Bible. We know we should read our Bibles, and we feel guilty when we don't. So, we hurry through the words, and don't think about what they mean. We gobble up the Scriptures and swallow them quickly.

How should we read the Bible? We should read it slowly and ask questions when we don't understand something. It's a good idea to have someone who knows the Bible well close by to help in difficult spots. There may be a word you do not know, so take the time to look it up in the dictionary. Our stomachs need us to chew our food well before swallowing it, and we can learn a lesson from that about how to read our Bibles. We need to study the words and think about them. Pray and ask God to help you understand the message He has for you in His Holy Word.

Now, give the children the other half of their piece of bread to eat slowly. You may want to provide jelly or some other topping.

☞ Bible Activity for Older Children: Hymn-ercize
○ RECORDED UPBEAT HYMN OR CONTEMPORARY SONG

In order to keep our bodies healthy we need regular exercise. It doesn't do much good if you only exercise once in awhile. Our bodies are made up of all kinds of muscles that have a variety of jobs, but all of them need to be strong to keep our bodies functioning the way they should. It's good to keep our bodies healthy, but our spirits and minds need to exercise, also. Name some things we need to do regularly to keep ourselves healthy spiritually.

Divide the children into groups of three or four to design an aerobic exercise routine to go along with the music you have picked out. Once they get it all together, encourage them to share their routine with the other groups—everyone on your feet to hymn-ercize! (If you have trouble getting the boys excited about this, give them hand weights to incorporate into their hymn-ercize.)

Enrichment Activity for Younger Children: Old Faithful
○ A PICTURE OF OLD FAITHFUL

Note: You can also go to the Web site *www.yellowstonenationalpark.com* for the Web cam picture of the next eruption.

Has anyone ever heard of Old Faithful? Do you know what Old Faithful is? (Most of them probably will not know about this famous landmark.) Old Faithful is what we call a geyser. Show the picture or Web cam of the geyser. A geyser is when water gets trapped underground against very hot rocks. The water turns into steam and builds up pressure. There is finally so much pressure that it has to explode. The underground water finds a hole in the ground above it and pushes water and steam out of the hole. Old Faithful is one of these geysers. It got this special name, because it erupts about every 45 minutes. You can count on it! The water spews into the air 60 to 100 feet high.

What can we learn about ourselves from learning about Old Faithful? What kind of things does God want us to do regularly? He wants to count on us regularly talking with Him in prayer, regularly worshiping Him because He is God, and regularly studying the words in the Bible He has given us to learn more about Him. God wants us to be "Young Faithfuls" in our prayer time, worship time, and study time.

Enrichment Activity for Older Children: The "I Can" Can
○ EMPTY CANS   ○ CONSTRUCTION PAPER   ○ TAPE   ○ MARKERS

In order to grow into the believer that God wants us to be we need to regularly work at moving in God's direction. List several disciplines the children need to begin as they grow into the person God intends them to be. Each child will write each of these disciplines on a strip of paper and roll them up. Place them in the can. Cover the outside of the can with a piece of construction paper and the words *I CAN Be More Like Christ!*

Once the cans are put together, instruct the children that at the end of each day they are to pull out one of the rolls of paper from their cans. If they have done what is written on the paper sometime that day, then return the rolled paper to the can and draw a star on the outside of the can. (If they haven't done what was written there, then just roll the paper and return it to the can for another day.) You may choose the same paper several times, but that's OK, because we need to work on some things a whole lot! After a couple of weeks and working on several of the disciplines that you need to develop, your can should have decorated itself with stars.

Memory Verse: 1 Timothy 4:13 (ICB)

"Continue to read the Scriptures to the people,
strengthen them, and teach them."

Alternate Version: 1 Timothy 4:13 (NKJV)
"Till I come, give attention to reading, to exhortation, to doctrine."

Get in Shape!

By Ivy Beckwith

Scripture: Hebrews 12:1

Lesson Aim: The children will understand that getting our spiritual lives in shape requires exercise and discipline the same way getting our bodies into shape requires exercise and discipline.

Memory Verse: 1 Timothy 4:13

Preparation

Gather together some simple exercise equipment—some weights, an exercise video or DVD, a jump rope or other pieces that denote some kind of exercise. Write *fasting, solitude/silence,* and *simplicity* on three separate slips of paper and put them in a bag or a basket.

Show the children the various pieces of exercise equipment. Ask of each piece: **What does exercising with this piece of equipment do for your body?** (If they are stumped you might turn to the congregation and ask them about the piece of equipment in question.)

Ask the children what other kinds of exercise they know about and wait for responses. Let's do some exercise right now. Lead the children in some simple exercises such as jumping jacks or stretches. If you are really brave, invite the congregation to stand and do these exercises with you. After you've done some of these exercises, ask the children to sit down. **Why do people exercise?** Many people exercise to make their bodies stronger and healthier. Some people exercise so they can do things like run a long race or lift something very heavy. Some people who have been sick exercise so they can get better from the effects of the illness. Exercising is very important if we are to have a healthy body.

But, did you know that in order to be a healthy Christian we need to exercise, too? Today's Bible verse tells us that following Jesus is a lot like running a very long race. (Read the day's Bible verse.) If we want to be able to run the race well, we need to be in healthy spiritual shape. So, just like we need to exercise our bodies so they can be healthy, we need to exercise our souls so they can be healthy, too. What kinds of exercises do you think you need to do to help your souls be healthy? We need to read our Bibles and pray. These will help make our souls healthy. There are some other actions the Bible and other Christians tell us are important for healthy souls. We're going to talk about three of them today.

(Hold up the bag or basket and ask a child to pull one of the slips of paper out of it. Read the slip of paper and talk about it.) **Who can tell me what it means to "fast?"** When a person fasts it means that person doesn't eat for a period of time. It might mean skipping a meal or skipping all the meals for one day. Then, the person uses those meal times to pray or gives the money he would have spent on those meals to charity. I wouldn't recommend you skip meals at your age but you could, say, give up dessert for a day and use that time to read your Bible, pray, or help someone.

(Have another child pick another slip of paper out of the bag or basket.) Ask: **How would a few minutes of silence or time spent being alone help make your soul healthier?** Sometimes our lives get so noisy we can't hear God talk to us. So, people who follow Jesus find if they get away from the noise and craziness of their lives they can hear God better. Hearing what God has to tell us helps make our souls healthy and strong. We can exercise our souls by being silent and listening to God.

(Ask another child to pick the last slip of paper out of the bag or basket.) **What does simplicity mean?** It means we don't let our lives get too busy and we don't spend lots of money buying a lot of stuff we don't need. **How can doing the exercise of making our lives simpler help make our souls stronger and healthier?** When we aren't crazy busy all the time we have more time to spend with God, more time to listen to God, more money to give to people who don't have as much as we have, and more time to do things at church and for other people. Doing all these exercises helps to make our souls healthy and strong.

Just like we have to exercise consistently to have a healthy and strong body, there are exercises people who follow Jesus need to do consistently in order to have strong and healthy souls.

Song Suggestions

"Lord I Give My Heart" by Mark Thompson from *Yes Yes Yes!* (Markarts, 2000)
"Say Thank You" by Mary Rice Hopkins from *Miracle Mud* (Big Steps 4 U, 1995)
"Outta Sight" by Dean-O from *Soul Surfin'* (FKO Music, Inc., 1997)
God's Power Songsheets published by CEF Press, P.O. Box 348, Warrenton, MO 63383

Craft for Younger Children: Jump Rope
○ ROPES ○ COLORED TAPE
Note: white rope at home improvement stores is good for this craft.

Demonstrate for the children how to wind colored tape around the ends of the rope creating the handles of the jump rope. Show the children how to use the jump rope, and don't forget to laugh at yourself!

This is a fun way to get exercise for our bodies! **What is a fun way to get exercise for our minds?**

✍ Craft for Older Children: Weights

- ○ PAPER ○ TAPE ○ MARKERS AND OTHER DECORATING MATERIALS
- ○ 1-LITER SODA BOTTLE

Fill the bottle with as much water as you want to lift. Make a cover out of paper and tape it around the bottle. Decorate the paper using markers, crayons, stickers, etc.

Demonstrate to the children how to properly lift the weight. Lifting weights helps to get our bodies in shape, doesn't it? How can you get your soul in shape?

🍿 Snack: Healthy Food

- ○ GRANOLA TYPE BARS ○ CUT VEGGIES

Today we are going to have a snack that will make you think of being healthy. **Why does eating these foods make you think of health? Why does eating sugary snacks make you think of eating something "not healthy"?** God wants us to be healthy. If you could choose one food as the healthiest food ever, what would it be?

✒ Memory Verse: 1 Timothy 4:13 (ICB)

"Continue to read the Scriptures to the people, strengthen them, and teach them."

Alternate Version: 1 Timothy 4:13 (NKJV)
"Till I come, give attention to reading, to exhortation, to doctrine."

📖 Memory Verse Activity

- ○ JUMP ROPES OR WEIGHTS MADE IN CRAFT TIME

Let children jump rope or lift weights as they chant the verse.

🙏 Prayer Focus

Dear God, thank You for all that You do for us. Thank You for giving us the holy Scriptures, because they teach us so much!

Who Are Your Friends?

By Tina Houser

> **Scripture:** Proverbs 12:26
>
> **Lesson Aim:** The children will be reminded that God wants us to have friends and to be good friends.
>
> **Memory Verse:** Proverbs 12:26

☞ Bible Activity for Younger Children: About My Friends
○ SCRAP PIECES OF PAPER ○ PENCILS

Give each child three pieces of scrap paper. On each paper they will write the name of one of their very good friends. Once done, the children will sit in a circle on the floor and place their friends' names in the center of the circle. As you go around the circle, each child will tell one thing that makes their friend so special to them. Then, the child will turn that piece of paper over so the name can no longer be seen. Continue going around the circle until all the children get to share one special thing about each of their three friends and all the papers are turned over.

☞ Bible Activity for Older Children: Stick with Your Friends
○ A SUPPLY OF WHITE MAILING LABELS FOR EACH CHILD ○ FINE POINT MARKERS

Why do you think God made us so that we would want and need friends? Why are friends so special? Tell about a time when a friend made you feel better when you weren't having a good day.

Give each child about ten white mailing labels. They are going to make stickers from these labels. Instruct the children to write encouraging statements on the stickers and decorate them with bright colors. Before starting, brainstorm with the children some phrases they could put on the stickers and write them on the board. *(Good Job, You're Terrific, You're a Winner, You're a Star, Have a Great Day, I'm Glad I Know You, Go Get 'Em, Do Your Best)*

During the upcoming week, give your friends a sticker to let them know that you think they're great or to encourage them through a bad day. When you give them their sticker label say, "Good friends 'stick' together!"

Enrichment Activity for Younger Children: A Friendship Quilt
○ SAME SIZE PICTURE OF ALL THE CHILDREN   ○ HOLE PUNCHES   ○ PIECES OF YARN

Before class, take a digital picture of all the children and process them so the photos are all the same size.

The children will work together to make a picture quilt. Each child will use a hole punch to make a hole in each corner of their picture. Use small pieces of yarn to tie the corners of different pictures together. Encourage other classes to do the same and then join the small photo quilts to make a larger one.

The yarn is holding our pictures together. **What holds our friendships together? What do we need to do to have strong friendships? What can we say to one another that would make our friendships stronger?**

Enrichment Activity for Older Children: Learn from the Geese
○ A PICTURE OF GEESE FLYING IN FORMATION

Let's see what we can learn from the way geese work with each other as they fly in formation. Show the picture of geese flying in the "V" formation. After each fact about geese, discuss what we can learn that would make friendships between people stronger and healthier.

Fact #1: When geese are flying in formation, the ones toward the back honk to encourage the ones up front to keep going.

Fact #2: There is one goose at the point of the "V." When that goose gets tired he goes to the back of the "V" and another goose becomes the lead goose.

Fact #3: The flapping of the bird's wings helps lift the bird behind him. They can fly much further when they fly in the "V" formation, because they lift each other.

Fact #4: If a goose gets sick or is wounded, two other geese drop out with it until it's ready to fly again. They fly together until they catch up with the others.

God put some special qualities in the geese so they could survive the long flights they make each fall and spring. God also gives us friends to enjoy and to help us through difficult times. Good friends encourage us and teach us about ourselves.

Memory Verse: Proverbs 12:26 (ICB)

"A good person takes advice from his friends,
But an evil person is easily led to do wrong."

Alternate Version: Proverbs 12:26 (NKJV)
"The righteous should choose his friends carefully,
For the way of the wicked leads them astray."

Who Are Your Friends?

By Ivy Beckwith

Scripture: Proverbs 12:26

Lesson Aim: The children will learn the ways friends can influence them.

Memory Verse: Proverbs 12:26

Preparation

Gather together pictures of you and friends or find magazine pictures depicting friends doing things together. Write out on separate strips of poster board the following phrases: *Helps you obey your parents; Dares you to do something you think is wrong; Helps you love and follow Jesus; Encourages you to make fun of other people; Works with you to help other people.*

Raise your hand if you have a friend. Most of us have friends. These are people we like to spend time with and do things with. Friends are people we can talk to about the things that make us sad and about the things that make us happy. (Show the pictures. If these are pictures of you and your friends you might want to speak specifically about who these friends are and the things you like to do with these friends.) These are pictures of people who are friends doing things together. **What do you like to do with your friends?**

Do you know God cares about who our friends are? In the Bible God tells us that we should choose our friends wisely, because they can help us follow Jesus or they can lead us away from Jesus. Our Bible verse today is from the book of Proverbs in the Old Testament, the first part of the Bible, and it is about the kinds of people we should choose as friends. (Read the verse.) **How does this verse say we should choose our friends?** (Cautiously.) The second part of the verse tells us why we should choose our friends cautiously—because if we choose bad friends they will lead us away from God and Jesus.

But sometimes it is not always easy to tell if we have good friends or not. Sometimes people seem like a lot of fun, but really the fun they want us to have is not something that honors God. So we're going to look at some things friends ask us to do and, then, I want you to tell me if that would be a friend who would help us get closer to God or one that would ask us to do things that would make God sad.

(One by one show the poster board strips. Read the phrase on each one and ask the children to comment on what kind of a friend would ask you to do what was written on the poster board.)

Friends who help us do things like obey our parents and help others are the kinds of friends we want to have and the kind of friends God wants us to have. But, friends who ask us to do things that make God sad are not the friends we want to have. As you go home today I want you to think about your friends and begin to decide if these are friends who help you to do good things or bad things.

 ## Song Suggestions

"I Open My Heart" by Mark Thompson from *Yes Yes Yes!* (Markarts, 2000)

"Day by Day" by Jana Alayra from *Jump into the Light* (Montjoy Music, 1995)

"Rad-Dude Attitude" by Dean-O from *You Got It All* (FKO Music, Inc., 1997)

"Sharing Comes Round Again" by Mary Rice Hopkins from *15 Singable Songs* (Big Steps 4 U, 1988)

Hallelujah Ballad Songsheets published by CEF Press, P.O. Box 348, Warrenton, MO 63383

Craft for Younger Children: Friendship necklaces
○ CORD   ○ BEADS   ○ OVEN-HARDENING CLAY   ○ HEART COOKIE CUTTER

Let children roll out the clay and cut out a heart. Children then cuts their hearts into two halves. Poke a hole in the top of each half. Bake the clay pieces. When cool, let children make two necklaces, stringing one heart onto each necklace. Add beads to complete.

Say: **Friends are fun to have! Give one of your necklaces to your friend and you can wear the other. This is called a "friendship" necklace because when you wear your half of the heart you think about your friend who is wearing the other half!**

Craft for Older Children: Friends Poster
○ CONSTRUCTION PAPER, PEOPLE SHAPES CUT FROM CONSTRUCTION PAPER

Note: Each child will need one shape for each other child in the class. If class is too large, divide the class into groups.

Let each child choose some people shapes. (They should have one shape for each child in the class.) Let the child decorate the shapes as they wish, and write their names on the shapes.

Say: **We are going to make a Friends Poster. Each of you give a shape that you have decorated to each other child. Then glue all the shapes onto your paper—when you are finished you will have a poster that shows all your friends!**

Snack: Sharing Snack

○ PEANUT BUTTER   ○ JELLY   ○ BREAD

Let children form pairs and make a sandwich. Share the sandwich. (Be sure that there are no peanut allergies in the group first.)

Having friends to share with is a wonderful gift, isn't it? It is a gift from God!

Memory Verse: Proverbs 12:26 (ICB)

"A good person takes advice from his friends,
But an evil person is easily led to do wrong."

Alternate Version Proverbs 12:26 (NKJV)
"The righteous should choose his friends carefully,
For the way of the wicked leads them astray."

Memory Verse Activity

Before class, write the verse on a piece of paper; one for every two children. Cut each verse paper in half but do it creatively so that each half looks different from the others.

Give out one half of the verse paper to each child and then they will find the person that "fits" with their half of the verse paper. **This is a great way to make a new friend, isn't it?** God wants us to have lots of good friends.

Prayer Focus

Dear God thank You for our good friends. Help us to be friendly so that more people will want us to be their friends.

Honor God with Your Body

By Tina Houser

Scripture: 1 Corinthians 6:19–20; 1 Peter 2:11

Lesson Aim: The children will understand God cares about how they treat their bodies and part of following Jesus is taking care of one's physical body.

Memory Verse: 1 Peter 2:11

☞ **Bible Activity for Younger Children:** Harming My Favorite Thing
- ○ DRAWING SUPPLIES

The children will draw a picture of the activity they enjoy the most. The leader should also draw a picture or prepare one before class.

When the pictures are completed, give each child a short time to tell about the activity they have drawn and why they enjoy it so much. The leader will then share about his or her activity. Drinking alcohol and taking drugs changes our bodies. It harms our coordination, destroys some of our organs, and confuses our brains. Describe how drinking alcohol or taking drugs would hurt your enjoyment of your favorite activity. **Do you need good coordination to do your activity? Do you need to be able to figure things out or concentrate? Do you need to be quick?** Your special activity would never be as good as it could've been if you let drugs and alcohol into your body. Rip YOUR paper in two or mark a large black mark across the picture. Alcohol and drugs NEVER make things better; they always destroy.

☞ **Bible Activity for Older Children:** Hidden Pinata Surprises
- ○ PIÑATA ○ BOTTLE CAPS ○ STICK ○ BLINDFOLD ○ MASKING TAPE
- ○ A PIECE OF CANDY FOR EACH CHILD

Before hanging the piñata, fill it with the plastic bottle caps (or other lightweight objects that will mask as candy). Do not put candy in the piñata. After hanging the piñata, mark off a safe zone with masking tape. No one, other than the person swinging the stick, can cross the safe zone line. Make sure the line is back far enough that the swinging stick cannot reach anyone. Take turns blindfolding the children. Each child will be spun around a couple of times and then can take three swings at the hanging piñata. If the child makes contact with the piñata, then they are asked to tell one reason why drinking and taking drugs is a bad idea. Write these comments in a place where everyone can see them. When someone finally swings hard enough to break open the piñata, the children are going to be surprised when the bottle caps fall out instead of candy.

God made our bodies special and He wants us to take care of them. Piñatas were made to have candy inside of them, not bottle caps. It was a disappointment when we found out that there were bottle caps in the piñata. God did not make our bodies to have drugs and alcohol in them. **Do you think God is disappointed when we put things in our bodies that He did not intend to be there? Why do you think He's disappointed?**

Give each of the children a piece of candy for being patient with the surprise piñata.

Enrichment Activity for Younger Children: Get M.A.D.D.
○ WHITE POSTER BOARD   ○ MARKERS

In 1980, a woman named Candy Lightner started an organization called M.A.D.D. **Do you know what MADD stands for?** (Mothers Against Drunk Driving) Candy Lightner took a horrible event in her life and let something good come from it. Because of an accident caused by a drunk driver, Candy's 13-year-old daughter was killed. The person who was driving drunk had already been charged several times with driving while under the influence of alcohol. Just two days before this deadly accident, the driver had been released after a hit-and-run crash he had caused. Candy Lightner was angry, but she let her anger lead her to start an organization that would help make a huge number of changes, so other people would not die because of drunk drivers. The goal of MADD is to educate the community about the dangers of drunk drivers. They want to prevent people, like Candy's daughter, from dying in these horrible accidents. MADD has been responsible for many new laws. Since MADD started, about 290,000 lives have been saved because fewer people are driving while drunk. There are still about 17,000 people who are killed each year because of alcohol-related accidents, but each year the number gets smaller and smaller.

Make a poster about drunk driving. MADD is an acronym, because each letter stands for something, and then makes a new word. Try coming up with your own acronym, like MADD, to use on your poster. (For example: SADD—Students Against Drunk Driving.)

Enrichment Activity for Older Children: Trojan Horse Virus

Most of you are familiar with computers. **Can someone tell me what a computer virus is?** A virus is a piece of computer code that attaches itself to your computer files and causes damage to your file. It can spread from that one file to all of your computer files and really be a big problem.

There is a special virus called the Trojan Horse Virus. It is named after a story that the Greeks told thousands of years ago about a humongous horse that was given as a gift to the enemy city of Troy. It turned out to be filled with soldiers who attacked the city of Troy and destroyed it. The computer virus that is named after this made-up horse is called that because information looks like it's OK, but really it can be very harmful. The people of Troy thought the horse was just a nice gift. Boy, were they surprised! The soldiers jumped out of the horse and attacked them. The computer virus claims to be something useful that you would want to have for your computer, but when you open it, there's nothing but trouble! If you get the Trojan Horse virus it is very easy to pass it on to the people you e-mail. Your problem now becomes their problem, also.

How are the Trojan Horse of the Greek story and the Trojan Horse virus like how people get involved in taking drugs and drinking alcohol? What trouble can drugs and drinking cause the person who gets involved with them? What trouble can their involvement cause the people around them?

Memory Verse: 1 Peter 2:11 (ICB)

"Dear friends, you are like visitors and strangers in this world. So I beg you to stay away from the evil things your bodies want to do. These things fight against your soul."

Alternate Version: 1 Peter 2:11 (NKJV)
"Beloved, I beg you as sojourners and pilgrims, abstain from fleshly lusts which war against the soul."

Honor God with Your Body

By Ivy Beckwith

Scripture: 1 Corinthians 6:19–20

Lesson Aim: The children will understand God cares about how they treat their bodies and part of following Jesus is taking care of one's physical body.

Memory Verse: 1 Peter 2:11

Preparation

- ○ BAKING MIX (CAKE, BROWNIES, ETC.) ○ BOTTLE OF DISHWASHING DETERGENT
- ○ CONTAINER OF TALCUM POWDER ○ BOTTLE OF DRAIN OPENER

Show the children the baking mix. **If I follow the directions on this package what will I be able to make?** I'll get something really good to eat, but I have to follow the directions and only put the right ingredients into the mix. (Look at the box and read some of the ingredients.) If I put all these ingredients in this mix and follow the directions I'll end up with something really yummy.

But, what if I decided to experiment a little bit and didn't follow the directions? Let's say I decided to add some of this to the baking mix. (Hold up the dishwashing detergent.) **What do you think would happen?** I think I'd bake something that didn't taste very good. **Or what if I decided to put a cup of this into the baking mix?** (Hold up the talcum powder.) **What do you think would happen?** I don't think my final product would be very tasty if I did that. **What do you think would happen if I added a little bit of this to the mix?** (Hold up the drain opener.) Not only would it not taste very good, it would probably make you very sick if you ate it because drain opener is poisonous. So, when you want to make something really good to eat you have to be careful about what you put into the mix. You need to make sure you follow the directions.

Well, God created our bodies to work better when we put good things into them rather than bad things. Because God lives in people who want to follow Jesus, God wants us to treat our bodies well out of respect for Him. Our Bible verse for today tells us this. (Read the Bible passage.) **So what kinds of things can we do to treat our bodies well and honor God with our bodies?** (Make sure they touch on things like eating good food and getting enough sleep and exercise.) When we do those things it's like we are following the directions on the package of baking mix. Our bodies will stay well and we'll be healthy. **What kinds of things do we do to our bodies that are like adding things like dishwashing detergent and talcum powder to the baking mix?** (Make sure they touch on things like eating too much junk food, not getting enough exercise, smoking, etc.) When we do those things we're not following God's directions for our bodies and honoring God with our bodies.

God created our bodies and knows what is best for keeping them healthy. And when we follow Jesus, God comes and lives in us. That makes our bodies even more special. Just like we need to follow the directions in the recipe and not add bad stuff if we want something good to eat, we need to follow God's directions for what we put in our body if we want to be healthy and live as God wants us to.

Song Suggestions

"Purest of Gold" by Kurt Johnson, a.k.a. MrJ from *Pure Gold* (Mr. J Music, 1995)

"Believe His Promises" by Dean-O from *Soul Surfin'* (FKO Music, Inc., 1999)

"Do Not Fear" by John J.D. Modica from *Ablaze with Praise* (Revelation Generation Music, 2000)

What a Mighty God We Serve Songsheets published by CEF Press, P.O. Box 348, Warrenton, MO 63383

Craft for Younger Children: Healthy Me!
○ WOODEN MOLDING PIECES 4 FEET LONG   ○ MARKERS

Using the wooden molding—measure each child's height. Mark their height and let them decorate the rest of the molding as they wish.

When you are healthy, you grow! This will help you to realize how much you are growing!

Craft for Older Children: Healthy Plant
○ ONE CUP OR CLAY POT FOR EACH CHILD   ○ SMALL SEEDLING PLANT   ○ SOIL

Plants need to be healthy to grow, just like we do! Let's decorate our pot (or cup) and then plant the seedling. **What do plants need to be healthy?** Then, be sure that your plant gets plenty of sun, water and soil to keep it healthy!

Snack: English Muffin Pizza
○ ENGLISH MUFFINS   ○ PIZZA SAUCE   ○ GRATED CHEESE

The children will make their own pizza by putting the sauce on the muffin topped by the cheese. Bake or broil, if possible, until cheese is melted.

God created our bodies and wants us to keep them healthy. This is a healthy snack to help us do just that!

"Dear friends, you are like visitors and strangers in this world. So I beg you to stay away from the evil things your bodies want to do. These things fight against your soul."

Alternate Version: 1 Peter 2:11 (NKJV)
"Beloved, I beg you as sojourners and pilgrims, abstain from fleshly lusts which war against the soul."

Memory Verse Activity

This is a great verse to make motions to. Write the verse on the board for all children to see. Say a phrase at a time and decide what the motion will be for that phrase. Put the verse together and say it with the motions.

Prayer Focus

Dear God, thank You for our bodies. Help us to take very good care of them!

The Quality of Mercy

By Tina Houser

Scripture: Psalm 57:1

Lesson Aim: Children will learn about mercy as an attribute of God and as a characteristic exhibited by those who try to follow Jesus.

Memory Verse: Psalm 57:1

☞ Bible Activity for Younger Children: Lopsided Ball

○ A BALL   ○ PACKET OF SAND

Tape the flattened packet of sand securely to the outside of the ball. The children will sit in a big circle with their legs spread apart. Each child will call out a name of someone in the group and then roll (or at least attempt to roll) the ball to that person. Because of the packet on the outside, the ball will roll in crazy directions.

God sees that we are in trouble and His heart hurts for us. Mercy is when you see someone else's hurt and reach out to help them. God reaches out to us to help us when we have lost our direction. Like our ball, we think we're headed one way and we get distracted and go a different direction.

Remove the packet from the ball and play the same game again. This time the ball will roll to the person aimed at. God reaches out to help those whose lives have lost their direction and are out of control.

☞ Bible Activity for Older Children: Mercy Mess

○ MISC. OBJECTS (SUCH AS: CLOTHES, CHAIRS, SUPPLIES, EMPTY 2-LITER BOTTLES)
○ BLANKET   ○ CONTAINERS (BOXES, LAUNDRY BASKETS)

Create a huge pile that is an absolute mess. These are all things that need to be put away today or the custodian is going to have to clean up this mess all by himself (or herself). He (or she) does so much already that it just doesn't seem right to leave this additional mess for him (or her). Don't you think it would be nice if we could help out? I've got a game that will make helping her a little more fun than just doing chores.

Label the containers with the categories of things you have in the mess (clothing, classroom supplies, garbage). Place these containers at the opposite end of the room from the messy pile. Choose two children to participate at a time. These two children will lie on the floor and roll as fast as they can to the pile. When they reach the pile, they will pick up one item and return it to the correct category box. That child chooses someone to take his or her place in rolling to the mess. The game is over when the mess has been relocated into organized containers. We have shown mercy to our custodian by helping in this way.

Mercy is seeing the hurt, or pain, or trouble that someone is in and caring enough to help them. When we get in situations like that, God sees our hurt. He cares about us and wants to help us. He also tells us that we are to be like Him. So, we should be anxious to show mercy to others. Our hearts should break when we see people hurting and we should want to help them, because God would want us to.

Enrichment Activity for Younger Children: Marble Painting
- ○ CARDBOARD TRAYS (LIKE VEGETABLE CANS ARE PACKED IN)   ○ MARBLES
- ○ CRAFT PAINT   ○ PAPER PLATES   ○ SMOCKS   ○ CARDSTOCK   ○ TAPE
- ○ LARGE POSTER BOARD STAR PATTERN

Draw around the star pattern onto a piece of cardstock for each child. The child will cut out the star and tape it in a cardboard tray by using one small pieces of rolled up tape on the back of the stars. Do not tape down the edges. Each child will roll a marble in one of the colors of paint and place it in the corner of their cardboard tray. Gently roll the marble around inside the tray, trying to get it to pass over the star cut-out as many times as possible. Do this several times with different colors of paint.

The tray looks quite confusing and messy when we look at it this way. Dislodge the star from the tray and display it for the kids. Once it has been removed from the messy tray, the star becomes something remarkably beautiful.

God sees our situations that are confusing and messy. He sees that we are hurting and He has mercy on us. God's heart breaks to see His creation suffer. In turn, He expects our hearts to break, also, when we see people suffering. He expects us to be His hands of mercy and to help those who need help. Showing mercy helps take a confusing and messy situation and make something nice out of it, just like our paint balls ended up making a beautiful star.

Enrichment Activity for Older Children: What Is Mercy?
- ○ LARGE PAPER

Mercy is when God sees our troubles, our hurts, and our pain. Because He cares for us so much He wants to help us and protect us. That's what mercy is. The Bible tells us that we should try to live our lives to be like God, using Jesus Christ as our example. If God shows mercy, then we should be like Him and show mercy, also.

Form groups of three or four children and give each group a large piece of paper and something dark to write with. Down the left side of the paper write *MERCY* in large letters. The groups will think of hurting situations people find themselves in, situations where God sees their trouble and wants to help them. Each idea should start with one of the letters in *mercy*. When they are finished, the groups should each have five situations, one for each letter. Take time to share their completed posters and talk about how mercy can be shown to these people.

Memory Verse: Psalm 57:1 (ICB)

"Be merciful to me, God. Be merciful to me because I come to you for protection. I will come to you as a bird comes for protection under its mother's wings until the trouble has passed."

Alternate Version: Psalm 57:1 (NKJV)

"Be merciful to me, O God, be merciful to me! For my soul trusts in You; And in the shadow of Your wings I will make my refuge, until these calamities have passed by."

The Quality of Mercy

By Ivy Beckwith

Scripture: Psalm 57:1

Lesson Aim: Children will learn about mercy as an attribute of God and as a characteristic exhibited by those who try to follow Jesus.

Memory Verse: Psalm 57:1

Preparation

You will need a tube of Ben-Gay and some Aloe Vera lotion. Make a large sign with the following definition of *mercy* written on it: *Relief of distress shown to a victim of misfortune.*

Show the children the tube of Ben-Gay and the Aloe Vera lotion. **Who can tell me what these are used for?** We use these when we've done something to make our bodies hurt. We use these when we've done too much exercise or, maybe, when we've burnt our fingers. These lotions help our bodies feel better. They soothe the places that hurt and make the pain go away.

Our Bible verse today tells us that God can help us in other ways when we hurt. (Read the Bible verse.) **What do you think the person who wrote this Bible verse was feeling?** (Read the verse again if you think it is necessary.) I think the person who wrote this verse was feeling scared and anxious about something, a disaster that was happening or about to happen. **What did the person who wrote the verse ask God to do for him?** The writer of this verse asked God to be a refuge for him. **Do you know what the word *refuge* means?** It's a place to hide, a place to be safe. The person who wrote this saw God as Someone who could keep him safe. If God answered this person's prayer, God would be showing that person mercy. Our Bible verse tells us our God is a merciful God; Someone who shows us mercy. **Does anyone know what the word *mercy* means?** (Show the poster with the definition of mercy written on it. Read the definition to the group.) When God shows mercy to us we are helping a person in a bad, difficult, or dangerous situation feel better and feel safer.

Can you think of some ways we can show mercy to other people? Can you think of some ways you can help people in difficult situations feel better or feel safer? There are lots of things we can do. We can give food to people who don't have enough to eat. We can give money to organizations that help people who don't have anywhere to live. We can give the toys we don't play with anymore to other children who don't have as many toys as we have. And we can give away clothes we've outgrown. Anybody at any age can show mercy to another person.

But it's especially important that people who follow Jesus show mercy to other people. **Does anyone know why that is?** Our Bible verse told us God is a God of mercy. Our God shows compassion and cares for people who are in difficult circumstances. In fact God shows mercy even to people who don't deserve to be taken care of because they got themselves into the mess in the first place. People who say they follow Jesus try to act in the same way God acts. So, if God shows mercy to others, we must show mercy to others, too.

Song Suggestions

"Change My Heart Oh God" by Eddie Espinosa from *Change My Heart Oh God for Kids* (Mercy/Vineyard Publishing, 1982)

I'm Not Too Little Songsheets published by CEF Press, P.O. Box 348, Warrenton, MO 63383

"Pure Heart" by Norm Hewitt from *Fired Up!* (Generation Ministries, 2002)

"You're in My Heart to Stay" by Jana Alayra from *Dig Down Deep* (Montjoy Music, 1997)

Craft for Younger Children: Lopsided Balloon Toy
○ SAND   ○ BALLOON

Funnel a little sand into the balloon before they blow it up. Blow up the balloon. You may decorate this "wacky balloon" if you wish.

When thrown or rolled, this balloon will "go wacky." Sometimes our lives feel a little wacky like this balloon, don't they? But God gives us "mercy" and we can feel better knowing that God is in charge of our lives.

Craft for Older Children: Memory Verse Plaque
○ PRINTED COPIES OF MEMORY VERSE   ○ PIECES OF WOOD (TO MAKE PLAQUES)
○ WHITE GLUE SOLUTION (3 PARTS GLUE—1 PART WATER)   ○ PAINT BRUSHES

Glue a copy of the verse to the wooden plaque. Using the paint brush, paint a covering of glue/water solution onto the verse. When dry this plaque will have a shiny finish that will keep for years.

This verse is a very good verse to memorize and have in your heart. It reminds us that God is merciful to us and protects us always.

Snack: Merciful Mix
○ PRETZELS   ○ CORN CEREAL   ○ NUTS   ○ FISH CRACKERS   ○ BAGGIES

Put all the ingredients out and let the children fill up their bags with the mix.

What does *mercy* mean? The children can discuss this while eating the snack. Mercy is something that God always gives to us and something we should always give to others.

Memory Verse: Psalm 57:1 (ICB)

"Be merciful to me, God. Be merciful to me because I come to you for protection. I will come to you as a bird comes for protection under its mother's wings until the trouble has passed."

Alternate Version: Psalm 57:1 (NKJV)
"Be merciful to me, O God, be merciful to me! For my soul trusts in You; And in the shadow of Your wings I will make my refuge, until these calamities have passed by."

Memory Verse Activity

The craft activity for older children also involved the memory verse. Using the plaques made in that activity, say the verse together. Talk about what it means to each child.

Prayer Focus

Dear God thank You so much for Your love and protection—You never leave us! We love You and we praise You.

Parents Are Important!

By Tina Houser

Scripture: 2 Timothy 1:5–8

Lesson Aim: The children will realize that who they are is greatly influenced by how their parents and grandparents live.

Memory Verse: 2 Timothy 1:5

☞ Bible Activity for Younger Children: Come on Down!
   ○ SEVERAL SLINKIES

What kinds of things are passed down to us from our parents and grandparents when we are born? You may have the same color of eyes as your father, and have your mother's blond hair. You may be tall and thin like your grandfather, and have long fingernails like your grandmother. These are all physical things. The Bible tells us that something more important is also passed down from our parents and grandparents— our faith in God. Write *Faith in God* on a piece of paper and attach it to a step on a stairway. **What other characteristics do our parents pass down to us?** (patience, tolerance, kindness, compassion) Write each response they give on a piece of paper and attach it to another step. God expects parents and grandparents to pass down the things that will make all of us more like Him. These things are passed down as we watch how our parents worship God, react to situations, and how they treat others.

The children will now take a Slinkie and start at the top of the steps. Bend and stretch the Slinkie to the next step, let go, and watch it go. Each step that it lands on, say what is written on that step.

* If you do not have a stairway available to you, steps can be made from bricks or boxes of different sizes.

☞ Bible Activity for Older Children: Brick Layers
   ○ CARDBOARD BRICKS

Attach pieces of paper with one of these words/phrases on it to each brick: *respect, self-worth, patience, trust, faith, belief, humility, pride, compassion, integrity, hope, gentleness, work ethic, kindness, contentment.* Place the bricks in a pile at one end of the room. The children will form a side-by-side line from the pile of bricks to the opposite side of the room. When the game starts, the person closest to the bricks will pick up one brick and pass it down the line until it gets to the other end. Once across the room, the end person will set the brick on the floor against the wall with the label showing. Leaving the brick there, that person will run to the pile at the other side of the room, pick up another brick and start it down the line. When the second brick gets to the end, it will be placed on top of the first one so that its label shows, and the end person will go to the pile to start another brick down. Continue doing this until all the bricks have been passed from one end to the other and now form one stack.

Name some of the physical characteristics we get from our parents. Even more importantly, our parents pass down these things that are listed on our bricks. Just like we have built this pillar of bricks, the characteristics that are written on them that our parents and grandparents pass down to us build us into the kind of person we are. **How does this work?** Take each of these characteristics on the bricks and ask someone to share one way this is passed down. (Examples: When our parents show patience when they have to wait for a long time, they are modeling patience for us. When the time comes, we are much more likely to show patience, also, because we have seen our parents and grandparents do so. When parents and grandparents live a great faith in God and their children see that modeled, then their children will be much more likely to live a life of faith, also.)

* How to make bricks: Use a half-gallon carton from milk or juice as the base of each brick. Rinse these out thoroughly, leave open, and let air dry. Once the cartons are dry, push in the top of the carton so the end is flattened. Hold this in with strips of duct tape. Wrap the carton with self-sticking shelf paper. (Many of these papers come in stone finish or brick finish that will make your fake bricks look more real.)

Enrichment Activity for Younger Children: Special Guests

Before class, ask several people to visit your group and bring along a family heirloom. An heirloom is something that is passed down from generation to generation to help the descendants in the family remember a certain person or something that happened in their family's history. We can learn a lot about ourselves by studying our family heirlooms.

Before your guests share the stories behind their family heirlooms, caution the children to not touch anything unless the visitor gives them special permission to do so.

We pass our special treasures down to our children and grandchildren, but much more importantly, parents and grandparents need to remember that they are also passing down their faith. When we see our parents relying on God to provide for them and to help them through their hurts and struggles, it gives us greater faith in God.

Enrichment Activity for Older Children: Time Capsule and Letters
◯ CONTAINER ◯ LINED PAPER ◯ ENVELOPES

You will need to contact the children ahead of time to bring in one thing from home that will symbolize what they would like to pass down to children in the future. Make sure they understand that this is something they will not be getting back. The children will place these in a container. Decide as a group when the container will be reopened (in one year, five years, ten years). As the children place their objects in the container, each one should tell what their object represents. Example: a bookmark, because I hope the children in the future will love to read the way I do.

Give out pieces of lined paper and envelopes. On the envelope each child will write their first and last names and today's date. On the paper write a short letter to someone in the future. Tell them about yourself and what you hope their lives will be like. Example: I gave my heart to Jesus and I hope you will want to do the same. Place the notes in the envelopes and seal them. Include them in the container before you close it.

Make sure the container is well marked with when it should be opened and place it somewhere it will be taken care of. Mark on the outside of the container the names of the children involved, so when the time approaches to reopen the container those children can be contacted.

Memory Verse: 2 Timothy 1:5 (ICB)

"I remember your true faith. That kind of faith first belonged to your grandmother Lois and to your mother Eunice. And I know that you now have that same faith."

Alternate Version: 2 Timothy 1:5 (NKJV)
"When I call to remembrance the genuine faith that is in you,
which dwelt first in your grandmother Lois and your mother Eunice,
and I am persuaded is in you also."

Children's Ministry Sourcebook

Parents Are Important!

By Ivy Beckwith

Scripture: 2 Timothy 1:5–8

Lesson Aim: The children will realize that who they are is greatly influenced by how their parents and grandparents live.

Memory Verse: 2 Timothy 1:5

Preparation

Bring in a picture of your parents (or you could substitute a photograph of people who look like they could be parents).

Show the children the picture of your parents. **Who do you think these people are?** These are my parents (or these are people who are parents). At this point, if you are using your own parents, you might want to tell the children a little bit about your parents: names, where they live, what they do, etc. **Why is it important we have parents?** God gave us parents to give us life, take care of us, to love us, and to help us grow into good and able grown-ups. God thinks being a parent is very important.

In fact, God thought parents were so important He made special mention of them when He gave Moses the Ten Commandments in the Old Testament. **Who can tell me what the Ten Commandments are?** God gave us the Ten Commandments so we would learn how to value the things God values. The fifth commandment tells us that God wants us to honor our fathers and our mothers. (Read Exodus 20:12.) We need to always remember how important our parents are. That is part of honoring them.

What else do you think it means when the Bible says we should "honor our fathers and our mothers?" It means that we should always remember these are the people who gave us life, love us, and give us the ability to live. So, we should always treat them kindly and with respect.

What are some things we can do to honor our parents? (You might want to share with the children some of the ways you honor your parents.) When we obey our parents, we are honoring them and showing them respect. When we show love to our parents, we are honoring them and showing them respect. When we spend time with our parents or remember their birthdays, we are honoring them and showing them respect. There are all sorts of things we can do to keep this commandment and honor our parents.

What are some things we do that aren't honoring to our parents? When we disobey them or talk back to them, we are not honoring our parents. When we take what they do for us for granted and don't thank them, we are not honoring our parents. When we forget that if it wasn't for them we wouldn't be here, we're not honoring our parents.

God thought respecting and remembering our parents was so important that He used a tenth of the Ten Commandments to let us know how important it was. I want you to think of one thing you can do this week to show one of your parents honor. Let's be quiet for a few seconds while we think of that one thing. (Wait a second or two.) **OK, does everyone know what they are going to do?** Let's pray, thanking God for our parents and asking God to help us honor them.

Song Suggestions

"Fingerprints" by Mary Rice Hopkins from *Juggling Mom* (Big Steps 4 U, 1999)
"Jesus Loves the Little Children" (Traditional)
"Turn It Over" by Dean-O from *God City* (BibleBeat Music, 2001)
Faith Is Just Believing Songsheets published by CEF Press, P.O. Box 348, Warrenton, MO 63383

Preparation

Craft for Younger Children: Family Tree

- ○ TREE SHAPE CUT FROM FUN FOAM (GREEN FOR TREE & BROWN FOR TRUNK)
- ○ 2-INCH FUN FOAM HEARTS (ONE FOR EACH MEMBER OF CHILD'S FAMILY)

Write *Our Family Tree* across the top of the fun foam tree. The children will tell you the names of their family members. Write one on each heart and let them place the hearts on the tree. **We love our families, don't we?** A family tree is a way to remember all the members of your family!

Craft for Older Children: Family Photo Album

- ○ FUN FOAM FOR COVER OF ALBUM   ○ SHEETS OF CONSTRUCTION PAPER

Make the book by attaching a fun foam cover to the front and back of several sheets of paper. Request ahead of time for children to bring family photos.

The children will write *My Family* on the front and attach pictures inside the album. When we keep photo albums, we remember special events in our families and how special our families are.

Snack: Family Ties

- ○ PEOPLE CRACKERS OR COOKIES   ○ FOOD DECORATIONS   ○ ICING

Decorate the people crackers or cookies to look like someone in your family. Tell which family member you made with your cookie. **We love all our family members don't we?** We thank God for them!

Memory Verse: 2 Timothy 1:5 (ICB)

"I remember your true faith. That kind of faith first belonged to your grandmother Lois and to your mother Eunice. And I know that you now have that same faith."

Alternate Version: 2 Timothy 1:5 (NKJV)
"When I call to remembrance the genuine faith that is in you,
which dwelt first in your grandmother Lois and your mother Eunice,
and I am persuaded is in you also."

Memory Verse Activity

Write verse onto the board and discuss what the verse means. Say the verse together several times.

Divide the group into four teams. Assign a phrase to each team. Say the verse again, letting each team say their phrase.

Prayer Focus

Dear God thank You for my family and all the faith that we have. You are an awesome God!

Love Will Keep Us Together

By Tina Houser

Scripture: 1 John 3:14

Lesson Aim: The children will learn that being reunited
with God is His desire and joy.

Memory Verse: 1 John 3:14

☞ Bible Activity for Younger Children: Match Cards
○ PICTURES OF ADULT ANIMALS AND THEIR BABY ANIMALS

The picture of the adult animal should be on one card and a picture of the baby animal
on another card. (You can get a deck of these at a discount department store or a
teacher supply store.) Lay all the baby animal cards face-up on the floor in one part of
the room. In another area, lay out all the adult animal cards face-up. Make the sound
of one of the animals. One child will run to the adult animal cluster of cards and choose
the card of the animal that makes that sound. Then, they will run to the baby animal
cluster and find the baby animal that goes with the adult animal card they picked up.
Continue doing this until all the cards have been matched.

Reconciliation is a big word, but it has a pretty simple meaning. It is the way that God
and humanity are brought back together. In our game the parent card went to the baby
card and then they were put together again. God is our Father (the parent) and we are
His children. God came to us so that we could be back with Him. The Bible tells us that
every person has sinned. God loves the sinner, but it is His nature that He has to judge
the sin and punish it. When we sin, we are separated from God. **How can we have reconciliation (being brought back together) between us and God?** It is only because of
Jesus that we can be brought back to God.

☞ Bible Activity for Older Children: Sole Searching
○ SMALL PIECES OF PAPER   ○ 2 CONTAINERS   ○ STOPWATCH

Write everyone's names on a piece of paper and put them in a container. Write numbers between 20 and 45 on the same number of pieces of paper as you have people playing.

The bigger the group, the more fun this activity is. If you have a small group of children, think about joining with another group or ask some adults to join you. Everyone
will take one shoe off. Make a pile of these shoes in a completely different area away

from the group. The group will sit in a circle away from the shoes. One person will draw a name from one container and a number from the other container. The leader will start the stopwatch for that number of seconds. The player who drew the papers out has that number of seconds to retrieve the shoe and get it on the person drawn out. If the player is successful in completing the task leave both pieces of paper out of the containers. If the player is unsuccessful in completing the task in the allotted time, then return the shoe to the pile and both pieces of paper go back in their containers. This game is full of laughs. Have fun!

How does this game remind you of being brought back to a right relationship with God? How does it remind you of true reconciliation with God? The shoe only had one person it would fit, and there is only one true God. We cannot be reconciled with any other god, except our Creator God. There is only one way to do that—through Jesus Christ. We do not know how long we have to give ourselves to our relationship with God. Each player had a different amount of time to complete their task. Some of us may live to be 100 years old; others will come to the end of their time here on earth much sooner. It is important to be reconciled with God now.

Enrichment Activity for Younger Children: Heavenward Bound—The Incredible Journey
○ THE MOVIE "HOMEWARD BOUND: THE INCREDIBLE JOURNEY"

Most of your children will be familiar with this movie, even though it came out in 1993. Show the end of the movie where the animals are reunited with their family.

When the animals were with their family, they were where they were supposed to be. There was nowhere else that was right for them. **How did the family act when the animals showed up? How did the animals feel when they saw the family?** There is only one place we are supposed to be in our lives and that is with God. No matter what else is going on, we need to be with our Master and Creator. The animals in the movie were so glad to be reunited with their family. There is a special joy in us when we are reunited with our Father God. The Bible tells us that all Heaven celebrates when one person is reunited with God. The joy that is in Heaven is even better than the joy of this family when Sassy, Chance, and Shadow returned.

Enrichment Activity for Older Children: Drawn Together
○ 2 BALLOONS   ○ STRING

(You may want to provide enough balloons and string for each child to try this.) Blow up both balloons and tie each to their own string. Rub the balloons against carpeting that will cause it to build up static electricity. Hold the ends of both strings and let the balloons hang. **What do you notice about the balloons?** (They don't touch each other.) Now, place your hand between the balloons and watch what happens. The balloons come together by clinging to your hand.

Reconciliation means bringing together those who have been separated for some reason. When we sin against God we separate ourselves from Him. When we put static electricity in the balloons they separate from one another. But, with the help of our hand between the balloons, they are brought back together. Think of your hand as Jesus. Jesus died so that we could be brought back to God.

Memory Verse: 1 John 3:14 (ICB)

"We know that we have left death and have come into life.
We know this because we love our brothers in Christ.
Whoever does not love is still in death."

Alternate Version: 1 John 3:14 (NKJV)
"We know that we have passed from death to life, because we love the brethren. He who does not love his brother abides in death."

Love Will Keep Us Together

By Ivy Beckwith

Scripture: 1 John 4:7

Lesson Aim: Children discover that one of the marks of a person who follows Jesus is the love he or she has for other people.

Memory Verse: 1 John 3:14

Preparation

Find a teaching picture of Jesus with His disciples at the Last Supper.

Gather the children together. Show them the picture of Jesus and His disciples at the Last Supper. This picture helps us remember one of the most important events in Jesus' life. **Can anyone tell me what this is a picture of?** This is an event in Jesus' life we call the Last Supper. This was the last meal Jesus ate with His friends, the disciples, before He was arrested and crucified. During that meal Jesus had a lot to tell His disciples because He knew He would be leaving them and He wanted them to remember all He had taught them.

One of the things Jesus did at the Last Supper was to pray for the disciples and give them some final words about how they should live their lives if they were really going to be His followers. That prayer and those words were written down in one of the Gospels found in the Bible. It was the Gospel that a disciple named John wrote. One of the very important concepts Jesus taught His disciples that night was that one way other people would understand the good news He brought to the world was if they could see how much His disciples loved each other. If people who didn't know Jesus saw the people who did know Jesus living in right and loving relationships with each other then they would want to know Jesus, too. Everyone wants to be with people who truly love them.

Later on, the same disciple, John, who told us about Jesus telling His disciples they need to love each other, wrote a letter to some people who were trying to follow Jesus by forming a church. They may have been having a problem loving each other and living in reconciled and right relationships with each other. In this letter John told them that if they were really lovers of God and followers of Jesus, they would act in loving ways toward each other. Let me read you what John wrote them. (Read the Bible text.) It's really important that people who follow Jesus show love to each other and to other people who don't know Jesus. People will understand Jesus' love when they are loved by others.

Just like Jesus' disciples and the people in the church John wrote the letter to, we need to love each other and other people who don't know Jesus. Let's think of some ways together we can show love to each other and to other people. Wow! These are wonderful ways we can show love to others. Now, let's see what the adults who are here in church today think. (Turn to the congregation and ask them to offer some ideas of ways we can show love to people at church and to those who don't know Jesus.) These are all great ideas, too. Now let's see if we can put them into practice this week.

Song Suggestions

"The Family of God" by Kurt Johnson, a.k.a. MrJ from *Kid Possible* (Kurt Johnson, 1995)
"No One Else I Know" by Mary Rice Hopkins from *15 Singable Songs* (Big Steps 4 U, 1988)
"This Is Love" by Dean-O from *God City* (BibleBeat Music, 2001)
What a Mighty God We Serve Songsheets published by CEF Press, P.O. Box 348, Warrenton, MO 63383

Craft for Younger Children: My Church
○ CRAFT FOAM CUT INTO SHAPES—SQUARES, RECTANGLES, TRIANGLES   ○ GLUE

The children will make a church from the shapes. Applaud their efforts. Say: **This is a beautiful church that you have made! The best part of the church is the people inside: the family of God!**

Craft for Older Children: Forming a Church
○ CRAFT STICKS   ○ GLUE

Demonstrate how to design their own church by gluing craft sticks together. Say: **You have designed a great church building! The best part of the church is the people inside!**

Snack: Family of God!
○ PEOPLE OR ELF SHAPED COOKIES   ○ CRACKER RECTANGLES
○ ICING FOR "GLUE"

Show children how to "glue" a person onto a church (rectangle) Say: **Being part of a church is very important for a Christian—it's where we see all our brothers and sisters in Christ!**

Memory Verse: 1 John 3:14 (ICB)

"We know that we have left death and have come into life.
We know this because we love our brothers in Christ.
Whoever does not love is still in death."

Alternate Version: 1 John 3:14 (NKJV)
"We know that we have passed from death to life, because we love the brethren. He who does not love his brother abides in death."

Memory Verse Activity

Divide the class in half. Write the verse on the board. Have each group repeat after you:

First half of the class	Second half of the class
We know that we have left death	and have come into life
We know this because	we love our brothers in Christ
Whoever does not love	is still in death

Prayer Focus

Dear God thank You for Your church. We love You and praise You for You have designed a great place for us to worship and be a family.

Chosen!

By Tina Houser

Scripture: Hebrews 2:11

Lesson Aim: The children will see themselves as people of significance, because they have been adopted into God's family.

Memory Verse: Hebrews 2:11

☞ Bible Activity for Younger Children: Cartoon Clues

○ SELF-ADHESIVE NAME TAGS

Before class, write the name of a popular cartoon character on each name tag. Do not let the children see these names. Place a name tag on the back of each student. The children will know which cartoon character everyone else is except themselves. By asking the other children questions that can be answered with either yes or no, the children will try to figure out what cartoon character they are. (Example of questions: Am I an animal cartoon? Am I a hero cartoon? Am I a bad guy? Do I live in outer space?) When a player thinks they know who they are, they can ask one of the other children, "Am I _____?" which can be answered with either yes or no.

Of course, you're not cartoon characters. But, it's important to know just who you are. People can give you all kinds of compliments—on your hair, about your grades, or noticing the way you act. The thing that should make us feel better about ourselves than anything is the fact that if we believe in Jesus Christ as God's Son and our Savior, then we are called brothers and sisters to Jesus. God has adopted us into His holy family. **Doesn't that make you feel good about yourself?**

☞ Bible Activity for Older Children: Riddle-Me-Ree

Have you ever tried to solve a riddle? A riddle gives you clues about the object or person being talked about and then asks, "Who am I?" or "What am I?" Here are some riddles for you to try.

The more of them you take of me, the more of me you leave behind. What am I? (footsteps)

I get wet when I'm drying? What am I? (a towel)

I go around and around the wood but never go into the wood? What am I? (the bark of a tree)

I met a man with a load of wood. The wood was neither straight or crooked. What kind of wood am I? (sawdust)

The more you take away, the larger I will become? What am I? (a hole)

I hold water yet I'm full of holes? What am I? (a sponge)

I belong to you but others use me more than you do? What am I? (your name)

Now, write a riddle that gives clues to who you are. Collect these when the children are done and then read them in any order. The children will try to guess who the riddle is talking about.

The most important thing that you are is part of God's family. He is proud to call you part of His family.

Enrichment Activity for Younger Children: Dots of Encouragement
○ TWISTER MAT   ○ BEAN BAGS

On small pieces of paper write 1, 2, 3, and 4. Prepare the Twister mat by taping the piece of paper labeled "1" to one of the blue dots. Tape the "2" to one of the yellow dots. Tape the "3" to one of the green dots. And, tape the "4" to one of the red dots.

Each child will stand back from the Twister mat and toss a bean bag at it. If it lands on one of the dots with a numbered paper on it, the rest of the group will respond with positive comments about the player. If the bean bag lands on the blue "1", then one person from the group will contribute a positive comment about the player. If the bean bag lands on the green "3" then three different people must contribute comments. The leader will need to set the example, maybe even contributing one comment for each child. ("I like the way you ...")

The way you think about yourself has a lot to do with the way others make you feel. If the people around you are always building you up with positive comments, then you will feel good about yourself. That leaves you with a big responsibility to help others understand how you feel about them and how God feels about them. You can contribute to making others feel good about themselves. After all, God thinks you're all pretty neat!

Enrichment Activity for Older Children: Imprints

Baby animals do something very interesting in the first moments of their lives that is called imprinting. Something inside them tells them that the first moving object they see is their mother. During those first few hours and days the baby learns exactly what its mother looks like, smells like, and sounds like. Even though they are tiny, they can easily pick out their mother in a flock or a herd.

Name ways you are like your mother. Name ways you are like your father. More importantly, name ways that you are like your Heavenly Father. We want to have God's imprint on our lives, so we know what God is like. We want to know His voice when He speaks to us and recognize His ways when we see Him working.

"Jesus, who makes people holy, and those who are made holy are from the same family. So he is not ashamed to call them his brothers."

Alternate Version: Hebrews 2:11 (NKJV)

"For both He who sanctifies and those who are being sanctified are all of one, for which reason He is not ashamed to call them brethren."

Chosen!

By Vicki Wiley

Scripture: Hebrews 2:11

Lesson Aim: The children will see themselves as people of significance, because they have been adopted into God's family.

Memory Verse: Hebrews 2:11

Preparation

○ STUFFED ANIMALS

How many of you have a pet? How did you get your pet? Was it given to you, or did you CHOOSE it?

Usually, when we get a pet, like one of these (show stuffed animals) we get to choose it. If these stuffed animals were pets and you were choosing a pet, which one of these would you choose? (Point out that there were different opinions; not all children chose the same one.) Sometimes choosing a pet and taking that pet home is called "adoption."

What is "adoption"? Adoption is also when you choose the one you want, or someone chooses it for you. When you "adopt" a baby, the parents either choose the child that they want to have in their family, or someone else chooses the child for them and they take it home and make it their own. The child that was adopted becomes a part of their family.

You are part of a very special family. You were either born into that family or chosen to be part of it through adoption.

God's family is like that too! God chose us, or adopts us, too! He chooses us and puts us in His family. Everyone that is chosen by God becomes part of the family of God. God loves us because He chose us and we are very special to God!

Song Suggestions

"The Family of God" by Kurt Johnson, a.k.a. MrJ from *Kid Possible* (Kurt Johnson, 1995)

"No One Else I Know" by Mary Rice Hopkins from *15 Singable Songs* (Big Steps 4 U, 1988)

"This Is Love" by Dean-O from *God City* (BibleBeat Music, 2001)

What a Mighty God We Serve Songsheets published by CEF Press, P.O. Box 348, Warrenton, MO 63383

✂ Craft for Younger Children: Proud to be Me!
○ POSTER BOARD   ○ STICKY BACKED MAGNET   ○ BLACK MARKERS

Trace around each child's right hand with a marker and make a handprint on the poster board. Do the same thing with their left hands. Cut around the outside of both handprints.

Write the possessive form of the child's name on one hand and followed by "Masterpiece" (as in Katie's Masterpiece). Put a piece of sticky-backed magnet on the back of each hand. Show children how to use these handprints on your refrigerator to hold up their school and art work. **How many of you bring home pictures from school? Are you proud of the art work?** Of course you are! You bring home pictures that only you can make! God made you just the way you are and loves the work that you do!

✂ Craft for Older Children: Imprints
○ PLASTER OF PARIS   ○ STIRRER (FOR THE PLASTER)   ○ LARGE PLASTIC BOWL (I.E. COTTAGE CHEESE CONTAINER)   ○ AN ALUMINUM PIE PLATE OR A PLASTIC LID ○ LARGE PAPER CLIP   ○ PERMANENT MARKER

Mix the plaster in a large plastic bowl, as needed, and have a wide container ready (like an aluminum pie plate or a plastic lid) to mold the handprint in. The plaster should be stiff, but creamy.

Pour the plaster into the flat container. The child will make a handprint (or a footprint) in the plaster. Before the Plaster of Paris hardens, push a partly unfolded paper clip into the plaster to make a hanger—or use a straw to make a hole in the plaster. The plaster will be completely dry in about a day, but you can take it out of the molding container after about 20 minutes.

This is your handprint, only yours. No one has the same one that you do. God makes us all differently, but puts us all in one family!

🍿 Snack: Choose Your Own Snack
○ SEVERAL TYPES OF SNACKS; FRUIT ROLL UPS, COOKIES, CRACKERS   ○ PLATTER

Put everything on a platter. Today you get to choose your own snack. Here are several to choose from. Let the children choose what they would like to eat. It's fun to choose your favorite snack.

God chose you to be a part of His family! **Are you glad that you were chosen?** God chose you because God knew you were the best!

"Jesus, who makes people holy, and those who are made holy are from the same family. So he is not ashamed to call them his brothers."

Alternate Version: Hebrews 2:11 (NKJV)

"For both He who sanctifies and those who are being sanctified are all of one, for which reason He is not ashamed to call them brethren."

Memory Verse Activity

Cut people shapes from construction paper. Write one word from the verse onto each shape. Write the verse on a white board and then let children try to put the "people shape words" into the correct order to form the verse.

Say the verse together.

Prayer Focus

Dear God, thank You for letting us be part of Your family; thank You for adopting us. Help us to serve You and love You.

God Is the King!

By Tina Houser

Scripture: Psalm 139:1–2; Psalm 47:7–8

Lesson Aim: Children discover an attribute of God—that God is King over all of the earth and creation.

Memory Verse: Psalm 139:1–2

☞ Bible Activity for Younger Children: Mystery Sack
○ 5 OBJECTS ○ PAPER LUNCH SACK

Place the five objects in the paper lunch sack and staple it shut. (The objects could be things like: a toy metal car, a candle, an action figure, a pacifier, a piece of candy. You just need a variety of shapes.) Give each child a set amount of time, perhaps 20 seconds, to feel the sack, trying to figure out what its contents are. It is not necessary to have them write their guesses down. Once everyone has felt the bag, ask the children to share their thoughts on what the items are. After you have exhausted their ideas, open the bag and pull the items out one by one.

Are there things hiding inside you that you think no one else knows about? When we think about God we have to realize that He knows everything, even if the people around us don't. He knew what was in the sack. He knows what is in your heart, even if you don't say it out loud. No person on this earth can know everything about you like God can.

☞ Bible Activity for Older Children: Fruity Guesses
○ JAR ○ FRUIT LOOPS CEREAL

Fill the jar with the Fruit Loops cereal. As you fill it, count the number of pieces that you put in the jar. Keep this number a secret. (You can also do this with small pieces of candy, fish crackers, or anything yummy that would take lots of them to fill the jar.) The children will guess how many Fruit Loops are in the jar. The person who gets closest without going over will win the jar and its contents. After they have all made their guesses reveal the correct number and award the prize.

Isn't it an awesome thing to think that God knew how many Fruit Loops were in this jar? He also knew what numbers you would choose. He knew who would win the jar and how they would react. Sometimes we think that our parents, our best friend, or our teachers know all about us, but there are still things about you that they don't know—

lots of things! God not only knows about you, but He also knows about each of the other 6 billion people who He created in this world. Isn't God amazing!

Enrichment Activity for Younger Children: Give God a Hand
○ PAPER

Take each child aside where the others cannot see and draw around their hand onto a piece of white paper. Try to get the children to lay their hands in a similar position so there isn't much difference between them. Make sure you lightly write their name on the back of each paper, so you know who the silhouette of the hand belongs to.

Hold the pictures up one at a time and ask the children to guess whose hand you are holding up. If you think this is your hand, raise that hand in the air so we can see it.

If was difficult to figure out whose hands these were. Many of you didn't even know which hand was yours! Isn't is amazing to think that God knew which hand was which and He even knows us better than we know ourselves!

Enrichment Activity for Older Children: Waxy Situation
○ WHITE CANDLES   ○ HEAVY WHITE PAPER   ○ CRAFT PAINTS   ○ BRUSHES

Before class, water down a few colors of craft paint in some disposable cups.

Give each child a white candle and a piece of white paper. The child will write "God" in large thick letters on the white paper. You will not be able to see the writing unless you look very carefully. Using the watered-down paint, brush paint over the entire piece of paper. When you do this, you will be able to see the white letters. The letters were there all along, but we weren't able to see them clearly.

God is always there. He never leaves us. Sometimes we can't see Him clearly, but He is still there. The paint revealed the letters on the paper. The situations we go through reveal God's presence in our lives.

Memory Verse: Psalm 139:1–2 (ICB)

"Lord, you have examined me. You know all about me. You know when I sit down and when I get up. You know my thoughts before I think them."

Alternate Version: Psalm 139:1–2 (NKJV)
"O Lord, You have searched me and known me. You know my sitting down and my rising up; You understand my thought afar off."

God Is the King!

By Ivy Beckwith

Scripture: Psalm 139:1–2; Psalm 47:7–8

Lesson Aim: Children discover an attribute of God—that God is King over all of the earth and creation.

Memory Verse: Psalm 139:1–2

Preparation

Find pictures of kings and queens from countries around the world and a picture of their country to match them with. For example, look for a picture of Queen Elizabeth to match with a picture or map of England. If you have trouble finding pictures of current monarchs, look for pictures of kings and queens from history and pictures of the countries they ruled. Three examples should be enough. Also find pictures of the earth taken from space and other pictures of the solar system (sun, Milky Way, etc.).

Gather the children together. Show them the first picture of the king or queen. Ask them who it is in the picture. Show them the picture of the country where that person is or was the king or queen. Talk about how that person is or was in charge of ruling that particular place or country. Repeat this for each of the pictures. Talk with the children about what kings and queens do. Each of these people was very important in his own country and, maybe, they were important to some of the countries surrounding their country, because they were the king or the queen. But none of them was as important a king or ruler as God is.

One of the things we know about God is that God is the King over everything. God is the King over all these countries we looked at and God is even the King over all the other kings and queens. (Show pictures again when you say this.) And God is the King not only over the whole earth (show pictures of the earth), but of everything out there in space, the whole universe. (Show the pictures of the various things found in the universe.) God is King over everything ever created.

Our Bible passage today tells us God is the King over everything. It's from the book of Psalms and it is part of a song God's people would sing to praise God for being the King over everything. Listen to what the poet said about God. (Read the Bible text.) Those Bible verses make God sound really important and He is.

If God is King over the whole earth and over all the universe and even over universes we might not even know about, what does that mean for how we should think about God? When people met the kings and queens we saw pictures of earlier, they would need to act in special ways. They would use certain kinds of words and phrases and they would bow and curtsy to show respect. When the king or queen would pass by in a parade the people would cheer and clap to show their love for him or her. And when the king or queen passed a law the people had to obey it or they would be in big trouble. Because God is our King we need to worship Him. We need to praise Him and we need to obey Him.

Song Suggestions

"He Is Really God!" by Dean-O from *You Got It All* (FKO Music, Inc., 1997)
Did You Ever Talk to God Above Songsheets published by CEF Press, P.O. Box 348, Warrenton, MO 63383
"Purest of Gold" by Kurt Johnson, a.k.a. MrJ from *Pure Gold* (Mr. J Music, 1995)
"Believe His Promises" by Dean-O from *Soul Surfin* (FKO Music, Inc., 1999)
"Do Not Fear" by John J.D. Modica from *Ablaze with Praise* (Revelation Generation Music, 2000)

Craft for Younger Children: Crown for the King

○ CROWNS CUT FROM PAPER (OR FROM A FAST FOOD RESTAURANT)   ○ SEQUINS
○ GLUE

The children will decorate their crowns. God is the King of our lives! We will wear this crown to remind us of that!

Craft for Older Children: "God Is King" Banner

○ CRAFT FOAM SHEETS   ○ CROWN CUT FROM CRAFT FOAM   ○ MARKERS

Write "God is King" across each crown. Glue to the top of the banner. The children will decorate the banner with things that God is King of: creation, themselves, etc.

God is the King of our lives and the King of creation! We praise Him because He is a good King!

Snack: Kings and Castles

○ SUGAR WAFER COOKIES   ○ ICING

Show the children how to build a castle using sugar wafer cookies. (Use them as though they were large "bricks" attached together with icing.)

In some places, kings live in castles. Our King is God, who lives in Heaven!

✒ Memory Verses: Psalm 139:1–2 (ICB)

"Lord, you have examined me. You know all about me. You know when I sit down and when I get up. You know my thoughts before I think them."

Alternate Version: Psalm 139:1–2 (NKJV)
"O Lord, You have searched me and known me. You know my sitting down and my rising up; You understand my thought afar off."

📖 Memory Verse Activity

Make up motions to this verse and teach both the verse and the motions.

Lord (make sign for Lord: with right hand form an "L" with thumb and first finger— starting at your left shoulder bring it down across your body)
You have examined me (pretend to "search" by shading eyes with hand and searching)
You know all about me (point to head and then to self)
You know when I sit down (point to head and sit down)
And when I get up (stand up)
You know my thoughts (point to God—point up)
Before I think them (point to head)
who can understand that? (lift both hands at sides as if to say "what?")

🙏 Prayer Focus

Dear God, You know all about me and You love me! Thank You for Your love! I love You too!

Children's Ministry Sourcebook

Follower of Christ

By Tina Houser

Scripture: 1 Peter 2:21

Lesson Aim: The children will understand that being a follower of Christ means becoming more like Him throughout their lives.

Memory Verse: 1 Peter 2:21

☞ Bible Activity for Younger Children: Follow Jesus Tag

Play a game similar to "Duck, Duck, Goose," but with the words "I … can … follow … Jesus … NOW!" The children will sit in a circle with their legs crossed. One child will walk behind the circle, tapping each player on the head and saying one of the words in the sentence "I can follow Jesus NOW!" You can tap some heads without saying a word. When the player taps a person on the head and says "NOW!" then that player jumps up to chase the tapper around the circle. The child tagged tries to catch the tapper before he or she can make it around the circle and sit in the place vacated by the tagged child. If the tapper is tagged, he or she has to tap some more. If the tapper sits down before tagged, then the person tapped becomes the new tapper.

The Bible says that we should follow in Jesus' steps. It doesn't say that we need to wait until we're adults to do that. Jesus calls all His believers, young and old, to follow Him, NOW!

☞ Bible Activity for Older Children: Pattern Toss
○ 2 BALLS

The children will make a huge circle. The ball is given to one player who throws it across the circle to anyone he or she chooses, calling that person's name as it is tossed. That person, in turn, throws it to another person across the circle as that name is called. The ball continues going back and forth through the circle until everyone has had possession of the ball, but no one has gotten the ball twice. The last person to get the ball then throws it back to the person who started the game. Start the rotation over again, throwing to the same person that you threw to the first time. When the ball gets about halfway through the rotation, start the second ball following exactly the same pattern. (If the group is real large you may want to start a third and fourth ball.) Enjoy playing with one ball following the other through the pattern several times.

The first ball was the example for the second ball to follow. **What would've messed up the game?** (If someone changed who they threw to. If someone had stopped passing the ball. If one of the balls got dropped.) Jesus set an example for us to follow and He commands us to follow that example. His instructions are plain and simple. He doesn't say that we can change His instructions, but tells us to do as He did.

Enrichment Activity for Younger Children: Shadow Animals
○ OVERHEAD PROJECTOR (OR OTHER SOURCE OF INTENSE LIGHT)

Darken the room and turn on the overhead projector so that the square of light shines brightly on a plain wall. Playing with shadows is always great fun. There are all kinds of animals you can make by holding your hands different ways in front of the light. The image is thrown on the wall. Choose one child to make an animal shadow on the wall. Each child will follow by trying to make the same animal that was demonstrated. Create as many different shadow animals as your time or ideas allow.

Jesus came to set the example of how we are to live. Name one characteristic of Jesus. (He cared about people.) If Jesus cared about people, then we need to follow His example and care about people, also. Continue naming attributes of Jesus, emphasizing that we are to use His example to model our lives after.

Enrichment Activity for Older Children: Apprentices
○ CHILDREN'S PLASTIC HORSESHOE TOSS GAME

An apprentice is someone who is learning a trade or a job. Because there were no special schools for learning these jobs in colonial days, young men would watch and practice along with someone who was a master in the trade. Divide the children into pairs and ask them to come up with two things they would need to learn from the master if they were going to learn one of the following jobs in colonial times:

Blacksmith (someone who works with iron to make farming tools, pots, nails, and horseshoes)
Cooper (someone who makes buckets, barrels, and tubs by bending strips of wood)
Cobbler (someone who makes shoes)
Miller (someone who grinds grain at the mill)
Tailor (someone who makes clothes)

If we are going to be a follower of Christ, our lives are like an apprenticeship. We learn about Christ by following His example and practicing the way He wants us to live. Get out the play horseshoe game. The children will take turns trying to get the horseshoe around the peg. Each time someone succeeds they will tell the group something that we learn so we can be more like our master—Christ.

"That is what you were called to do. Christ suffered for you. He gave you an example to follow. So you should do as he did."

Alternate Version: 1 Peter 2:21 (NKJV)

"For to this you were called, because Christ also suffered for us, leaving us an example, that you should follow His steps."

Follower of Christ

By Vicki Wiley

> **Scripture:** 1 Peter 2:21
>
> **Lesson Aim:** The children will understand that being a follower of Christ means becoming more like Him throughout their lives.
>
> **Memory Verse:** 1 Peter 2:21

Preparation

○ WHITE BOARD OR LARGE WHITE PAPER ○ MARKERS

Do exactly what I do! (Lead the children in a series of motions that they can follow and do, such as snap, clap, hit knee, clap, touch head, touch nose.) Repeat and then change the motions.

Was that difficult? It was pretty easy to follow me, wasn't it? Now what if I told you to follow me and I climbed up a mountain? Would that be harder? What if I asked you to follow me on a surf board? What about following me as I ran in a marathon? Those things would be really hard, wouldn't they? Even if I did it first, it would be hard to follow my example.

Let's do something that will be easier. I am going to draw something and what I draw will be an example for you. (Draw a simple shape, such as a heart.) **Would anyone like to follow my example and draw the same thing that I drew?** (Allow a child the opportunity to try.) Good! You followed my example very well!

When you follow an example, you copy or follow what the other person does. You followed my example by copying what I drew. **What if I asked you to follow my example in how I lived? What would that mean?** (We would be nice like you. We would teach children like you do.)

Jesus asked us to follow His example. **What do you think He meant by that? What was Jesus like?**

Jesus asked us to love our neighbor and love God with all our hearts, souls and mind. Jesus didn't just TELL us to do that, Jesus led us by His example. Jesus did it first and now He wants us to follow His example and do it, too!

What can you do to follow Jesus' example? How will you act? Following Jesus is a way to be sure that you are following the best example you could ever follow!

 Song Suggestions

"No Need to Worry" by Jana Alayra from *Jump into the Light* (Montjoy Music, 1995)
"Pray, Pray, Pray" by Mary Rice Hopkins from *Good Buddies* (Big Steps 4 U, 1994)
Let the Lord Have His Way Songsheets published by CEF Press, P.O. Box 348, Warrenton, MO 63383
"I Will Obey You" by Cindy Rethmeier from *I Want to Be Like Jesus* (Mercy Vineyard, 1995)

Craft for Younger Children: "I Will Follow Jesus" Poster
○ CONSTRUCTION PAPER   ○ SCISSORS   ○ MARKERS

Demonstrate to the children how to trace around their foot to make footprints. Cut out two per child. Write *I Will Follow Jesus* on the top of a piece of construction paper. The children will then glue the footprints onto the paper.

This poster will help you remember to follow Jesus your WHOLE life!

Craft for Older Children: Footprint Magnet
○ MAGNET STRIPS   ○ CRAFT FOAM   ○ SHARPIE MARKER

Draw around your foot to make a pattern. Reduce the pattern so that it is only about four inches long. Make several copies of the foot pattern.

The children will cut a foot shape for themselves from craft foam. Write *I will follow Jesus* on the footprint. Glue the magnet on the back of the footprint.

Put this magnet on your refrigerator or other surface to remind yourself that you will always follow Jesus!

Snack: Sandals
○ PEANUT BUTTER SANDWICH COOKIES (IN FOOTPRINT SHAPE)
○ LICORICE STRINGS   ○ ICING

Make a sandal by "gluing" (icing glue) the licorice strings to the "footprint" cookies. As we are eating these sandal cookies, we can remember that we should always follow Jesus!

Memory Verse: 1 Peter 2:21 (ICB)

"That is what you were called to do. Christ suffered for you. He gave you an example to follow. So you should do as he did."

Alternate Version: 1 Peter 2:21 (NKJV)

"For to this you were called, because Christ also suffered for us, leaving us an example, that you should follow His steps."

Memory Verse Activity

○ CONSTRUCTION PAPER CUT INTO FOOTPRINT SHAPES

Write one or two words on each shape and lay them out in order for the children to read while they step on them. They will go through the steps a few times until they learn the verse.

Prayer Focus

Dear God thank You for giving us a great example of how to live. Thank You for Your Son, Jesus. We thank You and we praise You!

Sift out the Sin

By Tina Houser

Scripture:	2 Corinthians 7:1b
Lesson Aim:	The children will respect that God wants them to be pure.
Memory Verse:	2 Corinthians 7:1b

☞ Bible Activity for Younger Children: Peel Protection

○ BANANA   ○ PERMANENT BLACK MARKER

Show the children the banana. Ask them to name things in the world that God does not want in our lives. Each time they name something, write it on the banana peeling. Try to completely cover the banana with black writing. When you are done writing, talk to them about these being the things that Satan would really like for us to put in our lives. But, God wants our lives to stay pure and not let them in. Knowing God's Word and having a relationship with Jesus Christ protects us from those things. **What protected this banana?** The skin kept the writing from getting to the banana. When we peel away the skin, we find the banana, untouched and still pure even though all those things were happening just outside.

☞ Bible Activity for Older Children: Tub of Trouble

○ LARGE TUB   ○ NEWSPAPERS   ○ ROPE

Set the tub in the center of the room. Choose one child to guard the tub. Indicate a large circle around the tub by laying down a rope. The other children will make paper wads out of the newspaper and they must stay behind the rope. At the signal, the children behind the rope will start trying to throw their paper wads in the tub, while the child in the center tries to guard the tub by deflecting the paper wads. Give different children the opportunity to guard the tub.

This game was fun and occasionally someone was able to get a paper wad into the tub. God wants us to keep our lives pure. **What can we learn from this game about keeping our lives pure?** Satan will send temptations at us from all sides. Sometimes we get distracted by what is going on in one part of our lives and we let down our guard in another part of our lives. Satan is sneaky. We have to work harder at times to keep impure thoughts and actions out of our lives. Others times, it isn't quite as difficult.

Enrichment Activity for Younger Children: Fruit Culls

○ OLD MAGAZINES   ○ PIECE OF POSTER BOARD   ○ SCISSORS   ○ GLUE

The children will work together to create a poster of a bowl of fruit by cutting pictures of fruit out of old magazines. Draw a bowl on the poster board before the children begin, and then they will glue on the pictures they have found to fill the bowl.

What do you notice about this fruit? Do you see any bruises? Are there any bug holes?
These are beautiful, unblemished, pure pieces of fruit. We are going to learn a new word today. The word is *cull*. A *cull* is a piece of fruit that has bruises, worm holes, or some kind of blemish on it. These pieces of fruit are set aside and do not go to the grocery stores for use in your lunch or a recipe your mom is fixing. The culls are thrown into the back of a semi-truck and carried off to a factory where they are made into things like baby food, canned fruit cocktail, or squeezed into juice. What the farmers are really wanting is the perfect fruit, but they can still use the culls.

God wants us to be pure, not letting Satan talk us into doing things that put stains on our lives. But, sometimes we listen to Satan anyway. When we let others talk us into smoking, cursing, drinking, shoplifting, taking drugs, and many other things, our lives are no longer pure. God's plan is that you never let any of these things make you impure. Think about that before you take a step to participate in any of these things.

Enrichment Activity for Older Children: God's Filtering System

○ BOWL FOR EACH CHILD   ○ FOOD COLORING   ○ MAP OF THE WESTERN US
○ PICTURES OF LAKE TAHOE'S SKY-BLUE WATERS

Look at a map and locate Lake Tahoe on the California/Nevada border. The water in Lake Tahoe is 99.7% pure; that's as pure as the water you get through a water filtering system at your house. The water is so pure that when a white dinner plate is dropped into it, you can still see the plate when it is 75 feet down into the water. The lake is a beautiful sky-blue color that over 4 million people come to see every year. It gets this gorgeous color because it is so deep, and the deeper the lake is, the bluer it looks. Lake Tahoe is almost 1,600 feet in some places. It is also blue because its purity helps reflect the bright blue sky above.

A terrible thing happened about 50 years ago that threatened the purity of Lake Tahoe. There were huge wetlands around the lake, and a developer decided to get rid of them and build houses, instead. But, the wetlands were the main way the lake stayed pure. The rain would fall on the wetlands and the water would slowly work its way through the soil. As it did, the soil would remove everything from the water and leave it pure when it reached the lake. These marshes and wetlands were wonderful filters. The developer got rid of the way God had set up to purify the lake water. This has been corrected now, and people are working hard to keep the lake as pure as it ever was.

Let's see how easily something pure can become something impure. Give each child a small bowl of water. Ask them to gently squeeze the food coloring bottle to drop only one drop of coloring into their water. Be patient, and in the next few minutes observe what happens to the water.

When we let something impure into our lives, it slowly spreads to affect other parts of our lives. God intended for our lives to be pure, just like He intended Lake Tahoe to be a pure body of water. Knowing His Word and being dedicated to Him helps us filter out the things that threaten to make our lives impure.

Memory Verse: 2 Corinthians 7:1b (ICB)

"So we should make ourselves pure—free from anything that makes body or soul unclean. We should try to become perfect in the way we live, because we respect God."

Alternate Version: 2 Corinthians 7:1b (NKJV)
"Let us cleanse ourselves from all filthiness of the flesh and spirit, perfecting holiness in the fear of God."

Sift out the Sin

By Tina Houser

Scripture: 2 Corinthians 7:1b

Lesson Aim: The children will respect that God wants them to be pure.

Memory Verse: 2 Corinthians 7:1b

Preparation

○ FLOUR   ○ SIFTER   ○ AQUARIUM ROCKS   ○ SMALL BOWL   ○ LARGE BOWL
○ SPOON

When we sin we add things to our lives that God does not want there. The sin keeps us from being the person God created us to be. God wants us to keep our lives pure. **When you think of something that is pure, what do you think of?** I think of water that is so clear, you can see the fish in the bottom. And, I think of a newborn baby. There's nothing polluting the water, and the baby isn't old enough to have done anything wrong.

Pour the flour into the small bowl until it is about half full. Give each child several small aquarium rocks. Put one of your rocks in the bowl of flour if you have ever told a lie, no matter how small. Lying makes our lives impure. (Allow the children the opportunity to place their rocks in the bowl after each command.) Put one of your rocks in the bowl of flour if you have ever taken something that did not belong to you. Stealing makes our lives impure. Put one of your rocks in the bowl of flour if you have ever disobeyed one of your parents. Put two rocks in the bowl if you have ever disobeyed both of your parents. Not showing honor to our parents makes our lives impure. Put one rock in the bowl of flour if you have ever gotten really angry. Anger makes our lives impure. Put one rock in the bowl of flour if you have ever thought something mean about someone. Even our thoughts can make our lives impure. Now, ask the children to add to the list of things that make their lives impure. **What kinds of things do we do to our bodies that make our bodies impure?** Don't forget that God wants you to take care of your body, your mind, and your spirit. Encourage the children to be specific in their comments (Example: Instead of saying, "I was jealous", encourage them to say, "I was jealous when my friend got so many cool things for his birthday.")

Now that the flour is quite lumpy with all these rocks in it, it's going to be difficult to get them all out by just using our fingers, without making a huge mess. I sure wouldn't want to try making cookies with this flour! The rocks have to be removed to make the flour what it's meant to be.

When we ask God for forgiveness and He forgives our sin, God gets rid of each and every one of these sins that have made our lives impure. God purifies us once again and makes us like brand new.

Enlist one of the older children to hold the sifter over the large bowl. Each child will dip the spoon into the flour and rock mixture and move that spoonful to the sifter. As they pour the flour and rocks into the sifter, ask them to repeat, "God's forgiveness makes me pure again." After each addition to the sifter, gently shake the sifter so the flour comes through. If it's a larger container you are sifting into, and you feel a little daring, you can give each child an opportunity to shake the sifter after they pour in their spoonful.

Where are the rocks? They stay behind, so we can throw them away. When we ask God to purify us, He takes our sin and gets rid of it. Throw the rocks away. Our challenge today is to not put the rocks in the flour in the first place—don't do things that keep your life from being pure.

*If you are in a position that would make it possible to break the children into small groups, they would each get to experience more of the sifting activity personally.

Song Suggestions

"Pure Heart" by Norm Hewitt from *Fired Up!* (Generation Ministries, 2002)
"You're in My Heart to Stay" by Jana Alayra from *Dig Down Deep* (Montjoy Music, 1997)
"Treasure of My Heart" by Jana Alayra from *Jump into the Light* (Montjoy Music, 1995)
"It's Jesus Love" by Dean-O from *Game Face* (Biblebeat Music, 2003)

Craft for Younger Children: Pure Heart Necklace
○ CORDING ○ BEADS ○ CRAFT FOAM HEARTS (PUNCH HOLE IN TOP)

Show the children how to string the heart and beads to make a necklace. When we have a pure heart we feel good, we can be close to God. God loves a pure heart. **When you don't have a pure heart, do you know what to do?** Ask God to forgive you for your sin, then you will have a pure heart again!

Craft for Older Children: Pure Heart
○ RED CONSTRUCTION PAPER ○ LAMINATING SHEETS ○ DRY ERASE MARKERS

Before class, attach the laminating sheets to the construction paper and then cut large heart shapes out of the resulting laminated sheet.

Give each child a laminated heart and marker. The children will write things on the hearts that they know are wrong, such as: lying, stealing, being mean. Then, show them how they can "wipe" the words away.

When you do something wrong and ask God for forgiveness the wrong thing you did is "wiped" away. You have a pure heart again, just like you do on this heart.

Snack: Fruit Cup
○ DIFFERENT KINDS OF FRESH FRUIT ○ ROCKS

Give the children different kinds of fresh fruit that they can slice or chop to add to a bowl for a fruit cup. When they finish, tell them that you have one more ingredient to add. I think I'll just add a cup of rocks to our fruit salad. The children will protest, because that would ruin it.

There are lots of wonderful things that God wants us to include in our lives. But, there are many things that He doesn't want in our lives. We wouldn't put rocks in our fruit salad, and we don't want to put sin in our lives.

Memory Verse: 2 Corinthians 7:1b (ICB)

"So we should make ourselves pure—free from anything that makes body or soul unclean. We should try to become perfect in the way we live, because we respect God."

Alternate Version: 2 Corinthians 7:1b (NKJV)
"Let us cleanse ourselves from all filthiness of the flesh and spirit, perfecting holiness in the fear of God."

Memory Verse Activity
○ RED POSTER BOARD

Cut a large heart from the poster board. Write the verse on the heart and cut it into puzzle shapes. The children will work the puzzle and say the verse together several times until they learn it.

Prayer Focus

Dear God, thank You for loving us so much that You made a way for us to have a pure heart. Thank You for Your love and forgiveness. Amen.

No Throw Aways!

By Tina Houser

Scripture: Zephaniah 3:5

Lesson Aim: The children will recognize that God has to judge our sin, but He also provides Jesus to take our punishment if we choose to believe.

Memory Verse: Zephaniah 3:5

☞ **Bible Activity for Younger Children:** Court in Session

○ BLACK ROBE ○ MALLET ○ CANDY BAR ○ KNIFE

Put on a black robe and carry in the mallet. Hit the mallet against the table and call the court into session, "The Honorable _____ presiding."

Give the candy bar to two children to share. Tell them you want them to have equal shares of the candy bar. **How do you ensure that they both are happy?** If I give the candy bar to the first child, he might cut it in two, but then take the half that was bigger. **What is our solution?** A wise judge would come up with a fair way to take care of this situation. Let's have the first child cut the candy bar, but the second child gets to choose first which half he wants. That way, the person cutting it will want to get it as even as possible, because he wants to make the situation fair for himself.

God is a just and fair Judge. When we have a question about what is right and wrong, or what we should do, we need to ask God for His help, because He will help us know what is just and fair. Finding solutions to our problems, may force us to be creative in the way we think.

☞ **Bible Activity for Older Children:** Fair Judgments

Read the statements below one at a time. The children will respond to each one. If it seems to be a fair statement, then they will go "ding, ding, ding." If it seems unfair, then they will make the sound of a foghorn.

You were grounded for 20 weeks, because you forgot to feed the dog.
You have to stay home from your school trip, because you have a temperature.
You have to pay for a toy someone else broke.
You have to taste one bite of everything your mom puts on your plate.
You have to go to the dentist twice a year.

Ask the children to contribute their own statements, and let the others respond to them. Bring this activity to a close with this last statement, "People dishonor God by the way they live even though He loves them." God created us out of His love. We also must understand that God cannot tolerate being with sin. The bad news is that God can have no part of our sin, and so we leave Him no choice but His punishment. The good news is that Jesus came to rescue us and to take our punishment, so that God judges us "forgiven" and welcomes us back into His family.

Enrichment Activity for Younger Children: To Jail!
○ MALLET

Give the children a topic (love, peace, patience, self-control). Each child (or with a partner) will create a scenario where that topic is either displayed or not displayed. Choose one child to be the judge. After each scenario, the judge will pound the mallet against the table and say "Good Job!" to the scenarios that have shown love. He will pound the mallet and say, "To jail!" to those who have given examples where love was not shown. For each new topic, choose a different child to act as the judge.

God knows exactly what is going on in our hearts. He is the judge that we have to answer to in Heaven. We cannot hide our sin or make excuses for ourselves when we're talking to God.

Enrichment Activity for Older Children: Warning! Warning!
○ LARGE CONSTRUCTION PAPER   ○ SAMPLES OF WARNING SIGNS

Show the children the warning signs you have and help them identify the warning that is being given. When it has been raining a lot and the water is over the road, there will be a warning sign that the road is closed. **What will happen if you don't pay attention to the warning sign?** Your car will stall in the middle of the high water. A yellow sign is at the entrance to the grocery store on a rainy day that says, "Slippery." **What is it warning you of? What could happen if you don't pay attention to that warning?** You could slip and fall. The warning light comes on in my car that says I'm low on gasoline. **What happens if I decide to ignore that warning?**

Warnings are given for our own good. The Bible has given us a warning about God. The Bible warns us that if we choose to dishonor God with the way we live that He has to punish us. God cannot live in a life that is full of sin. Because He hates what sin does to us, He has to punish us for living with sin. **Is that fair?** God could've left it there, but He had great mercy on us. He sees us in our sin and offers us a way to get rid of our punishment. Jesus died so that He could take our punishment and so that we would live without sin in God's presence.

Provide supplies for the children to create their own warning signs. When the signs are completed, the children will share them with the rest of the group.

"But the Lord is good, and he is there in that city. He does no wrong. Every morning he governs the people fairly. Every day he can be trusted by his people. But evil people are not ashamed of the bad things they do."

Alternate Version: Zephaniah 3:5 (NKJV)
"The Lord is righteous,
He is in her midst,
He will do no unrighteousness.
Every morning He brings His justice to light;
He never fails,
But the unjust knows no shame."

No Throw Aways!

By Tina Houser

> Scripture: Zephaniah 3:5
>
> Lesson Aim: The children will recognize that God has to
>   judge our sin, but He also provides Jesus to
>   take our punishment if we choose to believe.
>
> Memory Verse: Zephaniah 3:5

Preparation

○ WHITE BOARD   ○ PERMANENT RED MARKER   ○ MARKER REMOVER
○ ERASER   ○ RAG

Have you ever done anything wrong and gotten in trouble for it? As the children name these things, write them in large letters with a red permanent marker on the white board. Fill the board with the things the children have mentioned. Also, ask them what their punishment was for doing wrong. My goodness, my board is so full, I think I'm going to have to erase it so I can write some more of your ideas. Try to erase the words and act surprised that they won't erase. Get frustrated and say that you guess you'll just have to throw the board away. Then, notice the bottle of white board cleaner. Spray it on the board and let it set for a few seconds. The red marker writing will begin to run as it lifts from the board. **What does that look like?** The children will automatically think that it looks like blood.

When we sin God doesn't just throw us away. He offers a way to get rid of the sin and that is through Jesus' blood. Through our sin we did terrible wrong by disobeying God, and someone has to take the punishment for that. God is holy; He is perfect. Because of that, He cannot be in a place where there is sin. But, God loves us so much He just hates the fact that He's separated from us. Jesus stepped in and offered to take our punishment. God's Son offers to take our punishment! All God asks is that we say yes to Jesus' offer, that we come back to loving Him and that we begin again to follow His commands.

Are there any people in the Bible stories you have heard that sinned and then accepted Jesus' love and sacrifice? How about Paul? Paul not only sinned in his own life, but then he tried to find followers of Jesus and punish them for following Him. He was just about the rottenest man ever! Then, when he met Jesus, he knew that God's love was real. He understood that God was not happy with the way he was living. He also understood that without Jesus he was going to have to be punished all on his own. Paul decided to change his life and accept Jesus' offer to take his punishment. The crazy thing is that, when he accepted Jesus' offer, God rewarded him for his decision. God gave Paul a brand new, clean life and He helped him become a completely different person. God can give you a brand new life, also, and when you do He will help you become the person He had in mind when He created you.

Song Suggestions

"Pure Heart" by Norm Hewitt from *Fired Up!* (Generation Ministries, 2002)
"You're in My Heart" to Stay by Jana Alayra from *Dig Down Deep* (Montjoy Music, 1997)
"Treasure of My Heart" by Jana Alayra from *Jump into the Light* (Montjoy Music, 1995)
"It's Jesus Love" by Dean-O from *Game Face* (Biblebeat Music, 2003)

Craft for All Children: Treasure Can
  ○ CIRCULAR CHIP CAN   ○ ART SUPPLIES   ○ STICKERS

Clean the inside of the cans and air dry them before the children begin working on them. Cover the outside by wrapping it with sticky-back paper or construction paper. Decorate the can with stickers or draw pictures.

This can didn't look like much when I gave it to you. In fact, I was thinking about throwing it away, because it was just garbage. When we sin against God, we might think that there's no way we'll ever get on track again. We might think that there's nothing we are good for. God doesn't throw us away. When we ask for forgiveness, we are given a brand new life and a new purpose. This is no longer a used up chip can, it is now a great place for you to store your treasures. When you accept God's love and forgiveness, we are His treasure. Oh, how I love to be God's treasure!

Snack: Good Mix
  ○ ALL KINDS OF LEFTOVERS

Hold up one baggie that has a few pretzels in it. Mrs. Elkin was going to throw these away, but I told her I'd like to have them. Pour the pretzels into a bowl. Hold up a box of cereal that's almost empty. Jeffrey was about to throw out the rest of this, because it doesn't make an entire bowl, but I told him I'd like to have them. Pour the cereal into the bowl with the pretzels. Pastor was getting rid of these chocolate candies, because he's on a diet, and I stopped him before he threw them out. Add the candies to the bowl. Continue holding up the items and telling how you rescued them from the trash. Look at this mixture! I think we have something that looks really yummy now, and all those people were just going to throw those things away! I think there's enough here for us all to have a nice snack.

When we go against the ways God has set down for us to live, He really should punish us. After all, God made us and He knows what's best for us. Jesus offers to take our punishment and rescues us from our punishment. And then, He makes something brand new out of our lives!

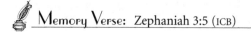

Memory Verse: Zephaniah 3:5 (ICB)

"But the Lord is good, and he is there in that city. He does no wrong.
Every morning he governs the people fairly. Every day he can be trusted by his people.
But evil people are not ashamed of the bad things they do."

Alternate Version: Zephaniah 3:5 (NKJV)
"The Lord is righteous,
He is in her midst,
He will do no unrighteousness.
Every morning He brings His justice to light;
He never fails,
But the unjust knows no shame."

Memory Verse Activity
○ WHITE PAPER   ○ MARKERS

Write two or three words on each piece of paper. As the children are sitting in a circle, give out the papers. Let them read their words in order. Keep going around the circle until the verse is said several times.

Prayer Focus

Dear God, thank You for not giving us what we deserve. Thank You for offering us a way to come back to You.

Spiritual Warfare

By Tina Houser

Scripture:	Ephesians 6:12
Lesson Aim:	The children will know that they have to protect themselves from Satan's attacks on their lives.
Memory Verse:	Ephesians 6:12

☞ **Bible Activity for Younger Children:** Protect Yourself

○ UMBRELLA ○ BASEBALL MITT ○ PAIR OF SHOES ○ SAFETY GLASSES ○ LOCK
○ SUNSCREEN ○ EARMUFFS ○ GLOVES ○ HELMET

Hold each item where the children can see it. For each item ask two questions: **What is this?** and **What does this protect you from?**

All of these things protect our bodies and keep us from getting hurt. The Bible tells us there are some other things we need to protect us. These are even more important than the items we have seen today, because these items protect us from the attacks of Satan. The Bible tells us that there is a spiritual armor that we need to help us fight Satan's lies. Wear the belt of truth around you. Put on the breastplate of righteousness. Wear shoes of peace. Hold tight to the shield of faith. Take the helmet of salvation and grasp the sword of the Spirit, which is the Word of God. We don't really put on a belt or hold onto a sword to fight a battle with Satan, but if we make all of these the most important things in our lives, then Satan won't be able to win us over. Let's all wear the armor of God!

☞ **Bible Activity for Older Children:** The Chase Is On

You will need a large running area for this game. Divide the children into three equal groups and put them in different locations to start the game. Each group will come up with a name for themselves. Take one child from each group and put them in the middle. To start the game, call out one group's name. That group will chase the 3 players in the middle. When you call a different group's name, then the first group will freeze, while the next group chases the 3 players. Continue doing this back and forth, so that no one knows which group will actually be chasing the 3 players. Whenever one of the original 3 players gets tagged, the two switch roles.

How was this game like the spiritual battles Satan sends our way? Are we always fighting against the same problems? When it seems we've escaped one temptation that Satan has thrown our way, then he sends something else to chase after us.

Enrichment Activity for Younger Children: Protect Yourself with Pizza
O ROUND PIZZA BOARDS   O TWINE

Before class, poke two holes in the center of each pizza board with a sharp object. These should be about four inches apart.

The Bible says that we can protect ourselves from the attacks of Satan's "fiery darts" by using our shield of faith. **What are these "fiery darts"?** Satan will lie to us, but our shield of faith will protect us from believing those things. Let's make our own shield of faith.

Pizza boards can be obtained from your local pizza place (usually donated). Each child will create an emblem that will represent their belief in God to decorate one side of their pizza board. Run a piece of twine through one hole and back through the other hole. Tie the ends together up against the board and cut off any extra twine. The children will be able to slip a hand in between the board and the twine to make a handle.

Enrichment Activity for Older Children: What's a Javelin?
O HEAVY DOWEL ROD   O HULA HOOP

Before class, find an open place to hang a hula hoop. The children will be throwing a makeshift javelin through this, so make sure that nothing is close by.

Do you know what a javelin is? A *javelin* is another name for a spear and was a common weapon in Bible times. It is a long stick with a sharp metal point at one end. Usually, a spear was bigger and heavier than a javelin. Soldiers could jab with the javelin or they could throw it long distances at a target. In the Old Testament, the spear is mentioned when Saul was angry with David and threw one at him. Sometimes in the Bible, the javelin or spear was also called a throwing stick.

The Bible tells us that we should fight against Satan with the "sword of the Spirit, which is the word of God." The Word of God teaches us God's way to live. We must know the Word of God to protect ourselves. Our faith must be strong to fight against the spiritual wars that Satan will bring against us.

Add a construction paper arrow to the end of a heavy dowel rod. The children will take turns trying their hand at hitting the hula hoop target with the javelin. It takes practice to get good at this skill. To keep our faith strong we need to put it into practice daily.

"Our fight is not against people on earth. We are fighting against the rulers and authorities and the powers of this world's darkness. We are fighting against the spiritual powers of evil in the heavenly world."

Alternate Version: Ephesians 6:12 (NKJV)

"For we do not wrestle against flesh and blood, but against principalities, against powers, against the rulers of the darkness of this age, against spiritual hosts of wickedness in the heavenly places."

Spiritual Warfare

By Vicki Wiley

Scripture: Ephesians 6:12

Lesson Aim: The children will know that they have to protect themselves from Satan's attacks on their lives.

Memory Verse: Ephesians 6:12

Preparation

○ SPORTS PROTECTION EQUIPMENT SUCH AS HELMET, KNEEPADS, ETC.

When you get in a car, do you put on a seat belt? Why do you do that? (Because it protects us.) Show protective equipment. **Do you ever wear any of these things? Why?** (Let the kids tell their stories as time permits.)

It is always good to protect ourselves any way that we can. Today, I want to tell you a story about someone who decided NOT to wear protective equipment and not to use the best weapons available to him. Instead he chose to trust in God!

Back in Bible times, there were a few different types of weapons. David was a young boy—the youngest boy in his family. His brothers were all out fighting a battle against the Philistines, some people who were enemies of God's people. So far, the battle wasn't going very well and God's people, the Hebrew people, were having trouble with a giant named Goliath.

Goliath was "taunting" them. That means he was making fun of them. They didn't like it, but they couldn't stop him—no one was brave enough. No one, that is, except David. David had come to bring some food to his brothers when he heard the giant Goliath. He asked, "Why doesn't someone do something?"

Then David decided that HE was the one that should do something! He was the one to fight the giant! He told everyone what he wanted to do and they went to get the protective armor for him to put on. David tried it on, but he decided that he didn't want to wear it and he took it off. Everyone was shocked!

Goliath had lots of armor and he also had a sword and two spears. David didn't hesitate to put the armor down, even though everyone else thought that he wouldn't be safe.

David said to him, "I come to you in the name of the Lord All-Powerful, the God of the armies of Israel! You have spoken against him and made fun of him, so today you will die."

What happened in this story next? Did David pick up the armor and spears? No! David took stones and a slingshot and with them he killed the giant Goliath. God answered David's prayers and kept David safe.

David knew that his fight was not really against Goliath, but against people that don't believe in God, people who loved evil. He knew that armor would not protect him against that.

God can protect you against evil like this. God can protect you against Satan because God is more powerful than Satan. All you have to do is pray and ask!

Song Suggestions

"Pure Heart" by Norm Hewitt from *Fired Up!* (Generation Ministries, 2002)
"You're in My Heart to Stay" by Jana Alayra from *Dig Down Deep* (Montjoy Music, 1997)
"Treasure of My Heart" by Jana Alayra from *Jump into the Light* (Montjoy Music, 1995)
"It's Jesus Love" by Dean-O from *Game Face* (Biblebeat Music, 2003)

Craft for Younger Children: Pumpkins

○ BROWN LUNCH BAGS   ○ NEWSPAPER   ○ GREEN FELT (CUT IN LEAF SHAPES)
○ GREEN CHENILLE STEMS   ○ ORANGE & BLACK PAINT   ○ MARKERS

Color or paint the bag orange leaving the top 1–2 inches of the bag brown. Cut leaf shapes out of the green felt. Cut the chenille stem in half.

Next, stuff the bag with newspaper and twist the top together with half of the green chenille stem. Twist in the bottom part of a felt leaf to hold it in place. Twist the other half of the chenille stem around a crayon or pencil to form a curly vine and attach the end to the green chenille stem wrapped around the bag.

A pumpkin reminds us of fall harvest and all the good things that God does for us. Put this somewhere where you can see it and thank God every time you look at it!

Craft for Older Children: Pumpkin

○ MASON JARS WITH LIDS   ○ GREEN TISSUE PAPER
○ GREEN CURLING RIBBON   ○ CANDY IN ORANGE WRAPPERS

Show the children how to fill the jar with the orange candies and then put on the lid. Cut a piece of green tissue paper long enough to wrap around the top of the lid and overlap an inch or two; it should be about 5-inches tall. Fold up one of the long edges to get a smooth edge. Wrap the tissue paper around the jar lid so it covers the lid completely. Gather the top of the tissue paper and tie with a 12-inch piece of curling ribbon. Use the sides of the scissors to curl the ends of the ribbon.

Put this jar where you can see it to remind you of God's great grace!

Snack: Pizza Protection!

O ENGLISH MUFFINS   O CHEESE   O PIZZA SAUCE   O MICROWAVE OR OVEN

Earlier we had an activity about pizza protection. Now we are going to make little pizzas to remind us of that activity.

Show the children how to grate cheese and top an English muffin with pizza sauce. Bake or microwave until the cheese is melted.

Memory Verse: Ephesians 6:12 (ICB)

"Our fight is not against people on earth. We are fighting against the rulers and authorities and the powers of this world's darkness. We are fighting against the spiritual powers of evil in the heavenly world."

Alternate Version: Ephesians 6:12 (NKJV)
"For we do not wrestle against flesh and blood, but against principalities, against powers, against the rulers of the darkness of this age, against spiritual hosts of wickedness in the heavenly places."

Memory Verse Activity
O LARGE CIRCLE CUT FROM POSTER BOARD

Write the verse on the poster board and cut as a pizza is cut. Let the children put the pizza together and say the verse together several times until they learn it.

Prayer Focus

Dear God, thank You for Your love and protection, especially Your protection from evil in the world. We love You! Amen.

Drawn to God

By Tina Houser

> **Scripture:** 2 Peter 3:9
>
> **Lesson Aim:** The children will be assured that God wants them as part of His holy family.
>
> **Memory Verse:** 2 Peter 3:9

☞ **Bible Activity for Younger Children:** What's Missing?
   ○ AT LEAST 20 SMALL ITEMS   ○ BOX OR A BAG

Lay the items out on the table. They can be anything at all—toys, office supplies, household items, gardening tools. The children will look at all the items and then close their eyes and turn their backs to the table. While the children have their backs turned, take one of the items from the table and place it in the box where it cannot be seen. When you signal the children to open their eyes and turn around they will try to figure out which item is missing. (So, the more items you have on the table, the more fun this will be, and the bigger the challenge.) If they get stumped, offer some clues about the missing object.

Our Bible verse today says that God doesn't want one person to be lost. When we could not figure out what had been removed from the table, we could've just said, "Forget it." But, we didn't. We kept thinking and working with the clues I gave you, so we could figure out what had been taken away. When we are away from God and have turned our backs on Him, He keeps trying to get us back to a right relationship with Him. God doesn't give up on us.

☞ **Bible Activity for Older Children:** Beach Towel Drag
   ○ 2 LARGE BEACH TOWELS

Divide the children into two groups. The groups will be at one end of the room. Choose one person from each group to start the game. These two players will go to the other end of the room. Indicate a stay-behind line (for the rest of the group) and a finish line (by the two lone players) with masking tape on the floor.

The two chosen children (one from each group) should be of similar strength. When the leader signals, each of these children will take the towel to the other end, lay it down, and one of the players from their group will get on the towel. The first player has to drag the other player to the finish line on the towel. Once they have crossed the finish line, then both of them can go back after one more person from their team. The next time all three can help bring someone back. With the added strength they will be able to retrieve players quicker. If they want to put more than one player on the towel at a time, that's OK. The game is not over until both teams have completed bringing everyone down to the finish line.

How does this game resemble the way God pursues us, how He keeps trying to bring us to Him? God pursues us and He doesn't quit. He utilizes people who have been drawn to Him to draw others to Him. Sometimes He uses one person at a time, and other times He uses groups of people.

Enrichment Activity for Younger Children: A Guiding Hand
◯ BLINDFOLDS

Set a few large things out in the room, like a chair, a garbage can, and a cardboard box. Review with the children what path you want them to take through the room, going around the objects and trying not to touch them. Blindfold one child and set them loose to try to walk the path you have designated for them. When they make it through or give up, then choose another child to go to them and get them back on the path. They now have someone who can guide them through the path without running into everything.

Which way was easier? How does this exercise remind you of how we live our lives? God has a plan for us, a path He wants us to follow. When we try to do it without His help, it's like being blindfolded and trying to walk the path in the dark. When we ask for His help, then it's like walking through the path with the assistance of someone who could see exactly where we were supposed to go. God patiently waits for us to ask for His help. He comes alongside us and helps guide us through our lives. He doesn't want you trying to live without Him.

Enrichment Activity for Older Children: Thomas Edison
◯ LARGE PIECE OF LIGHT YELLOW POSTER BOARD

Here's a quote from a famous inventor: "Genius is 1 percent inspiration and 99 percent perspiration." **What do you think that means?** It means that having the idea is just a small part of inventing something new. Finding a way to make that idea happen is where most of the work lies. By the way, the famous inventor who said that was Thomas Edison.

Thomas Edison lived in the late 1800s and early 1900s. One of his most famous inventions was the light bulb. When he first had the idea, he told someone that he thought he would have a light bulb working within a few weeks. Those few weeks turned into over two years! Before being able to get light from his new invention he would try over 6,000 different ways of making it. He was determined to make it work and would not give up on his idea. His persistence in inventing a light bulb has made a huge difference in the way people live today.

God has the wonderful idea that He wants you to be part of His family and spend eternity with Him in Heaven. God pursues anyone who isn't part of that family and refuses to give up. Sometimes He sends special people into our lives to help direct us back to Him or He makes a miracle, hoping that a person away from Him will come back. God never gives up on His perfect idea to have everyone He created join Him in Heaven one day.

Draw (or ask one of your talented children to do it) a huge light bulb on the light yellow piece of poster board. Cut out the light bulb and display it on the wall. Across the top of the light bulb write, *God Pursues You Because He Loves You!* The children will write their names inside the light bulb. Keep the light bulb on display to remind the children in upcoming weeks that God will always pursue them, because He loves them.

 Memory Verse: 2 Peter 3:9 (ICB)

"The Lord is not slow in doing what he promised—the way some people understand slowness. But God is being patient with you. He does not want anyone to be lost. He wants everyone to change his heart and life."

Alternate Version: 2 Peter 3:9 (NKJV)
"The Lord is not slack concerning His promise, as some count slackness, but is long-suffering toward us, not willing that any should perish but that all should come to repentance."

Drawn to God

By Tina Houser

Scripture: 2 Peter 3:9

Lesson Aim: The children will be assured that God wants them as part of His holy family.

Memory Verse: 2 Peter 3:9

Preparation

- PAPER CLIPS
- MAGNET
- LARGE METAL COOKIE SHEET
- SMALL PIECES OF PAPER
- PENCILS

There is a very familiar Bible story that I'd like for you to help me tell. I am going to leave out some of the words and I want you to help tell the story by filling in the word that I left out. I call this a "Pfffft" story! (You make the sound by pressing your lips together tightly and blowing, like you would if you were blowing into a trumpet. The kids absolutely fall in love with this storytelling technique! This works well and keeps the story flowing, but if you can't get the knack of it, use a kazoo or ring a bell.) Each time you hear "pfffft," you know that I am calling for your help. Just yell out the word that fits in that place. Sometimes you may have to complete your sentence before the children figure out the word from the context. The story I want you to help me with is the story of Jonah. Wet your whistle and have fun!

God asked Jonah to go preach to the people of Nineveh. The people there were known for not following God and for being a wicked town. Jonah didn't like the idea much. Instead of going to Nineveh, Jonah headed the other "pfffft" (direction). Jonah was hiding from "pfffft" (God). Jonah got to the sea and decided to get on a "pfffft" (boat). The boat set sail. Jonah was so relieved to be away from God that he went to the bottom of the boat and fell "pfffft" (asleep). When the boat got out to sea, a terrible "pfffft" (storm) came up and tossed the boat violently in the water. The sailors woke Jonah and told him to pray to God for help. Jonah didn't want to pray to God. He was running away from "pfffft" (God). When Jonah told the sailors that he was running away from God, they decided that God must be angry with Jonah, so they threw him "pfffft" (overboard) into the waves. Immediately, the waves got "pfffft" (still). When he fell into the water, he was swallowed by a great "pfffft" (fish). For three days Jonah stayed in the fish and he prayed to the Lord. He told God that he was sorry for not going to Nineveh. God heard Jonah's prayer and had the fish spit Jonah up on the "pfffft" (shore). God pursued Jonah and wouldn't let him get away. He loved Jonah too much to let him run away. When Jonah came back to God, he gladly went to Nineveh to preach to the people there about God's forgiveness and love.

Make a large label for one end of the cookie sheet that says, *God*. Ask all the children to write their names on a small piece of paper. Then, attach a paper clip to each paper. Talk about how God wants each of us to come to Him just like He wanted Jonah to come to Him. Each child will place their paper with their name on it at one end of the cookie sheet. Place the magnet under the cookie sheet and drag your name to the other end of the cookie sheet that is labeled *God*. The magnet may disconnect sometimes and the movement stop, but repeated tries will get each child's name to God. As each child works the magnet and paper clip down the cookie sheet, say to the child, "God will never stop pursuing _____" and add the child's name to the sentence.

Jonah followed God, then he stopped following God, and then he followed God again. God kept pursuing Jonah and He pursues us, also. He pursues us, even though sometimes we may feel disconnected from Him. He still reaches out to us, waiting for us to come back to Him.

Song Suggestions

"Purest of God" by Kurt Johnson, a.k.a. MrJ from *Pure Gold* (Mr. J Music, 1995)
"Miracle" by Mary Rice Hopkins from *Juggling Mom* (Big Steps 4 U, 1999)
"He's Got Plans" by Dean-O from *Soul Surfin'* (FKO Music, Inc.,1999)
"You're in My Heart to Stay" by Jana Alayra from *Dig Down Deep* (Montjoy Music, 1997)
Good News Songsheets published by CEF Press, P.O. Box 348, Warrenton, MO 63383

Craft for Younger Children: Pasta Necklace

○ PASTA WITH HOLES FOR STRINGING   ○ RUBBING ALCOHOL
○ FOOD COLORING   ○ PAPER TOWELS   ○ CORD FOR STRINGING THE PASTA

Before class, prepare the pasta. For each color, mix one tablespoon of food coloring with 2 tablespoons of rubbing alcohol. Make several different colors. Stir the macaroni into the colored solutions and spread it on the paper towels to dry.

Lay out the colored pasta and let the kids string the pasta on the cords. When they are finished they will have a beautiful necklace!

God wants us to stay close to Him, just like these pretty colors stay on the pasta. Remember to stay close to God, God loves you very much!

Craft for Older Children: Loving God

○ CRAFT DOUGH

Make the dough by mixing 1 cup of salt, 2 cups of flour, and 1 cup of water. Mix salt and flour. Add the water a little at a time, mixing to form a ball. Add red food coloring to make red dough. Knead for 7 to 10 minutes. (Food coloring can also be added to the water before combining the ingredients, but you may have to add more if the color is not dark enough.)

Let the children form their dough into a heart shape. Then, push the magnet into the back of the heart and let dry.

This heart will help you to remember that God loves you and wants you to stay close to Him. Put this magnet on your refrigerator so you will never forget!

Snack: Heart Cookies
○ HEART SHAPED COOKIES

Serve the cookies and tell the children that the heart shape stands for love and reminds us of love. **When you love someone what do you do?** You spend time with them and let them know you love them! It's the same with God. God wants you to spend time with Him and love Him.

Memory Verse: 2 Peter 3:9 (ICB)

"The Lord is not slow in doing what he promised—the way some people understand slowness. But God is being patient with you. He does not want anyone to be lost. He wants everyone to change his heart and life."

Alternate Version: 2 Peter 3:9 (NKJV)
"The Lord is not slack concerning His promise, as some count slackness, but is long-suffering toward us, not willing that any should perish but that all should come to repentance."

Memory Verse Activity
○ POSTER BOARD

Write the verse onto the poster board in large letters. Cut the poster board into a puzzle shape. The children can then work the puzzle to learn the verse.

Prayer Focus

Dear God, thank You so much for Your love. Thank You for letting us be so close to You.

Persecution

By Tina Houser

Scripture: Matthew 5:11

Lesson Aim: The children will become aware that perse-
               cution exists in our world today.

Memory Verse: Matthew 5:11

☞ Bible Activity for Younger Children: Where's the Bible?
   ○ STICKER OF A BIBLE   ○ ONE DOMINO

Place the Bible sticker on a domino (or something else that is small and substantial). One child, the guesser, will leave the room while the other children sit in a circle, passing the Bible domino. The domino will be hidden in one child's hand when the guesser returns to the room. The guesser will try to figure out who has the Bible. Play several times, giving as many children as possible the chance to be the guesser.

There are countries in our world that cannot have a Bible out in the open without getting in trouble for it. They have to hide their Bibles and then read them when no one is around. This is one way people in our world today are persecuted. The Bible tells us that God blesses the people who are strong in their faith and refuse to let anything stop them from their relationship with Him.

☞ Bible Activity for Older Children: Persecution Paint
   ○ CRAFT PAINTS   ○ 2-IN. PAINT BRUSHES   ○ BLACK PLASTIC GARBAGE BAG
   ○ PAPER PLATES   ○ SOMETHING TO COVER THE FLOOR

Prepare a black plastic garbage liner by cutting a hole in the bottom seam just big enough for a child to get his or her head through. Do not cut holes for the arms.

Select one of the children to be your victim—no, I mean your volunteer. Pull the plastic bag over them to completely cover their clothing, and ask them to stand on the floor covering you have prepared. Squirt several colors of craft paint onto separate paper plates. Each color should have its own brush.

Briefly talk about the meaning of persecution. Ask the children to mention how people are persecuted throughout the world. They will come up with things about how Bibles have to be hidden and people are thrown in jail. Now, let's think about how people in the United States are persecuted for being Christians. Each time one of these ideas is shared, the child sharing the idea will choose a color and paint a couple of swatches on the black plastic liner covering your volunteer. Encourage them to think about how students make fun of others at school for their beliefs or for going to church. Maybe they are called a name like "Miss Goodie Twoshoes." Some students have been asked to not wear T-shirts that have Christian messages on them. A coach keeps you from playing in a game, because you missed a practice when you were attending church. The little things can mount up and be a big mess just like our coverall has become. Remove the coverall carefully.

No matter what kinds of attacks are made on us because of our beliefs, we can be sure that God will be happy when we stand up for His truth, and that we will feel good about ourselves for doing it. It is always satisfying to know you have done what is pleasing to God.

Enrichment Activity for Younger Children: Persecution Birdies

O FEATHERS   O QUARTERS   O CIRCLES OF LIGHTWEIGHT FABRIC (4 IN. IN DIAMETER)
O THREAD

Two children will need to work as partners, but they will each need to make one of the weighted birdies. Give each child a quarter and a piece of the fabric. Place the quarter in the center of the fabric circle. Pull the edges together. Push 3 feathers down into the center where the edges are drawn up. With the fabric up around the feathers, tie a piece of thread around it to hold it in place. You should end up with something that looks like a little sack with 3 feathers sticking out the top.

Ask the children to share mean or hurtful things that kids say about each other. Each time something is shared the children will gently toss their birdie into the air. Another hurtful thing is shared and they all toss their birdie. **Are there mean things that people say to you (or you've heard other kids say) because of your belief in God?** Toss the birdies again.

What have you noticed about the way your birdie lands every time? Does it ever land on the feathers? No, it always lands with the feathers up. That's because the body of the birdie is weighted with the quarter. The Scriptures tell us that even when people say mean things against us because we are followers of Christ, God will never leave us. He is the weight in our lives that keeps us grounded. When people say mean things about us because of our beliefs, God doesn't go and hide. He stays there with us and helps us come through it happily, because we know that we have obeyed God Almighty.

Enrichment Activity for Older Children: Sudanese Prayer Wall

O GLOBE   O BANNER   O LINED PAPER

Sudan is a name of a country in Africa, right under Egypt. It is the largest country on the continent of Africa and is about one-third the size of the United States. **Can you locate Sudan on the globe?**

Children's Ministry Sourcebook

Sometimes we think that persecution happened years ago, even hundreds and thousands of years ago. But, persecution still happens today and it happens in horrible ways. In 1997, a report was given to one of the United States Senate subcommittees that persecution was going on in the country of Sudan.

The government in Sudan does not want Christians in their country and many of the people there are Christians. In fact, at one time more people were becoming Christians in Sudan than in any other country in the world. It's hard to believe that these things are happening in our world today, but the government of Sudan regularly burns villages to the ground where there are a lot of Christians living. They take the children away from their parents to become slaves. The cattle they depend on for food are being killed. When pastors of churches are found, it is not uncommon for them to be thrown into a well, doused with gasoline, and set on fire. The people are beaten and parts of their bodies amputated.

Why would the government of Sudan treat the Christians this way? They are trying to get them to give up their belief in Jesus Christ by making life miserable for them. We need to pray for the people of Sudan, because they are also our brothers and sisters in Christ.

Make a banner that says, *Our Prayer Wall for Sudan.* Ask the children to write prayers to post under the banner. You may want to divide the prayers into categories: pray for the government of Sudan, pray for the mothers and fathers, pray for the United States government will help if they can, pray for the ministers who continue to preach Jesus Christ, pray for courage.

Memory Verse: Matthew 5:11 (ICB)

"People will say bad things about you and hurt you. They will lie and say all kinds of evil things about you because you follow me. But when they do these things to you, you are happy."

Alternate Version: Matthew 5:11 (NKJV)
"Blessed are you when they revile and persecute you, and say all kinds of evil against you falsely for My sake."

Persecution

By Tina Houser

Scripture: Matthew 5:11

Lesson Aim: The children will become aware of persecution in their world today.

Memory Verse: Matthew 5:11

Preparation

○ WORLD MAP MOUNTED FLAT   ○ BRIGHT-COLORED PUSH PINS   ○ ENVELOPES
○ THREAD

*Note: Open Doors puts out a wonderful 3-minute eye-opening DVD about persecution in our world today. The DVD is free for the asking, along with a packet of information, by contacting them at *OpenDoorsUSA.org*. This DVD would be an excellent addition to this lesson because it gives a heart-wrenching visual lesson.

Before class, prepare an envelope with a fact statement in each (listed below).

We're going to talk about a big word today that may be new to many of you. The word is *persecution*. **Does anyone have an idea what *persecution* means?** *Persecution* is when someone tries to make you so afraid that you stop doing what you are doing, even if what you are doing is right. Christians all over the world are faced with being afraid to worship Jesus Christ. Right now, more people are persecuted for their belief in Jesus Christ than any other time in the history of our world. **That's scary, isn't it?** Over 200 million Christians in 60 different countries live with the fear that something terrible will happen to them because they read the Bible and worship Jesus Christ.

One of the amazing things about these people who are being persecuted is that when they ask the rest of the world to pray, they do not ask for things to be easier for them. They ask people to pray that they will be strong and keep spreading the word of Jesus. They ask people to send more Bibles—the very Bibles that are going to get them in trouble. These people know that Jesus was persecuted, and as followers of Jesus, He told us that we would be persecuted, also.

Persecution happens all over the world. Before the lesson begins, give out the envelopes you have prepared. If you are in a setting where there is a congregation of adults, enlist them to stand and read the fact statements from their seats. Then ask one or two of the children to join them. If your setting is with the children only, give the envelopes to older children. Each time a different envelope is opened, help one of the children identify the location of that country and put a push pin on the map to mark it.

When all the fact statements have been read and the countries have been marked, make sure you clarify that these are not the only countries where persecution is happening.

Hold up a piece of thread. This represents one person somewhere in the world who is being persecuted because of his belief in Jesus. Snap the thread. We can make that person stronger with our prayers. Bring out another whole piece of thread. Add other pieces to it. Each time a thread is added say, "_____" (the name of one of the children) is praying that persecuted Christians will stay strong in their faith. After several threads have been added, attempt to break the thread again. Our prayers help to strengthen people on the other side of the world, just like these added threads helped strengthen that one thread that was all by itself.

End your time together by asking all the children to go stand with one of the people who read a persecution fact. While these small groups are together, ask them to pray for the country that is represented by that group.

Additional information for the presenter (not to be read to the students)
Fact Statements:
   In Egypt, people are shocked with electricity if they believe in Jesus.
   In Saudi Arabia, people have been beheaded because they believe in Jesus.
   In Sudan, entire villages where Christians worshipped have been burned to the ground.
   In China, people have been beaten to death because they believe in Jesus.
   In Vietnam, the government refuses to give permission for a church to meet.
   In Laos, people having a Bible study had the windows and doors nailed shut so they couldn't leave. For three days they were there without food or water, while their persecutors threatened to set the house on fire.
   In India, people have been thrown in jail for believing in Jesus.
   In Nigeria a pastor and the congregation were attacked and killed. The church was burned down.

Song Suggestions

"Believin' On" by Jana Alayra from *Believin' On* (Montjoy Music, 2002)
"Little Is Much" by Mary Rice Hopkins from *15 Singable Songs* (Big Steps 4 U, 1988)
"Faith Will Do" by Dean-O from *You Got It All* (FKO Music, Inc., 1997)
God's Power Songsheets published by CEF Press, P.O. Box 348, Warrenton, MO 63383

Craft for Younger Children: Corn Cob Decoration
   ○ SCISSORS   ○ GLUE   ○ POPCORN KERNELS   ○ POPPED POPCORN
   ○ YELLOW AND GREEN CONSTRUCTION PAPER

Cut out a corncob shape from yellow construction paper and cut out some leaves from green construction paper.

Put glue all over the corn cob section, then glue unpopped or popped corn (or both) to the cob. Add leaves and let dry.

This is a corncob, which is a symbol of 'plenty" or having plenty. We have so much in our country. This Thanksgiving be sure to thank God for all that we have! Let this corncob remind you of the blessings God has given you.

Craft for Older Children: Thanksgiving Turkeys

- O WOODEN HEARTS (TURKEY "FEATHERS") O WIGGLE EYES O GLUE GUN
- O SMALL WOODEN BALLS (TURKEY BODY) O YELLOW CRAFT FOAM
- O RED CRAFT FOAM O PAINT (RED, ORANGE, BROWN) O GLUE

Before class, paint the heart red and the wooden balls brown. Glue the wooden balls together; one on top of each other with a glue gun.

The children will glue the red heart behind the body of the turkey to form the feathers, glue the wiggle eyes to the front of the head. Cut a beak and gobbler from the craft foam. Your turkey is finished!

At Thanksgiving we show God and others how thankful we are for everything that God does for us. This will help you remind yourself of how thankful you are!

Optional Craft: Pine Cone Turkey

- O PINE CONE O ACORN OR ELONGATED SMALL NUT
- O 2 (10 MM) WIGGLE EYES, LOW TEMP GLUE GUN OR TACKY GLUE
- O RED CHENILLE STEMS O ORANGE CHENILLE STEMS O WIRE CUTTERS
- O BIRD FEATHERS O SLICE OF DEAD TREE BRANCH OR OTHER PIECE OF WOOD FOR BASE (ABOUT 1/2" THICK AND 3" ACROSS) O GOLD SPRAY PAINT

Lightly spray the pine cone with gold spray paint and let it dry. Cut the orange chenille stems into 2 (3-in.) pieces. Fold the first orange chenille stem into half, twist about 1/4" from the end and open up the ends to make the feet. Repeat with the second orange chenille stem.

Stick the orange feet in the turkey a little less than 1/2 way from the largest end. Glue in place. Glue the turkey body (pine cone) with feet down to the piece of wood. Glue the acorn to the smallest end of the pine cone. Glue the feathers in the pine cone closest to the largest end. Glue the wiggle eyes on the head (acorn). Cut a tiny piece of red chenille stem to use as the waddle and glue below the eyes.

Snack: Popcorn!

- O POPCORN KERNELS AND POPPER (OR PRE-MADE POPCORN)

The children can enjoy eating the popcorn. This popcorn will help you remember how much we have and how lucky we are. It will remind you how much we can help. A little bit of popcorn kernels became this whole bowl of popcorn! It's the same with helping others—a little bit of help will fill a whole heart!

Memory Verse: Matthew 5:11 (ICB)

"People will say bad things about you and hurt you. They will lie and say all kinds of evil things about you because you follow me. But when they do these things to you, you are happy."

Alternate Version: Matthew 5:11 (NKJV)
"Blessed are you when they revile and persecute you, and say all kinds of evil against you falsely for My sake."

Memory Verse Activity

Make enough turkey feathers from different colors of construction paper so that you can write a few words of the verse on each feather. Use a paper plate as the body of the turkey and glue the feathers around the edge so that the words can be read in order. The children will say the verse and then pluck one of the feathers. Continue removing the feathers until the children have memorized the verse.

Prayer Focus

Thank You God for all we have. Thank You for being in our lives. We love You!

God's Provision

By Tina Houser

Scripture: Psalm 107:1–2

Lesson Aim: The children will be assured that God is the Great Provider.

Memory Verse: Psalm 107:1–2

☞ **Bible Activity for Younger Children:** Build a Clubhouse

Provide the children with a variety of materials with the instruction that they are to work together to build a little clubhouse. Be creative in the supplies you offer them: card table, blanket, boxes, inner tube(s), laundry basket, buckets, flower pot, piece of material, etc. I have provided you with everything necessary to build a clubhouse.

Were you able to put a clubhouse together? When it was finished, was it exactly as you had pictured in your mind at the very beginning? God provides us with everything we need to build our lives. God provides us with what we NEED to build the life HE has in mind. Sometimes we think we have to have something in our lives, but we find out that it's just something we WANTED. God provides our needs, and sometimes He throws in some unexpected delights.

☞ **Bible Activity for Older Children:** A–Z Gratitude

○ SET OF ALPHABET CARDS

(If you have platform scooters, they would be a fun alternative to running for this game.) Spread the cards out on the floor face-down. The children will form two equal-size groups. One person will run down and pick up a card. (This is where the scooters would come in—roll instead of run.) Bring the card back to your group and show the letter. The group will decide on something they are grateful to God for providing them that begins with that letter. Write that at the bottom of the letter card, then send another member of the group to get a new card. Both groups are using from the same deck of alphabet cards. If a card is retrieved that no one has a suggestion to put on it, then it has to be returned to the other end of the room. BUT, another card cannot be picked up on that trip. A different player will have to go get a new card.

When all the cards have been retrieved, the groups will share their answers with one another by proceeding through the alphabet.

Enrichment Activity for Younger Children: Blanket Protection
○ A LARGE BLANKET

When the eggs hatch, little chicks get their first view of the world. They are not able to take care of themselves, so God has put the instinct in them that they know to stay close to their mothers. The mother hen shows them where the food is, leads them away from danger, and protects them from the weather. When she senses that something could harm her chicks, she raises her wings and all the little chicks scurry under her wings. She, then, gently lays her wings down around the chicks. She covers them on hot summer days when the sun is too hot for the chicks to be out. Her wings become an umbrella for the little ones when the rain is pouring down.

God provides protection for us. When something threatens us, He is there to go through it with us. He wraps His arms around us and keeps us close. I'm grateful for God's protection. **How about you?**

Let's play a little game to help us remember that God provides protection and companionship for us. Hold the blanket around you. Walk around the room with the children following you. Yell out, "Danger!" and raise the blanket over your head. All the children will huddle around you. Bring the blanket down around them as they crouch at your feet.

Enrichment Activity for Older Children: Pumpkin Prayers
○ SMALL PUMPKINS OR GOURDS   ○ PERMANENT MARKERS

On each pumpkin or gourd write one of the verses listed below. If you have more children than verses, then duplicate the verses on the pumpkins. (The real thing is fun for the children, but you can also use pumpkin or fall cut-outs.) Each child will choose a pumpkin and look up the verse indicated there. Each of these verses has to do with being thankful to God for His wonderful provisions. Take the pumpkins home and place them in a prominent place. Each time you pass them, be reminded that God has provided a wonderful world for you to enjoy and be part of. Say a "pumpkin prayer" of thanksgiving when you are reminded by your little pumpkin.

1 Timothy 2:1	Psalm 75:1	Ephesians 5:20
1 Thessalonians 5:18	Psalm 107:1	2 Corinthians 9:15
Psalm 100:4	Philippians 4:6	Colossians 3:15

Memory Verse: Psalm 107:1-2 (ICB)

"Thank the Lord because he is good. His love continues forever. That is what the people the Lord has saved should say. They are the ones he has saved from the enemy."

Alternate Version: Psalm 107:1-2 (NKJV)
"Oh, give thanks to the Lord, for He is good!
For His mercy endures forever.
Let the redeemed of the Lord say so,
whom He has redeemed from the hand of the enemy."

God's Provision

By Tina Houser

Scripture: Psalm 107:1–2

Lesson Aim: The children will be assured that God is the Great Provider.

Memory Verse: Psalm 107:1–2

Preparation

○ A VERY LONG ROPE

Hold the end of the rope in your hands as you begin talking with the children. Psalm 107:1 says to "Thank the Lord because he is good. His love continues forever." I wonder how long forever is. His loves continues (pull the rope through your hands as far as it will go from one outstretched hand to the other) and continues (pull the rope again) and continues (pull the rope again). Stop when there is still quite a bit of rope left on the ground. We can't even see the end of His love.

If God's love goes on forever, then our gratitude should go on forever, also. Ask each child to name something they are grateful to God for providing for them. The first child to name something will start at one end of the rope and stretch their arms as far as they will go on the rope. Hold onto that point. The next child to identify their gratitude will start at that point and stretch as far as they can. Each child will stay where they are, holding on to the rope. Our gratitude goes on and on just like God's love!

There was a movie out a couple of years ago called "Pay It Forward." The movie was about a boy who had to come up with a project for school that would change the world in some way. His plan was to change more than the little bit of the world around him; he wanted to change the whole world! He was going to do something BIG to help three people. Instead of them saying "thank you" or returning the favor to him, he wanted them to show their gratitude by doing something BIG for three more people. Each of those people would do three BIG things and so on and so on. He thought his plan had failed, but then he found out that people were "paying it forward" on the other side of the country. **What were they paying forward?** They were paying the debt of gratitude by helping someone else. The boy's gratitude plan had spread throughout the country and was affecting people just as he had imagined.

God provides for us in so many ways as our rope exercise demonstrated earlier. The best way to show our gratitude for what God has done for us is to share that with others. The Bible tells us that when you give someone a cold drink in the name of Jesus, then it is just as if you had given it to Jesus Himself. When we reach out to the people around us, that's like sending God a great big "Thank You" card!

Song Suggestions

"Say Thank You" by Mary Rice Hopkins from *Miracle Mud* (Big Steps 4 U, 1995)
I'm Not Too Little Songsheets published by CEF Press, P.O. Box 348, Warrenton, MO 63383
"Pure Heart" by Norm Hewitt from *Fired Up!* (Generation Ministries, 2002)
"You're in My Heart to Stay" by Jana Alayra from *Dig Down Deep* (Montjoy Music, 1997)

Craft for Younger Children: Thank You Card
○ CONSTRUCTION PAPER IN SEVERAL COLORS ○ MARKERS

Write *Thank You God* across the top of the paper. The children will make a thank you card for God. Today we are going to say thank you to God for all that God has done for us. **What can you thank Him for?** Write or draw it on the card.

Craft for Older Children: Thanksgiving Tree
○ CONSTRUCTION PAPER IN FALL COLORS (INCLUDING BROWN)

Show the children how to trace their handprints onto construction paper. Each child will need one brown hand print and several different colored handprints.

Make a tree by placing the brown handprint (with wrist) down on a piece of construction paper. This will be the trunk of the tree. Add the other colors as leaves on the tree.

Write something that you are thankful for on each of the leaves on your tree. Thank God for everything God has given you!

Snack: Thanksgiving Turkey Cookies

Make these cute snacks ahead of time and serve in class.
○ MICROWAVE ○ BAG OF CANDY CORN (BEAK AND EYES)
○ BAG OF CARAMEL CANDY SQUARES (BODY) ○ BAG OF DOVE CHOCOLATE (BASE/FEET)
○ BAG OF STRIPED CHOCOLATE COOKIES (TAIL AND FEATHERS)
○ THANKSGIVING CUP CAKE LINERS ○ MICROWAVABLE PLATE

Unwrap a piece of Dove chocolate to use as the base of the turkey. Place it on a microwavable plate. Unwrap a piece of caramel and stick it on top of the Dove chocolate bar for the turkey's body.

Take a piece of candy corn and push it down on top of the caramel (pointed end out). This makes the turkey's beak. Use another piece of caramel and push it down on top of the first caramel. This is the head of the turkey.

Break off the little white ends of two candy corns and push in the top caramel for the eyes. Take one striped chocolate cookie and apply to the back of the body to form the feathers. Put the turkey in the microwave for up to 8 seconds just so the candy and cookie can fuse together.

Memory Verse: Psalm 107:1-2 (ICB)

"Thank the Lord because he is good. His love continues forever. That is what the people the Lord has saved should say. They are the ones he has saved from the enemy."

Alternate Version: Psalm 107:1-2 (NKJV)
"Oh, give thanks to the Lord, for He is good!
For His mercy endures forever.
Let the redeemed of the Lord say so,
whom He has redeemed from the hand of the enemy."

Memory Verse Activity

Write the verse on the board so that all children can see the words. Divide the children into six groups and assign words to say as follows:

First group	Thank the Lord because He is good.
Second group	His love continues forever.
Third group	This is what the people
Fourth group	The Lord has saved should say.
Fifth group	They are the ones
Sixth group	He has saved from the enemy.

The groups will stand, say their part of the verse and sit down before the next groups stands to say their part. Continue doing this until the verse is memorized.

Prayer Focus

Dear God, we thank You because You are so good! Your love lasts forever!

Loneliness

By Tina Houser

Scripture: Deuteronomy 31:6

Lesson Aim: The children will be reminded that God is always with them and they are never alone.

Memory Verse: Deuteronomy 31:6

☞ Bible Activity for Younger Children: Bucket Brigade

○ 6 BUCKETS   ○ BEAN BAGS   ○ MASKING TAPE

Label three buckets *By Yourself* and three buckets *With Others.* Line the buckets against the wall, alternating the labels. Mark a stand-behind line on the floor with a piece of masking tape. The children will take turns tossing a bean bag at the buckets. If the bean bag goes in a bucket labeled "By Yourself" they will tell an activity that you do by yourself. If the bean bag goes in a bucket labeled "With Others," then tell an activity that you like to do with other people. As the children make their comments write them where everyone can see the two lists. After everyone has had a couple of chances to toss and you have several things in each list, talk about what you have put together.

Are there things on the "With Others" list that you could do by yourself, you would just rather not? Which ones are they? Why would you rather do them with someone else? When do you like to do things by yourself? There are times when you would like to be with someone else, but there's no one around. You could be lonely at those times. The Bible tells us that if we believe in God we are never absolutely alone. God is always there. When you're all by yourself is a wonderful time to talk to God. When you're tempted to feel sorry for yourself because no one else is around, remember that God is with you. He thinks you're important enough to never leave you!

☞ Bible Activity for Older Children: I Sense You're There

○ BLINDFOLD

Blindfold one of the children. The leader will tap one of the other kids on the shoulder. That person will sneak up to the blindfolded person, as quietly as possible. When the blindfolded person thinks someone is within arm's reach, they will reach out to touch them. Give as many children as time allows the opportunity to be blindfolded.

There were times when we knew that someone was standing close by, but other times we weren't sure where the person was. Sometimes we can feel God's presence, and other times we have a difficult time sensing Him. We may be alone, but God is always there.

Enrichment Activity for Younger Children: Drama Pairs

The children need to form pairs to accomplish the following tasks. All activities are pretend and are meant to be done (imagined) together and never alone.

> Saw wood like a lumberjack.
> Jump on a trampoline.
> Walk through a muddy field.
> Roll like a log.
> Get caught in quick sand.
> Give a dog a bath.
> Take out the garbage.
> Crawl under a table.

When does God want to be with you? The all-powerful God wants to do everything with you. He wants you to be together when you play, when you eat, when you sleep, when you have a terrible cold, when you practice the piano, when you do your chores, when you are waiting for someone, when you study for a test, and when you go to a party. There's never a reason to be lonely when God wants to share everything with you.

Enrichment Activity for Older Children: Tied to Christ
○ STRIPS OF OLD SHEETING

Using the strips of sheeting, tie the children together in pairs, facing one another. Tie right hands to left hands. Give each pair a task to perform in your room. These tasks could include things like: arrange the chairs in a different configuration, wash the table with soap and water, look up the memory verse for this lesson and mark it with a bookmark, make a snake out of play dough, cut a heart out of construction paper, write your names on the board. Tailor your tasks to what is available in your space.

When we become a follower of Christ, we must remember that in everything we do, His Spirit is with us. We never do anything completely alone. As you completed the tasks, you were beginning to figure out how to work together in a better and easier way. As we follow Christ, we grow more like Him and understand what pleases Him. Following Him becomes easier the more we know about Him.

Memory Verse: Deuteronomy 31:6 (ICB)

"Be strong and brave. Don't be afraid of them. Don't be frightened. The Lord your God will go with you. He will not leave you or forget you."

Alternate Version: Deuteronomy 31:6 (NKJV)
"Be strong and of good courage, do not fear nor be afraid of them;
For the Lord your God, He is the One who goes with you.
He will not leave you nor forsake you."

Loneliness

By Tina Houser

Scripture: Deuteronomy 31:6

Lesson Aim: The children will be reminded that God is always with them and they are never alone.

Memory Verse: Deuteronomy 31:6

The main part of the Vietnam War took place in the 1960s and 1970s. The United States was involved in this war and many of our men became POWs. **Do you know what POW stands for?** (Prisoner Of War) Being a prisoner of war, or a POW, meant that you had been captured and were being held in an enemy prison. POWs did not have contact with their families, friends, or military commanders. Many times they were kept in cells all by themselves for years.

The POWS of the Vietnam War came up with what has become known as the "tap code." Each letter had a certain number of taps with a pause in the middle of it. The prisoners could send each other messages by slowly tapping out letters on anything that would make a noise. They could tap a message on a pipe, a pan, the wall, a door, or their food dish. It was not the same as Morse Code, because Morse Code had both long and short sounds. When you tapped on a pipe, you could only make one sound, so a new code had to be created. One of the main things they did through the tap code was to figure out who was in prison with them. This helped greatly if the men ever left the prison. They were able to tell the military, so they would know what happened to all the soldiers. But, most importantly, through the tapped messages they could encourage one another and keep their fellow prisoners from giving up on their situation. They knew they were not alone.

When they were allowed to be in the same room together, the POWs were not allowed to speak with one another. They used a blinking code, then, and could talk to each other by blinking the tap code. The North Vietnamese were never able to figure out how the code worked.

It's easy to see how being a POW could've been a terribly lonely situation. Having some-one tapping out messages every once in a while helped the POWs survive this horrible ordeal during the Vietnam War. The tap code was an unusual way to communicate. **How do we communicate with God?** Through prayer we talk with and listen to what God wants to share with us. Prayer is an unusual way of communicating. **Can you think of anyone else you talk to through prayer?** No. That's because it's a special way God created just to talk with Him. When no one else is around and you start to feel lonely,

God is with you and you can send God a message through prayer. The other POWs were just on the other side of the wall from each other and couldn't see one another. We can't see God, but He's not on the other side of the wall; He's right there with you! So, there's never a reason to feel lonely!

♪ Song Suggestions

"Lord I Give My Heart" by Mark Thompson from *Yes Yes Yes!* (Markarts, 2000)
"Say Thank You" by Mary Rice Hopkins from *Miracle Mud* (Big Steps 4 U, 1995)
"Outta Sight" by Dean-O from *Soul Surfin'* (FKO Music, Inc., 1997)
God's Power Songsheets published by CEF Press, P.O. Box 348, Warrenton, MO 63383

Craft for Younger and Older Children: Thanksgiving Memory Baskets

○ TINY TWIST PRETZELS ○ OYSTER CRACKERS ○ STICK PRETZELS
○ CANDY CORN ○ MINI-MARSHMALLOWS ○ FRUITY BALL-SHAPED CEREAL
○ TEDDY BEAR-SHAPED GRAHAM CRACKERS

Today we are going to make "memory baskets." As we get ready for Thanksgiving, we want to remember how good God is to us,

Tiny twist pretzels—The pilgrims believed in God and felt that they should be free to worship God the way they wanted to. They should be able to pick their own pastors and make their own laws. The pretzels represent praying hands. The pilgrims prayed for a place they could go to be free to worship God the way they wanted to. They prayed for God's protection on their trip across the ocean and for God to help them in the new land.

Oyster crackers or other dried bread and jerky—If the weather was bad on the Mayflower, the pilgrims had to eat cold biscuits and salted meat.

Stick pretzel—The pilgrims cut down trees and used logs to build their homes.

Mini-marshmallows—These remind us of snow and the first winter in the new land in which only half the pilgrims survived.

Candy corn and gold fish crackers—Squanto showed the pilgrims how to grow corn by putting four seeds into a little mound of earth and placing fish around the seeds.

Life Saver candies—God helped the pilgrims survive in the new land. He sent Squanto to help the pilgrims and show them how to find food. He was their life saver.

Teddy Grahams—The pilgrims had to learn to defend themselves against wild animals like bears.

Fruity cereal or other fruit shapes or dried cranberries—Squanto taught the pilgrims where to find wild berries and fruits and how to dry them for the winter.

 Snack: Memory Snacks

The children can eat the remaining ingredients of the memory basket as you remind them of what each one means.

✑ Memory Verse: Deuteronomy 31:6 (ICB)

"Be strong and brave. Don't be afraid of them. Don't be frightened. The Lord your God will go with you. He will not leave you or forget you."

Alternate Version: Deuteronomy 31:6 (NKJV)
"Be strong and of good courage, do not fear nor be afraid of them;
for the Lord your God, He is the One who goes with you.
He will not leave you nor forsake you."

📖 Memory Verse Activity
  ○ WHITE BOARD

Write the Bible verse on the board. All the players will stand and recite the verse with the Scripture reference, then they can all sit down.

Choose one player to erase one word of the verse. Then, ask all of the girls to stand and recite the verse inserting the missing word. Choose another player to erase another word of the verse. Ask all of the boys to stand and recite the verse inserting the missing words. Continue the game by erasing each word one at a time and having different groups of players. All of them who have a birthday in February stand and recite the verse, all those with blond hair, etc. When all of the verse has been erased, have a contest between the boys and the girls to see who can say it with the fewest mistakes.

🙏 Prayer Focus

Dear God, we thank You especially this week of Thanksgiving. We know that others suffer much more than we do and we pray for their safety. Thank You for all You do for us, we love You and praise You!

Advent 1—
He Will Be Our Peace

By Tina Houser

Scripture:　　Matthew 1:23b

Lesson Aim:　　The children will understand that peace comes from knowing Immanuel, "God with us."

Memory Verse: Matthew 1:23b

☞ **Bible Activity for Younger Children:** A Childlike Gift
○ WRAPPING PAPER　○ RIBBON　○ BOWS　○ TAPE　○ SCISSORS　○ CAMERA

Divide the children into groups of three or four, making sure there is a rather small child in each group. Give each group some gift wrapping supplies. They are going to wrap the smallest member of their group as if he or she were a Christmas gift. Take pictures as the children are working and then, also, when they have completed their project. The child being wrapped can stand or lay down, but will have to remain very still throughout the project.

God was giving the whole world a special gift in Jesus our Savior. But, God gave Mary and Joseph another special gift; He gave them the responsibility of being Jesus' earthly parents. At first that must have been very scary, but the angel assured both of them that God was in this wonderful event, and there was nothing for them to fear. Mary and Joseph were at peace with God's plan.

☞ **Bible Activity for Older Children:** A Surprise Package
○ VARIOUS SIZES OF BOXES WRAPPED IN BEAUTIFUL CHRISTMAS WRAP
○ ONE BOX WRAPPED IN BROWN PAPER

Point to each of the pretty boxes and ask the children to guess what might be in it. (There's nothing in any of them and you're not going to unwrap them, so it doesn't matter what their guesses are.) Now, point to the box covered in brown paper. **What do you think is in this brown one? If the UPS delivery man had brought all of these packages to your door, which one would you be most interested in? Which one would you be least interested in?**

People were expecting the Messiah, the Savior of the world, to come as a king. They expected Him to have fancy wrappings of jewels, a crown, and long flowing robes. They expected Him to be born in an expensive castle to parents who were well-known. But, Jesus didn't come as expected. He wasn't fancy at all. Tell some ways that were very ordinary about the way Jesus came to this world. (He was born in a stable. His mother and father were just ordinary people. The people who shared the joy over His birth were lowly shepherds. The town was crowded with strangers all around. His bed was made out of straw.)

When the angel told Mary and Joseph that they would be Jesus' earthly parents, they questioned why it would be them. After all, there wasn't anything special about them. God gave them a peace, though, a quietness and rest in their spirits, that His plan was not as people expected, and that Jesus would come in a very common, ordinary way.

Enrichment Activity for Younger Children: A Special Census
○ PACKAGE OF M&MS FOR EACH CHILD ○ SCRAP PIECES OF PAPER

Give each child a package of M&Ms, a piece of paper, and a pencil. Open the candies and pour them out onto the table. On their paper, the children will write all the different colors they find in their packages. Once they have written down the names of the colors, they will count each color. Write the number counted next to the color.

You have just taken a census of your candies. A census is when a special count is taken and usually means when citizens of a country are counted. Mary and Joseph went to Bethlehem for a census. The Roman government counted its people every 14 years and this was the time for that to be done. A census is usually taken for one of two reasons: to find out how many men there are for military purposes, or to find out how much is owed the government in taxes.

Enrichment Activity for Older Children: The Hula Hoop Hussle
○ HULA HOOPS ○ LARGE BOWL OF CEREAL (LARGER PIECES) ○ LARGE PLASTIC GLASS
○ MUSIC PLAYED AT HIGH SPEED

Place the bowl of cereal on the floor and the glass on the floor in a different place far from the bowl of cereal. In various places throughout the room place the hula hoops on the floor. Make groups of 5 children to get inside each hula hoop. When the leader indicates, all the groups will move to the cereal bowl at the same time where each player will have to bend down to pick up a piece of cereal. There is absolutely no order to this, and the more chaotic the better. The children should not be discouraged from pushing and bumping into one another. Once everyone in a hula hoop group has their piece of cereal, they will proceed to the plastic glass where each one will deposit their cereal. The groups will then return to their place of origin. (When the activity begins, the leader may want to play some Christmas music at high speed to increase the level of tension to the game.)

When Mary and Joseph got to Bethlehem it was crowded, because people from all over were visiting there for the same reason. They had all come because of the census. We know that it was crowded, because Mary and Joseph had a difficult time finding a place to stay. Even though Bethlehem was crowded and frantic with visitors, Mary and Joseph had a special peace; they knew that God was leading their lives. The baby that would come would bring peace to the world. Even the name Immanuel, which means "God with us," would bring a sense of peace.

At Christmastime, how is our town like Bethlehem was during the census? The hustle and bustle of buying presents, going to parties, putting up decorations, and more could make us feel frantic if we didn't know the peace that the Christ-child brought.

Memory Verse: Matthew 1:23b (ICB)

"'She will have a son, and they will name him Immanuel.'
This name means 'God with us.'"

Alternate Version: Matthew 1:23b (NKJV)
"Behold, a virgin shall be with child, and bear a Son,
And they shall call His name Immanuel, which is translated, God with us."

Advent 1—
He Will Be Our Peace

By Tina Houser

> **Scripture:** Matthew 1:23b
>
> **Lesson Aim:** The children will understand that peace comes from knowing Immanuel, "God with us."
>
> **Memory Verse:** Matthew 1:23b

Preparation
○ REFLEX HAMMER

Bring a child forward to sit in a chair, cross one leg over the top of the other and relax. Using a reflex hammer, gently tap right below the knee cap on the leg that is hanging free. If you tap in the correct place, and this is a healthy child, the child's foot should jump away from their body just a little. **What was the reaction to me tapping on his knee?** This reaction is called a reflex and you can't help but do it.

Listen for the reactions in this story.

An angel, Gabriel, was sent to a young woman named Mary who was engaged to a man named Joseph. When the angel appeared to Mary she didn't know what to think. The angel then told her that she was going to have a baby that would be the Son of God. She wondered how this could be. She was only engaged to Joseph; they weren't married yet. The angel then told her that God would be the father of this child and "nothing is impossible for God." When Mary heard the angel say this, she was at peace, because she knew God was using her for something wonderful. Right after that, Mary went to see her elderly aunt Elizabeth who was also going to have a baby. Elizabeth was much older than most women who were having babies. Seeing Elizabeth assured Mary that God could do impossible things. When Elizabeth saw Mary, the baby in Elizabeth jumped for joy. That was the way the Holy Spirit told Elizabeth that the baby Mary was carrying was from God and would be the Savior of the world. The Bible says that Mary praised God. Read Luke 1:46–49 (ICB). Here is Mary's praise:

"My soul praises the Lord;
My heart is happy because God is my Savior.
I am not important, but God has shown his care for me, his servant girl.
From now on, all people will say that I am blessed,
because the Powerful One has done great things for me.
His name is holy."

How did Mary react when the angel appeared? (frightened, startled, confused) **How did she react when the angel told her "nothing was impossible for God"?** (believed the angel, was at peace) **How did Mary react when Elizabeth got her message from God about the baby Mary was carrying?** (gave God praises) Mary's reactions were a reflection of her relationship with God. She knew in her heart that God could make the impossible happen, and because of that she had peace. She knew that her baby would be the Savior, and when Elizabeth realized that also, she sang praises and had peace about her mission for God.

Reread the verses of Mary's praise. Those sound like the words of someone who is at peace with what God is doing in her life! In our lives we get to choose how we react to different situations. The way we react tells other people a lot about our relationship with Jesus. Our reaction should become automatic as we grow in Christ that we would always consider what Jesus would do if He were here. We couldn't control our reaction to the reflex hammer; it was automatic. The longer we live with Jesus as our Lord, our reactions should become more automatically like Him.

Song Suggestions

"Wrap It All Up" by Mary Rice Hopkins from *Mary Christmas* (Big Steps 4 U, 1993)
"Glory" by Mary Rice Hopkins from *Mary Christmas* (Big Steps 4 U, 1993)
"Oh, Come Let Us Adore Him" (Traditional)
"Silent Night" (Traditional)

Craft for Younger Children: Angel Sack

  ○ WHITE LUNCH SACK ○ DOILIES ○ GOLD GLITTER ○ COFFEE FILTERS
  ○ CONSTRUCTION PAPER

Open the lunch sack out so it will stand on its own. Fold over the top and staple the sack shut. Fold a doily in half and place it over the top of the sack. Staple it in place. Cut out a circle from construction paper for the angel's face. Draw the features on the angel's face with a marker. Place a thin line of glue across the forehead and sprinkle with gold glitter to make a halo. Glue the face in place against the doily. For the wings cut another doily in half and glue the two pieces behind the face so they stand up.

Craft for Older Children: He Is Our Peace

  ○ WIDE RIBBON (2 FEET LONG EA.) ○ CRAFT FOAM ○ SEQUINS, ETC.
Note: This will be an ongoing craft that the child will add to all month.

Today we learned that Jesus is our PEACE. **What is the symbol for peace?** (peace symbol, dove, etc.) There are many symbols for peace. Jesus is also a symbol for peace. Jesus is true peace!

Write the word *PEACE* on the board for all to see. The children will design their own symbol for peace from the craft foam; they can also just cut the letters out to spell the word. Glue this onto the top of the ribbon. Each week another symbol will be added to the ribbon.

Snack: PEACE Crackers
○ LARGE ROUND CRACKERS   ○ SQUEEZE CHEESE

Gather children around and spread the crackers out on a plate. Write one letter on each cracker P-E-A-C-E. Continue until all crackers have a letter on them and then let the children spell PEACE with the crackers.

Jesus is our peace. Jesus gives us great peace in our lives when we believe in him. When Jesus is in your life you will have peace. Spell PEACE!

Memory Verse: Matthew 1:23b (ICB)

" 'She will have a son, and they will name him Immanuel.'
This name means 'God with us.' "

Alternate Version: Matthew 1:23b (NKJV)
"Behold, a virgin shall be with child, and bear a Son,
And they shall call His name Immanuel, which is translated, God with us."

Memory Verse Activity
○ CRAFT STICKS (8 STICKS FOR EACH SET)

For each set of memory verse sticks, write the following phrases on the sticks, one phrase on each stick

| She will | have a son | and they will | name Him |
| Immanuel | this name | means | God with us. |

Give out one set of sticks to each group of 4 children. Place the sticks face down on the table. Let the children turn the sticks over and place the sticks in the right order. Say the verse together.

Prayer Focus

Thank You God for the wonderful peace that comes from knowing You. We love You and we praise You.

Advent 2—
He Will Be Our Joy

By Tina Houser

Scripture: Luke 2:10

Lesson Aim: The children will celebrate the announcement of Jesus' birth.

Memory Verse: Luke 2:10

☞ Bible Activity for Younger Children: Crazy with Joy!
○ RED AND GREEN BALLOONS

(Note: Make sure you are aware of any latex allergies.) Give each child a balloon. Ask the children to mention something that brings them joy at Christmastime. Each time someone mentions something new, everyone will blow a big puff of air into their balloons.

What brought the shepherds joy that very first Christmas? Blow one last puff of air in your balloon and then let it go! Jesus came to bring us the greatest joy, and that's the joy of being close to our Heavenly Father.

☞ Bible Activity for Older Children: How Did It Happen?
○ RED AND GREEN BALLOONS ○ SMALL SLIPS OF PAPER

(Note: Make sure you are aware of any latex allergies.) Write each of the following sentences on slim pieces of paper and roll them up tightly.

• The shepherds were out in the field watching their sheep.
• An angel stood before the shepherds.
• The angel said, "Don't be afraid. The good news I bring will be joy to all people."
• The angel told the shepherds they would find the baby wrapped in cloths and lying in a manger.
• A large group of angels appeared, praising God.
• The angels left.
• The shepherds talked among themselves about going into Bethlehem.
• The shepherds left their sheep.
• The shepherds found Mary, Joseph, and the baby Jesus.
• The shepherds told everyone about the child.
• The shepherds went back to their sheep, praising and thanking God.

Insert the tiny roll into the mouth of a balloon until it falls into the belly of the balloon. Blow up the balloon and tie it.

Each child will choose a balloon to pop. When they pop their balloon they should retrieve the piece of paper that was inside it. (If you have more children than balloons, just blow up some balloons without clues, so that everyone has the joy of popping a balloon.)

Balloons mean fun and joy to me! How can you be sad when there's a balloon around? The children will work together to put the strips in the correct sequence. The story you have put together was a story of great joy! The angel said the news would bring joy to all people. **What was that good news?**

Enrichment Activity for Younger Children: Message in a Bottle
O EMPTY WATER BOTTLES   O DECORATING SUPPLIES

What ways could you use to get a message to someone? (write it in the sky with an airplane, send it tied to the leg of a carrier pigeon, write it on a paper airplane, leave it on their answering machine, put it in a bottle and throw it in the ocean, write them a letter, send them an e-mail, put it on a teleprompter at a ballgame) **How did God get a very special message to the shepherds?** He sent angels, His messengers, to tell them. **How would you feel if you got a message by way of an angel? That would make you feel pretty important, wouldn't it?** The message that God sent to the shepherds brought them great joy. **Then, how did the shepherds get the message to the people in the town of Bethlehem?** They went through the streets telling everyone they met about the baby they found in the stable who would be the Savior of the world.

Let's send the good news message of Jesus' birth by putting it in a bottle. The children will write their messages on a pieces of paper and then roll them up to insert into the bottles. Decorate the outside of the bottles with construction paper, sequins, ribbon, and if you dare, glitter! These bottles aren't actually going to be dropped in a river or the ocean because that would be considered littering, but if you put it on your dresser, it will remind you of the way the shepherds got their good news from God.

Enrichment Activity for Older Children: Sheepish Video
O COSTUMES (SHEPHERD, ANGEL, SHEEP)   O CAMCORDER

Have you ever just thought, "I wonder about that." Let's think about some "I wonder" questions.

- I wonder how they felt.
- I wonder what they said.
- I wonder if they believed.
- I wonder if they were scared.
- I wonder who was with them.

• I wonder if they felt important.
• I wonder what they did.

Write these "I wonder" statements, and any others the children come up with, in a place where everyone can see them. The children will get in small groups and choose either the shepherds, the angels, or the sheep to focus their "I wonder" statements around. Each group will create a monologue or a little skit that will answer some of those "I wonder" questions.

As the children get ready to share what they have put together, use the costumes to add some drama to their presentation and pull out the camcorder. They will love seeing themselves in their very own "I wonder" presentation.

Memory Verse: Luke 2:10 (ICB)

"The angel said to them, 'Don't be afraid, because I am bringing you some good news. It will be a joy to all the people.'"

Alternate Version: Luke 2:10 (NKJV)
"Then the angel said to them, 'Do not be afraid, for behold, I bring you good tidings of great joy which will be to all people."

Advent 2—
He Will Be Our Joy

By Tina Houser

Scripture: Luke 2:10

Lesson Aim: The children will celebrate the announcement of Jesus' birth.

Memory Verse: Luke 2:10

Preparation
○ JINGLE BELLS

When I jingle the bells it's time for our Bible lesson. (Jingle the bells.) The jingling of bells got your attention and announced that it was time for us to come together.

How does the Salvation Army get your attention to notice their kettle at Christmastime? (They ring a bell.) **How do the stores get your attention about their sales?** (They put ads in the paper.) **How do you find out about a Christmas party?** (You get an invitation.) **How does your teacher get your attention when she wants to begin class? How does your mom get your attention when you're watching television?** There are lots of ways to get someone's attention, and God had the grandest idea of all when it came to announcing the birth of Jesus.

Ask the children to lie down on the floor and look up at the ceiling. Imagine that you are out on a hillside. It's a quiet night and the sky is full of stars. It's a little cool, so you better pull the blanket up around you. Can you count the stars? My goodness, there are so many stars! You can hear the fire crackle; every once in a while it pops and sends a spark flying into the air. Now and then you hear one of the lambs let out a little baa as it nestles in closer to its mother. Oh, it is so peaceful, unbelievably peaceful.

Then, all of a sudden there is a bright light in the sky and an angel is right there over your head. (Everybody sit up!) You don't know what to do. Should you run? Should you hide? Should you pretend to be dead? Should you look up or look down at your sandals? While your mind is whirling in a panic, the angel speaks to you (freeze and look up) and says, "Don't be afraid. I bring you good news of great joy which will be for all people. Today, in Bethlehem your Savior has been born. You will find a baby wrapped in cloths and lying in a feeding trough." Just about the time you start breathing again, more angels appear and they are filling the air with their beautiful singing. They are singing songs of joy like you have never heard before.

When the angels leave, your heart is still racing. Without thinking, you just know that you need to go find this baby and see for yourself. Leaving the sheep there on the hillside that is now quiet and calm once again, you run (run in place) to the town to find this baby the angels have spoken of. There (stand still), right where they said you would find Him, is the baby in a feeding trough. All bundled up, and making sweet little baby sounds, you find Jesus. You are so full of joy yourself that you bow down to worship Him. (Everyone down on one knee.) As you leave to go back to the hillside and the sheep, you go through the town telling everyone about this joyful experience.

Jesus came to be our joy. When we believe in Jesus as our Savior, He gives us joy that is like nothing we have ever had before.

Song Suggestions

"On, Come Let Us Adore Him" (Traditional)
"Silent Night" (Traditional)
"We Three Kings" (Traditional)
"Follow That Star" by Mary Rice Hopkins from *Mary Christmas* (Big Steps 4 U, 1993)

Craft for Younger Children: Joy Chain
O RED & GREEN CONSTRUCTION PAPER (CUT INTO 1-IN. X 4-IN. STRIPS)   O TAPE

Write the letters in the word *joy*, one letter on each strip. Each child should have at least three sets (9 strips).

Today we learned that Jesus is our JOY! What does *joy* mean? Let's make a chain to remind us that Jesus is our joy. First, make a circle from the strip with the letter *J* on it. Then add the strip with the letter *O* and begin to make a chain. Add the letter *Y* and you have the first JOY in the chain! Continue until your chain says JOY three times! Joy! Joy! Joy!

Craft for Older Children: He Is Our JOY
O WIDE RIBBON (CUT 2 FEET LONG EA.)   O CRAFT FOAM   O SEQUINS, ETC.

(This craft is a continuation of the advent ribbon craft that the children will add to each week during advent.) Today we learned that Jesus is our JOY. **What is the symbol for joy?** (smiley face, balloons) There are many symbols for peace. Jesus is also a symbol for peace. Jesus is true peace!

Write the word *joy* on the board for all to see. The children will design their own symbol for joy from the craft foam; they can also just cut the letters out to spell the word. Glue onto the ribbon.

Snack: Overflowing Joy

○ LEMON-LIME DRINK   ○ STRAWBERRY FROZEN YOGURT
○ DESSERT PLATES   ○ SPOONS

Give each child a scoop of frozen yogurt in a cup that is sitting on a dessert plate. Pour room temperature lemon-lime soda over the top to fill the glass. If the foam has not already come over the top, when the children stick their spoons into the full glass, it will come over the sides. Our drink is overflowing, just like the joy of the shepherds overflowed!

The shepherds could not keep their joy inside when they saw the baby who was their Savior. **How did their joy overflow? What did they do to express their joy?**

Memory Verse: Luke 2:10 (ICB)

"The angel said to them, 'Don't be afraid, because I am bringing you some good news. It will be a joy to all the people.'"

Alternate Version: Luke 2:10 (NKJV)
"Then the angel said to them, 'Do not be afraid, for behold, I bring you good tidings of great joy which will be to all people.' "

Memory Verse Activity

○ 10-15 EMPTY CANS   ○ WRAPPING PAPER   ○ SMALL BALL

The children will wrap each can with wrapping paper. Assign a word or phrase to each child that they will write on a piece of paper and tape to a can. Place the cans about six inches apart on the floor in order so the entire verse CAN be read. The children will take turns rolling a ball at the cans. If a can is hit, it is removed from the sequence and everyone says the verse together. Continue tossing and removing cans until all the cans have been removed.

Prayer Focus

Dear God, thank You that we can call You our JOY! We thank You for being in our lives and loving us!

Advent 3—
He Will Be Our King

By Tina Houser

Scripture: Matthew 2:2

Lesson Aim: The children will participate in the story of Jesus' birth.

Memory Verse: Matthew 2:2

☞ Bible Activity for Younger and Older Children: Christmas Relay
- ○ TINSEL HALO ○ STRAW ○ SHEPHERD'S STAFF ○ CROWN ○ GIFT
- ○ STAR ○ MASKING TAPE

Kids of all ages love playing this game and will want to do it again and again. You can play this one child at a time, or make it into a relay with multiple teams. If you use multiple groups, remember to duplicate all the items for each group. Indicate a starting line with a piece of masking tape on the floor. About ten feet from the starting line lay the halo in the floor. In another ten feet, place a nest of hay. Another ten feet and place the shepherd's staff. And, lastly, in another ten feet place the crown and gift on the floor. Hang a star on any of the walls in the room where the children can see it. (A light-up star is really fun to have.)

One at a time, the children will run the course. The player will go to the halo, put it on, and yell, "Yo, Mary—you're gonna have a baby!" The player takes off the halo and lays it where he found it and runs to the next stop. Here, the player will sit in the straw nest, suck his thumb, and cry like a baby. The player then moves to the third stop, where he picks up the staff and says, "Here sheepy, sheepy, sheepy." After returning the staff to the place it was found, the player moves to the last stop where he will put on the crown, pick up the gift, and point at the star while commanding, "Follow that star!" Return the crown and gift to their places of origin, and run back to the group to tag the next player to begin through the course. Continue playing until everyone has had a chance to participate.

Enrichment Activity for Younger Children: Gift Clues
- ○ WATCH (1) ○ PIECE OF BREAD (2) ○ BABY DOLL (3) ○ BABY BLANKET (4)
- ○ COTTON BALLS (OR A TOY SHEEP) (5) ○ GOLD CHENILLE HALO (6) ○ HAY (7)
- ○ HEART (8) ○ STAR (9) ○ SCROLL (10) ○ MAP (11) ○ GIFT (12)

(Wrap each in gift boxes and number 1–12 in this order.)

Place the twelve gifts you have prepared under the tree or in a pile where the children can easily see them. Choose twelve children one at a time to come forward and choose one of the gifts before you start the activity. Tell the story of Jesus' birth using the twelve wrapped gifts as clues. Start with the box numbered 1. As you get to the number where the next clue gift is needed, ask the person who has possession of that gift to open it and show its contents. **What do you think this clue has to do with the story of Jesus' birth?**

Below are the key words from the Scripture and the order the gift clues will come.
- at that time (gift clue: watch)
- Bethlehem means "house of bread" (gift clue: piece of bread)
- a baby was born (gift clue: baby doll)
- wrapped Him in cloths (gift clue: baby blanket)
- sheep (gift clue: cotton balls)
- angel (gift clue: halo made from a gold chenille stem)
- manger (gift clue: hay)
- treasured them in her heart (gift clue: heart)
- saw the star (gift clue: star)
- it was written (gift clue: scroll)
- traveled (gift clue: map)
- gold, frankincense, myrrh (gift clue: 3 wrapped gift boxes)

Enrichment Activity for Older Children: What's the Word?
○ COPY OF THE STORY BELOW (ENLARGED)

Without the children knowing what you are going to do with the suggestions, ask them to give you the words that are recommended for each blank. Do not take these in order, because the children who are very familiar with the story of Jesus' birth will try to make sure they give you the right answer. (They will have opportunity to do that later.)

Caesar Augustus sent a decree to the entire kingdom that they should go to the country where they came from and be (past tense verb _____). So, Joseph and Mary went to (name a place _____), because Joseph was from there. Mary was expecting a (name a thing _____). While they were at (same place named before _____), it was time for Mary to have her (same thing named before _____). She wrapped Him in a (noun _____) and laid Him in a (noun _____).

There were (name an occupation _____) out on the (type of terrain _____). They were watching the (name of an animal, plural _____). All of a sudden (number _____) (name another occupation _____) came to them telling them not to be (emotion _____). The (same occupation _____) brought good news. They told them to go to (name a place _____) and find the (same noun _____). They went there and found the (same noun _____). Afterward, they told everyone what they had seen.

In (name a country _____) there were (number _____) (occupation, plural _____). They noticed a new (thing _____) in the sky. They followed it and it led

Children's Ministry Sourcebook

them. They gave the (thing named in first paragraph _____) gifts of (a noun _____), (a noun _____), and (a noun _____).

Now that you have filled in the blanks, read the new story to the children. It will be lots of laughs. (Don't be surprised if Mary and Joseph go to Walmart, and the shepherds are watching over giraffes!) After you have had your fun, go through the story once again and ask the children to fill in the blanks with the correct words from Scripture.

Memory Verse: Matthew 2:2 (ICB)

"'Where is the baby who was born to be the king of the Jews?
We saw his star in the east. We came to worship him.'"

Alternate Version: Matthew 2:2 (NKJV)
"'Where is He who has been born King of the Jews?
For we have seen His star in the East and have come to worship Him.'"

He Will Be Our King

By Tina Houser

Scripture: Matthew 2:2

Lesson Aim: The children will participate in the story of Jesus' birth.

Memory Verse: Matthew 2:2

Preparation

⭘ CARROT ⭘ SMALL PIECE OF STRING ⭘ CHRISTMAS LIGHTS ⭘ BIG BOW

Wear some of these peculiar things as you begin with the children: a string around your finger, a carrot sticking out of your pocket, a string of Christmas lights around your neck, a bow on your head.

Do you notice anything different about me today? When the children point out the carrot, comment that your mother put that in your pocket to get your attention. She wants me to pick up some carrots for our Christmas dinner. When they point out the Christmas lights, say that your husband hung those around your neck to get your attention. These lights don't work and he needs me to pick up another string for him. When they point out the bow on your head, then tell them that your sister put that there to get your attention, so you'd remember to pick up wrapping paper for that huge gift that's left to wrap. You want the string to be the last thing they notice, so if it comes up before then, just look at your finger with a puzzled expression, and shake your head like you don't know. After the carrot, bow, and lights have been acknowledged, then go to the string around your finger. By this time, you aren't sure why it's there, but you put it there yourself to get your attention to help you remember something! Wonder what it was?

God sent something very special that got the attention of the wise men. **Do you know what that was?** God put a new star in the sky. The star got the attention of some wise men, because they spent much of their time watching the skies and studying the stars. This new star was very obvious to them. Recognizing that it was something new and different, they took it as a sign from God that something spectacular had happened. As they traveled in the direction of the star, they let it lead them to where the baby Jesus was. Before they got to Jesus they talked to King Herod, who was curious about where they were going. The wise men said that surely there was a new king born to have such a beautiful star tell about Him. And, the Scriptures told of a leader who would come to lead all of Israel. Herod was consumed with jealousy, and told the wise men to tell him as soon as they found this new king. He lied to the wise men and told them that he would like to know where the baby was so he could also worship the new king.

The star pointed the way for the wise men and led them to Jesus, where the special visitors gave Jesus gifts of gold, frankincense, and myrrh. After worshiping the baby king Jesus, they left. Before they could get back to Herod, though, God warned them in a dream not to go back to Herod, so they returned a different way.

I wore this carrot to lead me to the grocery store, the lights to lead me to the hardware store, and the bow to lead me to the discount store. And, I still don't know why I have this string around my finger! **What did God use to lead the wise men to Jesus?** A new star was used to get their attention. Each one of you can be God's little "stars" and lead people to Jesus. You could be the "star" that leads them to their new King. Name some ways you can be a "star" and get someone's attention to bring Jesus into their Christmas. (Invite someone to a special Christmas service. Make them a gift that tells about Jesus' birth. Tell others that Christmas is about celebrating Jesus' birth.)

Now, I know the star pointed the wise men to Jesus and we can point the people around us today to that same Jesus!

Song Suggestions

"Oh, Come Let Us Adore Him" (Traditional)
"Silent Night" (Traditional)
"We Three Kings" (Traditional)
"Follow That Star" by Mary Rice Hopkins from *Mary Christmas* (Big Steps 4 U, 1993)

Craft for Younger Children: Jeweled Ornament

❍ 2 OLD CDS PER CHILD   ❍ RIBBON   ❍ TACKY GLUE   ❍ GLITTER PENS
❍ RHINESTONES

Cut a piece of ribbon that will act as the hanger for the ornament. Make a loop and glue the ends onto an edge of the label side of one CD. Glue the other CD on top of the first, with labels together. The plain silvery side of the CD should be showing on both sides. The children will then decorate one side of the ornament with glitter glue swirls and rhinestones.

Because the wise men who sought out Jesus were prominent men, we tend to think the gifts they brought were in fancy containers. Let this ornament remind you of the extravagant gifts the wise men brought to Jesus.

Craft for Older Children: He Is Our King!

❍ WIDE RIBBON (CUT 2 FEET LONG EA.)   ❍ CRAFT FOAM   ❍ SEQUINS, ETC.

(This craft is a continuation of the advent ribbon craft that the children will add to each week during advent.) Today we learned that Jesus is our KING. **What is a symbol for king?** (crown, jewels, purple, etc.) There are many symbols for king.

Write the word *king* on the board for all to see. The children will design their own symbol for king from the craft foam; they can also just cut the letters out to spell the word. Glue onto the ribbon under the "peace" and "joy" symbols. Each week another symbol will be added to the ribbon.

Snack: Cupcakes for a King
○ CUPCAKES   ○ ICING   ○ GUM DROPS   ○ SMALL CANDIES

The children will ice their own cupcakes. Decorate the cupcakes with gum drops and small colored candies to make a jeweled gift like the wise men gave Jesus.

Memory Verse: Matthew 2:2 (ICB)

"'Where is the baby who was born to be the king of the Jews? We saw his star in the east. We came to worship him.'"

Alternate Version: Matthew 2:2 (NKJV)
"'Where is He who has been born King of the Jews? For we have seen His star in the East and have come to worship Him.'"

Memory Verse Activity
○ A SMALL WRAPPED GIFT   ○ CHRISTMAS MUSIC

Instead of using a potato, use a gift to pass around the circle as you play a game of "Hot Potato." When the Christmas music stops, the person holding the gift will choose two other children. These three "wise men" will say the verse together. Each time the music stops the child holding the gift will choose two wise men. The combinations of three are huge.

Prayer Focus

Dear God thank You for the gift of Jesus. Thank You that He is our King. Help us to honor Him as a King.

He Will Be Our Salvation

By Tina Houser

Scripture: Luke 2:30–31

Lesson Aim: The children will understand the Christmas message of God's salvation for everyone.

Memory Verse: Luke 2:30–31

☞ **Bible Activity for Younger Children:** Treasure Search
- ○ TOOTSIE ROLL   ○ PACKAGE OF GUM   ○ BASKET   ○ NICKEL   ○ CUP
- ○ SUCKER   ○ GROCERY BAG   ○ CANDY KISS   ○ BUCKET   ○ BAG OF CHIPS
- ○ NAPKIN   ○ HERSHEY'S BAR   ○ MUSIC STAND   ○ STRIPS OF PAPER
- ○ CONTAINER

Write each of the following instructions on strips of paper, fold them up, and put them in a container. (Feel free to modify these instructions according to your facility.) One at a time the children will draw a strip of paper from the container and read it. Using the clues on the paper, go find the item it is leading you to. If your group is small, you can all go on the search together.

- You will find a Tootsie Roll on a window sill in the kitchen.
- You will find a package of gum in a basket on top of the refrigerator.
- You will find a nickel under a cup on the stairs.
- You will find a sucker in a grocery bag hanging from the coat rack.
- You will find a candy kiss in a bucket on the secretary's desk.
- You will find a bag of chips under a napkin on the video cart.
- You will find a Hershey's bar on a music stand by the men's restroom.

Simeon and Anna had been looking for the Savior all their lives. They had waited patiently for God to tell them where they would find Him. The Bible tells us that the Holy Spirit led Simeon to the temple the day the baby Jesus was brought there. Simeon's clue might have read: You will find the Messiah in the form of a baby at the temple today. Anna, who stayed at the temple all the time, was standing there when Simeon found the baby Jesus.

☞ Bible Activity for Older Children: A Special Invitation
- ○ AN INVITATION SEALED INSIDE AN ENVELOPE ○ PAPER ○ MARKERS
- ○ OLD CHRISTMAS CARDS

(Bring in an envelope addressed specifically to you.) I got this several days ago in the mail. Look, it has my name on it—just for me! I wonder what could be inside. It could be a bill, or—(Ask the children to suggest possibilities for what might be in the envelope, such as a letter, an invitation, a check, an advertisement, an application for a credit card.) I wish I knew what was in this. (Pretend to be flustered because you don't know what it contains. Keep going until one of the children suggests that you open it.) That's a great idea! Oh, wow, it's an invitation to a Christmas party. I imagine there will be lots of food and games and friends.

God wants everyone in this world to believe in Him, and to join Him in heaven one day. He has invited everyone. God doesn't send an invitation in the mail like this one. It's up to us to make sure everyone knows they are invited to be part of God's family and that they are invited to spend forever with Him. We are all invited to share in His salvation gift. God has sent His invitation to everyone, but they have to open their hearts and accept it. The invitation to the party wasn't any good until I opened it. Until we open ourselves to God's love, we don't really understand it.

Give each child a piece of cardstock to fold into a card. Decorate the front by cutting around pictures from old Christmas cards. Under the picture write: *You are invited* and on the inside write, *to be part of God's family this Christmas.* Sign this card and deliver it to someone who needs to know about Jesus.

Enrichment Activity for Younger Children: A Strange Gift
- ○ LARGE POSTER BOARD CUT-OUT OF A CROSS ○ LOTS OF STICKY BOWS
- ○ SHEETING STRIPS FOR BLINDFOLDS

Hang the poster board cross on the wall securely. One at a time, blindfold the children and give them a gift bow. Each child will walk toward the cross and stick the bow to the cross anywhere they can feel to do it. The object is for the group to completely cover the cross with bows.

We talk about the baby Jesus being God's Christmas gift to us, but really it's what Jesus did later that became the greatest gift. When Jesus took the punishment for our sin and died on the cross for us, that was the most wonderful gift He could give us—the gift of His sacrifice for our salvation!

Enrichment Activity for Older Children: Christmas Lights
- ○ SEVERAL STRINGS OF MULTI-COLOR CHRISTMAS LIGHTS

(Dim the lights in the room and drape the strings of lights across your shoulders.) I love Christmas lights, but they're not very pretty this way. **When do they get really pretty?**

When you plug them in, of course. The lights shine only when they are plugged in. These lights are like Christians. Christians come in many different colors. Every bulb has the same filament inside, but on the outside they are different colors. Even though people come in all colors, when we believe in Jesus as our Savior we all have the same Spirit of God within us. Each bulb is very pretty in its own way. Each person is a beautiful light when God shines through us. Electricity gives the Christmas lights power to shine. **Who is it that gives us the power to shine?** But, wait, there's darkness in the rest of the room. **What do you think that is?** The darkness is like all the people in our school, our town, our country, and our world who don't know about Jesus and that He can save us from our sin. Every time someone gives their life to Jesus, they aren't part of the darkness any longer; they also are one of the lights on this string. God wants to change our lives and take us from the darkness to being His light.

Recruit the children to help hang the strings of lights around your room. Let these lights be a reminder of the light God wants us to be for Him in our world.

Memory Verse: Luke 2:30-31 (ICB)

"'I have seen your Salvation with my own eyes.
You prepared him before all people.'"

Alternate Version: Luke 2:30-31 (NKJV)
"'For my eyes have seen Your salvation which You have prepared before the faces of all peoples.'"

Advent 4—
He Will Be Our Salvation

By Tina Houser

Scripture: Luke 2:30–31

Lesson Aim: The children will understand the Christmas message of God's salvation for everyone.

Memory Verse: Luke 2:30–31

Preparation

○ BOX OF FACIAL TISSUE   ○ COUGH SYRUP   ○ VAPORIZER   ○ HOT WATER BOTTLE
○ THERMOMETER   ○ COUGH DROPS   ○ COLD TABLETS   ○ BATHROBE
○ HOUSE SLIPPERS

Enter in a bathrobe and house slippers, carrying a box of tissues and a bottle of cough syrup. Stand before the children and talk with a heavy nasal tone as if you have a terrible head cold.

My throat is sore, my eyes are itchy, and nose is stopped up. I keep sneezing (achoo) and I can hardly breathe. When you have a cold, nobody wants to be around you, especially at Christmas. It's terrible! I just don't feel like celebrating. (Pretend to sneeze on one of the children.) **Are you afraid you're going to catch my cold? Why do you keep moving away from me?** When I get close to people, they just turn their heads and then they walk away. None of my family or friends want to be with me, and it's Christmas, for goodness sake. I've been taking this cough syrup and this cold medicine. When I go to bed I turn the vaporizer on. I check my temperature with this thermometer. I suck on these cough drops. And, I cuddle up with this hot water bottle. If I keep doing all these things, surely I'll get rid of this cold. I just want to get better in time to celebrate Christmas.

My cold reminds me of how sin is. My cold is separating me from the people I want to be around, and sin separates us from God. God loves us, but He can't stand to be around sin. We take our medicine to get rid of a bad cold, and then people want to be around us again. When we accept Jesus as our Savior, that gets rid of our sin, and then God is so happy to welcome us back. I'm doing my best to doctor this cold and get rid of it. God has a cure for our sin, too. He sent His Son, Jesus, to earth to be our Savior. Christmas is when we celebrate God sending the cure for our sin.

"Silent Night" (Traditional)
"Treasure of My Heart" by Jana Alayra from *Jump into the Light* (Montjoy Music, 1995)
"It's Jesus Love" by Dean-O from *Game Face* (Biblebeat Music, 2003)
"Wrap It All Up" by Mary Rice Hopkins from *Mary Christmas* (Big Steps 4 U, 1993)

✂ Craft for Younger Children: Christmas Wreath

- ○ PAPER PLATES WITH CENTER CUT OUT (FORMS A WREATH)   ○ RED RIBBON
- ○ GREEN CONSTRUCTION PAPER   ○ ASSORTED CONSTRUCTION PAPER

Cut a circle out of the center of the paper plates forming a wreath shape, cut leaves from the green paper, cut squares (presents) from the colored paper.

Show the children how to form a wreath by gluing the leaves onto the wreath, then adding the presents onto the wreath.

You have made a beautiful wreath! A wreath is used to celebrate Christmas. **What is inside your "presents" on the wreath?** The best present of all is the salvation that Jesus gives us!

✂ Craft for Older Children: He Is Our Salvation

- ○ WIDE RIBBON (CUT 2 FEET LONG EA.)   ○ CRAFT FOAM   ○ SEQUINS, ETC.

(This craft is a continuation of the advent ribbon craft that the children will add to each week during advent.) Today we learned that Jesus is our SALVATION. **What is the symbol for salvation? That one is hard isn't it?** The cross leads to our salvation so we will use the cross as a symbol today. Let each child cut a cross out of craft foam and glue it to the ribbon.

This week the craft is finished and children can take it home. Review what each symbol means

🍿 Snack: Christmas Cookies

- ○ ASSORTED CHRISTMAS COOKIES

These are special cookies. We make special cookies because it is Christmas. **What else do we do that is special because it is Christmas?**

We remember Jesus when we celebrate Christmas!

 Memory Verse: Luke 2:30-31 (ICB)

"'I have seen your Salvation with my own eyes.
You prepared him before all people.'"

Alternate Version: Luke 2:30-31 (NKJV)
"'For my eyes have seen Your salvation which You have prepared before the faces of all peoples.'"

Memory Verse Activity
○ A ROPE ○ DIFFERENT COLORS OF PAPER ○ CLOTHESPINS

Before class, string the rope across the room. Make a large paper light bulb for each word in the memory verse. Write one word of the verse on each bulb and place the bulbs face down on the table.

Say the verse together several times. One child will choose a paper light bulb and read the word printed there. Attach the light bulb to the rope in what they think is the appropriate place. If the word comes near the end of the verse, then they should use the clothespin to attach the bulb close to the end of the rope. Continue doing this until the verse has been put together on the rope. Each time a bulb is added the group should recite the verse together.

Prayer Focus

Dear God, thank You for this wonderful season which reminds us of Your precious gift—your Son Jesus. Thank You for the salvation that He gives to us.

When I Was Younger

By Tina Houser

Scripture: Proverbs 27:19

Lesson Aim: The children will find value in reflecting on what has happened in their lives this past year.

Memory Verse: Proverbs 27:19

☞ Bible Activity for Younger Children: Tic-Tac-Tell

○ MASKING TAPE   ○ BEAN BAGS

Create a giant tic-tac-toe board on the floor with the masking tape. In each section tape a piece of paper that has one of the following statements written on it:

Name somewhere you got to go.
Name someone you met.
Name something you learned at school.
Name something you learned at home.
Name something you learned at church.
Name some place you ate.
Name someone who visited you.
Name a book you read.
Name something you got to do.

Let's think about this past year. Lots of things have changed. **Are you exactly the same as you were this time last year?** You're not the same person. You've grown and learned so much in one short year. When we think about where God has taken us this past year, it gets us excited about what He will do in our lives in this coming year! Looking back at how God helps to assure us when we get in difficult situations. We know that He has helped us in the past and He will surely help us in the future.

The children will take turns tossing the bean bag at the tic-tac-toe board. Each time the bean bag lands completely (without touching lines) in a section, ask the child to respond to what is written there. Each response should be about something that happened in this past year. The challenge is to get them to only think about this year. (Understanding time is still difficult at this age, but they should know that they didn't learn how to walk and talk this past year!)

☞ Bible Activity for Older Children: My Real Reflection
○ HEAVY COLORED PAPER ○ ALUMINUM FOIL ○ LINED PAPER ○ HAND MIRROR

Give each child a piece of the colored paper. Use the hand mirror as a pattern to draw around to make your own mirror on the paper. Cut out the pattern you made on the paper. Now, cut a piece of aluminum foil to make the reflecting part of the mirror. On a piece of lined paper, write something you have learned about God this past year and glue it to the aluminum foil. As you look into the mirror you can see yourself in the foil and be able to read what you learned about God at the same time.

When we look into a mirror in the morning we see what a mess our hair is; we see if we missed a spot when we brushed our teeth; we can see if our glasses are on straight—we can see ourselves the way we really are. When we reflect and think about what has happened to us and what we have learned, it helps us see ourselves for who we really are and who we are becoming. Reflecting is a good mental exercise to get in the habit of doing.

Enrichment Activity for Younger Children: Mirror, Mirror on the Wall
○ DARK WIDE MARKER ○ PLAIN PAPER ○ 2 MIRRORS ○ PINS

Before the session, write a one-sentence encouraging statement about each child. Write their name in larger letters than the rest of the sentence. Example: I love to hear ANTO-NIO read.

Pin that special name tag to the child's back without them reading what it says. One mirror should be placed in a stationery place (and be as large as you can bring with you). The child will stand with their back to the stationery mirror and hold the hand mirror at shoulder height in front of them. They will look into the hand mirror and be able to read the statement that is pinned to their backs. Ask them to read out loud what they see.

The mirrors reflected the light so that we could actually see what was behind us. As we look back at the year that is coming to an end this week, it is time for us to reflect so we will appreciate what is behind us. **What does *reflect* mean when it's used this way?** Reflect means to stop and think about things that have happened. When we reflect we realize that a lot has happened. **What other things do we realize when we reflect?** We realize we have grown physically. We realize we have learned a lot. We realize we have met some new people, and said good-bye to others. It is good for us to reflect, because it makes us grateful for all the different parts of our lives.

Enrichment Activity for Older Children: Drawn In
○ SODA BOTTLE ○ BOWL ○ BALLOON

Fill the soda bottle with really hot water. Fill the bowl with cold water. Let them sit for a minute or two. Then, pour the hot water out of the bottle. Pull a balloon across the mouth of the empty bottle and stand it in the bowl of cold water. Watch what happens!

Children's Ministry Sourcebook

Let's explain what happened here. The hot water heated the bottle, so when the water was poured out, the heat that was in the bottle heated the air inside the bottle. When we placed the bottle in the cold water, it caused the air to contract, which means it took up less space. It needed more air to fill the bottle, so it pulled air in from the outside. The balloon got drawn in and was inflating inside the bottle.

As we come to the end of a year, it's nice to look back at what has happened to us, who we've met, and what we have learned. Each moment, each day, each month of this past year, you have been drawing things inside you. They have all become part of you and make you a more interesting person. The balloon was drawn inside the bottle, because the air inside the bottle needed it there. We need to take some time throughout the year and right now to think about what has become part of our lives. Thinking about those things will help us experience this coming year more fully.

Memory Verse: Proverbs 27:19 (ICB)

"As water shows you your face,
So your mind shows you what kind of person you are."

Alternate Version: Proverbs 27:19 (NKJV)
"As in water face reveals face,
So a man's heart reveals the man."

When I Was Younger

By Rev. Jim Miller

Scripture: Proverbs 27:19

Lesson Aim: The children will find value in reflecting on what has happened in their lives this past year.

Memory Verse: Proverbs 27:19

Preparation

○ A LARGE HANDHELD MIRROR ○ A LARGE BOWL OF WATER

I've got a mirror here. **When you look at yourself, what do you think of?** (Show it around.) A mirror can show you if you have food on your chin, or if you have something stuck in your teeth. It also shows you how you've gotten older in the last year. Reflecting in your mind is similar to the reflecting a mirror does.

Sometimes around this time of year, your parents might think about the year they just finished. They call this "reflecting," which is like what a mirror does, but a little bit different. It makes them say things like, "Where did the time go?" and "It sure goes by fast," and "Maybe I'll try that diet again."

You all are pretty old and wise now. **You'd have to think pretty hard to remember what you were like a year ago, wouldn't you?** Let's take some time to do some reflecting ourselves. **Tell me this—what's one fun thing you did in the last year? What's one important thing you learned since last year? What is something new you learned about God last year? What's one thing you want to do next year?** That's the kind of thing you think about when you're reflecting.

Now there's a deeper kind of reflection we can do. This kind of reflection is called CONFESSION. **Can everyone say that?** Confession is just looking back at everything you've learned in the last year, maybe even thinking about the mistakes you've made, and thinking about how you can do things differently the next time around. It's not thinking in a way that makes you feel bad, it's just thinking in a helpful way, so that next year is even better than last year. Then, you can tell God about all the things you're reflecting on.

The Bible says "As water reflects a face, so a man's heart reflects the man" (Proverbs 27:19 NIV). Water reflects the way a mirror does. Take a look in this bowl to see how much of your face you can see. The Bible says that in the same way this mirror shows what's on your face, your heart shows people who you really are. If, in your heart, you're reflecting on the things you've done and trying to do better the next time around, people will see that you're a nice person. And I know you all are. So it can be good to spend time reflecting on everything that has happened in your life this year. Let's pray. (Thank God for the chance to reflect together.)

Song Suggestions

"I Open My Heart" by Mark Thompson from *Yes Yes Yes!* (Markarts, 2000)
"Day by Day" by Jana Alayra from *Jump into the Light* (Montjoy Music, 1995)
"Rad-Dude Attitude" by Dean-O from *You Got It All* (FKO Music, Inc., 1997)
"Sharing Comes Round Again" by Mary Rice Hopkins from *15 Singable Songs* (Big Steps 4 U, 1988)

Craft for Younger Children: New Year Noise Maker

○ PAPER PLATES　○ CRAYONS　○ DRIED BEANS　○ STAPLER
○ CRAFT STICK　○ TAPE

Decorate the paper plates for New Year's Eve. Put one paper plate on the table, with the right side up. Tape a craft stick to the rim of the plate leaving out part of the stick for a handle. Place the other paper plate on top of the first one, right side down. This will make a gap in the middle. Start stapling the edges together. Leave an opening to slide a handful of dried beans in. Finish stapling it shut. Tonight, when you celebrate New Year's Eve, you can use this noisemaker!

Craft for Older Children: Time Capsule

○ POTATO CHIP CAN OR OTHER SIMILAR CONTAINER　○ DECORATIONS

The New Year is a fun time to remember how much you change through the years. Today, we will make a time capsule to record all the important things happening in your lives.

Decorate the can as desired. Send it home with instructions to fill it with some of the following: photographs (put them in a plastic baggie), ticket stubs, letters, pictures of your own room, list of your friends, papers from school, a letter to yourself in 5 years. After you fill your time capsule, put it somewhere and forget about it for a few years. Open it up later and see how much you have changed!

Snack: Happy New Year!

○ SMALL SQUARE RICE CEREAL　○ PRETZELS　○ SMALL CHOCOLATE CANDIES
○ BAGGIES

Place the ingredients out in the bowls, with small spoons in each one. The children will make their own Happy New Year mix by adding spoonfuls of each ingredient into their baggies.

December 31, 2006

Sometimes we have very special food to celebrate with, and sometimes people like to have this special mix. Tonight you will celebrate a Happy New Year and you can share your mix with your family.

Memory Verse: Proverbs 27:19 (ICB)

"As water shows you your face,
So your mind shows you what kind of person you are."

Alternate Version: Proverbs 27:19 (NKJV)
"As in water face reveals face,
So a man's heart reveals the man."

Memory Verse Activity

Write the verse on the board where all the children can see it. Go around the room and assign one word to each child. Say the verse together and then go around the room, having the children "pop up" and say their word in turn.

This game gets a little silly, but is a fun way to memorize a verse.

Prayer Focus

Thank You, God, for this new year. Help us to focus more on You, because we love You so much!

Feature Articles

Big Rocks

By Karl Bastian

If you have friends (or strangers) who forward you every e-mail they find even remotely interesting, then you've probably heard this story, but I think it's worth repeating. And, if you don't forward to ten of your friends, don't worry, nothing will happen to you!

But the story is of some college professor somewhere who displayed a large clear container to his class along with a pile of large rocks. He asks a student to fill the container with as many of the large stones as possible. After the last rock is in, the student declares it full, and the class agrees, until the teacher reveals a pile of smaller rocks and has another student fill in the gaps with those until he and the class agree that it is again full. To which the wise teacher responds by displaying a pile of yet smaller rocks. This process is painfully repeated in detail through the small rocks, then gravel, then sand and finally water. Only then does the sage agree that the container is indeed full.

He then asks the class, "If the container represents your life, what is the lesson here?" The story then goes on that some well-meaning schmuck (who, if this story is true, must be grateful his name was dropped!) stands up and declares, "It means that there is always room in your life for more!" The cries of despair and distain echo in front of computers around the world as the teacher kindly corrects the poor sap, saying, "No. The point is that if we hadn't put the big rocks in first, they would never have fit later."

Except to the one over-eager but misguided student in this story, the point is clear: we must make sure the most important things in our lives are included first before we allow the rest of life to fill in all the cracks.

How does that apply to your life and ministry? Are the gravel, sand, and water of ministry choking out the Big Rocks? Or you laughing and saying, "Big Rocks? Did you say BIG ROCKS! I can't even get the medium sized ones in!" If so, I've been there! In fact, I was there much this summer as I took on a few too many projects myself. Now that the fall is here, we all need to stop and think about the big rocks that may have been shoved out of the box by gravel! I share this with you, not as the mountaintop guru who has it all figured out and mastered, but as a fellow struggler in ministry who often wonders if the Big Rocks haven't been lost in the quicksand of ministry!

Don't just read this—Do it!

Let me challenge you to take a break this week, even just a lunch date with yourself and God. (He is always available for that, believe it or not, as important and busy as He is!) Take a blank piece of paper with you. No calendar. No contact list. No to-do list. No agendas or minutes or outlines or scope-and-sequences. Consider even leaving the Palm Pilot and cell phone behind. My own hands are now trembling!

Just like in grade school, number your piece of blank paper from one to ten. When you pray over your food, pray as well that God would show you over your lunch meeting with Him, TEN BIG ROCKS for your life and ministry. Don't worry about that order. Unfortunately, they won't come out in order, but get them on paper. Later you can rearrange the order of importance, but get the TEN BIG ROCKS written in ink on paper. There is POWER in writing something down. It brings it suddenly out of the realm of idea into the real world. When you see in your own handwriting, things you need to be doing, you are more likely to actually do them.

Things like "I need to pray for my students weekly"—"I need to visit the kids in my church in their homes"—"I should send out birthday cards to my students"—"I need to plan a date with my wife"—"I need to give an evening to my kids"—"I should read that book"—"I haven't written to some of my friends in awhile," etc. God will give you the ideas! Think about the things you WANT to do, SHOULD do, COULD do, WOULD do, if only you had the time. The fact is you have the time! You just have to put the Big Rocks in first!

After you have your list—the second step is to PLAN THEM into your life. First, schedule them! If you get sick, you suddenly have time in your busy life to sit in a doctor's waiting room. One of my secrets to getting something done I call the "Staff Meeting Principle." My pastoral staff meeting is Tuesdays from 2:00–4:00 p.m. No matter what is going on in my life—no matter how busy I am—no matter how stressed I am—no matter what deadlines I am struggling with—no matter what, unless I am out of town or deathly ill, I will be in Room 200 at 2:00 p.m. on Tuesday for staff meeting.

Believe me, there are days I do not want to be there. (Hope my boss doesn't read my Web site!) But I'm sure you've never had that experience. However, it always turns out to be a good thing I was there and helpful to my ministry. I call it the "Staff Meeting Principle" that no matter what, those two hours are committed to staff meeting, whether I like it or not. Why? Well, because I am required to be there by my boss. Think about this: Why is it we can be there 'no matter what' when it's our boss making us, but we can't be our own boss and schedule other things that we won't miss no matter what? You must schedule some of your high priorities and give them the same priority and 'no matter what' status as your staff meeting.

What are your Big Rocks? Lesson prep? Discipleship? Prayer? Visitation? Note writing? Phone calling? Whatever it is, schedule it! And treat it like staff meeting, even running if you are late!! Why? Because if you don't get the Big Rocks in first, they won't fit later. BLOCK OFF TIME SLOTS for your most important ministry duties. Here is a fact of ministry that if you haven't figured this out yet, it may be a relief to learn now: Every Week In Ministry Things Will Be Left Undone. Right up there with the Transitive Property and the Trichotomy Property is the To-do-next-week Property. Things WILL get left undone—but guess what? YOU CAN DETERMINE WHICH.

If you honestly CAN'T get the Big Rocks first, then you simply are doing more than God is asking you to, and you need to take a hard look at your life and ministry and do some heart-searching prayer about what God is asking you to do. And let some things go. *No* may be a word you need to practice, translated often as, "Wow, that's a great idea, but I'm sorry, I just can't do that right now, I've got some Big Rocks I need to deal with first."

I think a lot of ministries are covered in some very nice looking gravel, but it's still gravel, and some Big Rocks are missing. Determine your Big Rocks, and get those planned and scheduled first. The gravel can wait. There may, no, make that, there will be a lot of 'nice' things you won't get to, but in the end, few will notice or miss those little things, and you will feel so much better about what you are accomplishing overall. You'll feel better and you will be more satisfied with your life and ministry.

So grab your pen and a piece of paper, and take God to lunch. You'll both be glad you did.

Give It Back to God

"Too Blessed to Be Stressed" says a button I own, though I've never worn it out in public for fear that some stressed out person will give me a black eye for mocking their pain! But I do save it because I think it contains a pearl of wisdom. Stress is caused primarily by worry or overload—both of which are often optional. However, I do understand that is easier said than done! And I won't pretend to be one who lives daily in blessed stress-free bliss.

Quite to the contrary, with two full-time ministries I am quite familiar with stress and am afflicted with migraines most likely as a result. Overload is a daily battle as I am a high-energy, high-output, highly-motivated person whose brain seems to never stop. (Indeed, I am writing this at 30,000 feet when I could be sleeping like those on both sides of me—or watching the free Ben Aflick/J.Lo movie—nah.) But having said all that, if you are stressed out over your ministry, I'd like to share some things I've learned over the years, and perhaps soon you'll be able to say with me, "What?! Me? Stressed? No way! I'm too blessed to be stressed!"

1. Get it in your head: It's not your ministry!

This may sound harsh, but you've got to hear it, and I say it to myself as much as I say it to you: *It's not your ministry, it is God's, and He is quite capable of running it without you.* Listen to me—verily, verily, I say unto you: When you stress over your ministry you have taken the ministry away from God and have made it your responsibility to solve its problems.

So when the problem (or more likely volunteer openings) remains unsolved (or open) you feel as if you have failed, or worse, that God has failed you, as though He works for you, as a volunteer in your children's ministry. Let me say it again, it isn't your ministry. Now few would claim to disagree with that statement, but it is how you act on and implement this fact that can have a profound impact on your ministry!

Hear this please—you are merely the steward of God's ministry. If I seem to be over-emphasizing it, you're wrong, it can't be over-emphasized. The day you begin to feel underappreciated, taken for granted, frustrated, or like a failure is the day you cease to allow God to run His children's ministry. If you take the ministry from God, you become a hindrance to what He wants to accomplish. Now, of course, I don't mean you can just sit in your office and play video games while God runs the ministry! For a steward, there is work to do, and plenty of it (more than is possible, in fact), but at the end of day, after you've done your best, the results are up to God.

We often turn ourselves in to the "protector" (or "savior") of programs. If God wants a program to launch or continue, He will provide the leadership and workers. If He doesn't, it may be His way of suggesting something. The Bible doesn't lay out programs we must have, it just calls us to make disciples and reach the lost. Programs are fine, as long as they are means to an end, never the end in, and of, themselves.

For example, Vacation Bible Schools are wonderful! Many kids are led to Christ and they create lifelong memories for children. But if you can't get a director (or rather, God doesn't raise up a leader), then perhaps it is time to try a new approach to summer outreach. I could share many stories of times I let the ministry be God's and how He surprised me with how much better a job He could do than me! The bottom line—if you are stressed over "your" ministry, you may be out of touch with something God is trying to do in His ministry. If He is in something, He will provide!

2. Let others hear you talk about the ministry as God's.

When you begin to talk about the ministry as "God's ministry" and not allow yourself to be the band-aid for everything that goes wrong, people will get the message and begin to respond. Know this: People will let you do anything you are willing to do. Let's face it, most people will assume that you can do a better job than them, and they may even be right sometimes, but "better" is not always what is "best."

Ten people doing ten things their best is better than you doing the same ten things better. And all too often, even people who have felt God leading them to do something won't step forward until they are convinced that they are the answer to prayer. Out of fear, nervousness, or humility, they will wait to see if anyone else steps up first. If you decide, "Oh, I'll just do it" they will let you and you will never know the volunteer of God's choosing that you lost.

I can't tell you how many times it was after announcing the canceling of a program "because God has not provided the leader/teacher" that a person has answered, "No, God's been working on me, I'll do it, I'm sorry I waited so long." If you truly believe it is God's ministry and you act on that, you will see Him work in ways you never could!

Maybe it is time to give your ministry back to God. Here are some steps that might help. Hear this please—you are merely the steward of God's ministry. If I seem to be over-emphasizing it, you're wrong, it can't be over-emphasized. The day you begin to feel underappreciated, taken for granted, frustrated, or like a failure is the day you give the ministry back to God in prayer. Consider writing it out so you can be thoughtful and thorough. Confess acting like it is your job to fix everything, staff everything, and run everything. Confess it if you have treated God like a volunteer who needed to bless your plans and solve your problems.

Thank God for placing you as the steward of His ministry. Think about all the good things happening and thank Him for them—the children, faithful workers, a heritage of ministry, supportive leaders, your position.

Make a list of the needs and/or problems in God's ministry and pray about them. Not "God do this" or "God change that" or "God provide this." Instead, ask "God what are You doing? These are the needs I perceive, but I'm trusting You to reveal Your plans through answers to prayer, the no's as well as the yeses."

After giving the results of these things to God, make a list of the things YOU can do to work on them as God's steward. What visits, calls, or announcements can you make? How can you advertise, promote, or communicate the needs? Who can you invite to pray with you, for you, and for these needs?

For the things that God doesn't seem to be answering, pray and think about what God could be up to. Testing your trust? Suggesting a new strategy? Asking for changes?

The Mountaintop

By Mary Rice Hopkins

Have you ever climbed up to the top of a mountain? Have you been on top where you can see for miles? Once I took a tram ride to the top of a mountain in Oregon. It was a clear day where it seemed like I could see forever! Everywhere I looked I saw beautiful scenery; a lake over here and another mountain in the distance. It is so breathtaking to see! God's creation is so awesome!

Did you know that the Bible says our Lord searches the whole earth, His whole creation just to find faithful people to support? Isn't that an awesome thing? Our God wants to bless us just for being loyal and faithful to Him!

In 2 Chronicles 16:9, it says, "for the eyes of the Lord run to and fro throughout the whole earth to show Himself strong on behalf of those whose heart is loyal to Him." So next time you're in up in the sky in a plane or on a mountaintop looking at God's awesome creation, remember that God is looking at you. He knows your life and knows your heart and blesses you for being loyal and faithful.

Can God Use Me?

By Mary Rice Hopkins

God uses all kinds of people to do His work, even ordinary ones. At my concerts, I love to ask kids questions and hear their response; you just never know what they are going to say especially the wee little ones. One time I asked a little boy if he knew what his daddy did for work? He looked up at me and said, "No, what?"

I love the fact that when I ask the little ones about what they want to be when they grow up they have all sorts of answers. Most of them really have no limits about what they want to be, their dreams are so big! Little kids, in their fantasy world, usually feel they can do anything and be anything. But as they grow older they may think, "Oh I can't do that!"

It's not our place to decide what someone can or cannot do, but I do know beyond a shadow of doubt what God can do and cannot do; God can do anything. He is all powerful and almighty in all things. Have you ever caught yourself thinking, "I could never do that"? Have you ever put aside something or quit dreaming because you thought your dreams were impossible? When God shares His plans for your life with you it's normal to think you cannot do these things in your own strength. Guess what? You're right, you can't. But GOD is in the business of doing things that are impossible to us. And if you have faith in a big God to do big things, anything is possible. If you think your dreams are unrealistic, ask yourself the following question, "What is too Big for God to do?" Matthew 19:26 says, "with men this is impossible but with God ALL things are possible," and Luke 1:37 says, "for with God nothing will be impossible."

David was a man who felt small and not very important, but God used him to kill a giant. David stumbled in life but he got back up and God made him Isreal's greatest king. Joseph was thrown in a pit and sold into slavery, but later God used him to become a ruler of all of Egypt because he kept on dreaming. Jacob made mistakes but he got back up and became the father of the 12 tribes of Israel. Moses felt he couldn't talk and kept asking God to send someone else in His place. Rahab was a harlot but she later turned to God and is in the lineage of Jesus.

In Jesus' family tree there were all kinds of people. Some were kings and heroes dedicated completely to God but others were sinners in a BIG way. Many were ordinary people like you and I. So if you are ever wondering "how can God use me?" just remember that God is looking for imperfect people who depend upon an extraordinary God. He is looking for people who are dependent on a big God and are not willing to give up.

Converting the Childcare Model

By Rev. Barney Kinard

When you allow your children's ministry to be designated as a "childcare" program, you succumb to secularizing your ministry, which makes it more conducive to a "baby-sitting" service, than a legitimate ministry function that is complimentary to a church. Therefore, every minister in charge of children's ministry should be careful to convert every "childcare" program and avoid using such terminology in their ministry. I do understand that well-intentioned leaders want to assure adult attendance for their ministries by providing "something for the children." While this accommodates young families, it reframes the image of children's ministry, which makes it harder to change this sterotype to any legitimate ministry later. In order to convert any "childcare" opportunity, one should carefully consider the following:

Change the Name!
This is the first assignment: In order to convert any program from a *childcare* model, one must not use the words *childcare* for any legitimate ministry for children. To continue to use the word *childcare* for ministry further entrenches the function and makes it harder to convert it to real ministry. The best way to prevent it is to prevent it from getting started.

Pick a Catchy Name or Theme!
Create a program that can reach a broad base of children's needs and interests. Attach a catchy theme to the program. Call it something that reinforces that theme and/or what you will be doing in your ministry with the kids. This will be the new name that will replace the word *childcare* when referring to this program for children of any age.

Decide on Biblical Content!
Brainstorm some creative ministry approaches to convey a Biblical theme. This will lead to Biblical content or a curriculum that you can use. Some research is needed here, but it is a crucial step toward converting the *childcare* model to a ministry model. Be aware you may need to design your own program and/or write your own curriculum. Maybe you will decide to have a guest speaker, or a puppet program.

Orient and Train Your Workers!
All your team and volunteers must be oriented and trained to your new purpose, procedures and policies. You must orient your team of leaders and helpers about what you will be trying to accomplish. Of course, you will be doing the things required for good *childcare*, but from now on, you will not refer to this in such terms.

As you unfold the program and the order of things you will be doing, it will be clear ministry was your intention. As you will call upon your team to help you implement this vision, you will be asking them to "partner" with you in ministering to the children. Train them for team ownership!

Budget for Quality!
You can immediately tell by the allotted budget if this program is *childcare* or ministry. It should be more valuable to all your parents compared to the normal cost of *childcare.*

You can calculate "childcare model" budget by establishing a baby-sitting fee (cost per child). Multiply that amount (the cost per hour), times the number of children, then multiply by the number of hours served. Your ministry model should be worth more than the childcare cost you calculated per kid, per hour. If your ministry calculations are lower than reasonable "childcare" costs, your budget is too low. Make noises about "raising the bar" and doing more than childcare would cost. I would propose that you need to submit a revised budget that exceeds the value of a reasonable "childcare" estimate.

Create Ministry Goals!
There are many suitable program goals for your new children's ministry. Here are a few examples that might get you started toward the conversion of your childcare model:
1. Train your new workers.
2. Teach young believers.
3. Reach new kids for Christ and the church.
4. Disciple new converts in Christ.
5. Utilize your new resources and the room.
6. Solve a long-standing misconception.
7. Introduce a new curriculum.
8. Train children in new skills.
9. Promote a new outreach program.

Raise the Bar!
This means that you are not maintaining a program, but raising the standards of your children's ministries by responsible ministry, responsible child advocacy, and quality children's evangelism. The challenge is one of quality and ministry.

Promote Your Program!
The key to changing the program image is to use the new designated title exclusively when referring to that new children's program. This describes what your children's ministry is now and by omission, it is no longer childcare. Every public announcement, either written or oral, will now use this new program title, not some former "baby-sitting" type name. Design a new informative brochure that outlines your complete program with your plan of how it will work for children and their parents. Of course, your new program title is prominently displayed on the cover and throughout the piece. Signs at the entrances to the rooms would help too.

Although we all believe in childcare, we are not doing just *childcare*, we are doing far more than childcare. We are carrying on a legitimate ministry to all our children and those who come our way. Every minister to children should be poised to do children's ministry anytime, and thereby, able to convert every potential "child-care" opportunity into significant ministry to children. We become known for what we do!

15 Reasons Why I Believe in Object Lessons!

By Rev. Barney Kinard

1. They help the teacher to teach from "the known to the unknown." This is one of the "basic laws" of the learner, which employs the familiar to provide a basis to introduce a spiritual or an unknown lesson.

2. They help learners to move from "concrete" to "abstract" thinking. The younger the student, the more concrete the object lessons needs to become when teaching abstract truth. However, for older students, the object lessons can be more abstract and symbolic representing the truths of the Bible.

3. They can be helpful to reduce a complex subject into something simpler. Another advantage of an object lesson is its ability to be used to simplify a grand theological truth. Therefore, even the young can receive and relish the truth on their own level. **4. They assist in the integration and application of truth.** Object lessons can be used to clarify the nuances of truth, especially for the "visual" learner. The visualization of something complex results in the student getting the concept. For some, this is the only effective way they can learn. For them, all visual lessons are converted into mental pictures that are integrated with other known images already "on file" in their head. **5. They provide an "aid to the memory."** Object lessons are therefore, "mneumonic" devices, which means that they provide an "aid to the memory." They become like a mental framework to help learners remember by simple association involving the object and the lesson.

6. They provide a "basis" for review and testing for recall. Either by referring to an object or showing that object, the learner can recall the message and application that the teacher taught about that object. The student will then automatically associate the presented object with the "lesson taught." The object then becomes synonymous with the lesson taught and therefore easily retained.

7. They have a way of "fixing themselves" in your mind for years. Many adults give testimony of remembering object lessons learned from childhood. They seem to have a lasting impact, even years later. Once the mind has been fixed on these lessons, they have a way of being used by God in ones adult life. These past spiritual lessons, which are easily remembered, are testimony that the object lessons are still bearing fruit. It is always amazing when adults can relive object lessons they were taught as children.

8. They utilize the "eye gate," which accounts for 50% of what we learn. Research has shown that 50% of what a student remembers is from what he sees. Therefore using visual aids can help a student receive and retain what is being taught more effectively. Teachers using the eye-gate can substantially enhance what is being said.

9. They provide a focus to "hold the attention" by capturing the eyes of the learner. Object lessons are useful for giving the eye a visual reference. Therefore, it assists in holding attention while the teacher elaborates on the lessons that are inherent in the object's usefulness. This is particularly true with children, but especially, younger children.

10. They accommodate any "age level" by the teacher adjusting "age-appropriate language" in their teaching. Knowing each learners and what age-appropriate language to use, enables a sensitive teacher to fit the application of lesson to their developmental level. He knows what they are ready to hear and learn. The teacher should only use words that they can explain to the age of the children being addressed.

11. They can "peak" the curiosity of the learner, especially when the object is new or unusual to them. Especially with older learners, the teacher can expand their view of world by introducing new, unfamiliar or even strange objects requiring explanation. When the element of surprise is added, the object becomes even more unforgettable. Their curiosity is "peaked," and recall is enhanced by their new focus.

12. They facilitate "participatory" interaction between the lesson content and the speaker. A good teacher can skillfully evoke questions and answers about the usefulness and applications taught by the presented object lesson. This kind of participation stimulates more recall and more mental interaction with the lesson and their teacher.

13. They are like "windows to the soul" that let the light of God's Word enter. Children can easily understand the stories of the Bible because there are so many everyday objects used to illustrate its teachings. When the object illustrates the message it becomes like a window for the soul allowing the light of God's Word to shine brightly inside.

14. They were widely used by the Old Testament Prophets. The prophets were emphatically told by God to use objects in their preaching and teaching. The prophets were able to convey their message so clearly by using objects that it left the Jewish people (and leaders of other nations) without excuse. Their object lessons left a profound impact on their hearers. Even today, we acquire profound understanding from their symbolical pronouncements.

15. They were the "strategic teaching method" that Jesus used repeatedly in His ministry.

The teaching ministry of Jesus provides abundant evidence that He expounded truth by repeatedly using object lessons. His lessons would either clarify or confound. Jesus often drew a sharp contrast between what other teachers said and what His Father taught. But to those who have "ears to hear" and "eyes to see," they could learn lessons of eternal significance through His daily object lessons.

How to Start
A Children's Ministry Network in Your Area

By Rev. Barney Kinard

1. **Gather names and addresses of area children's leaders!** Your list should include anyone in your area involved in full or part-time Children's ministry, such as Children's Pastors, Directors of Children's Ministry, volunteer leaders and ministry specialists serving the local church. You will want to informally contact as many of these leaders as you can to poll their interest. Try to enter your list into a computer database to produce mailing labels.

2. **Mail a personal invitation to everyone on your list!** Invite those on your list to an information and orientation meeting about the new networking group on children's ministry. You will need to follow up with phone calls to confirm their coming and keep their interest alive.

3. **Host an introduction—orientation luncheon!** Once your network gets going, monthly meetings rotate among the local churches. For this first meeting, we have found that it is best to use a neutral restaurant site, rather than a church. It would be helpful at this meeting to go around the room and have each person introduce themselves and share what they are responsible for in children's ministry. During this first meeting, you will want to cover the following items:

    Briefly explain the benefits of networking, which includes, fellowship, prayer, topic of interest, mutual support in common ministry and question and answer time, and sharing what works and fails. This group cannot be dominated by the larger works in town. This group is a network that focuses on children and practical helpful ideas on how they can be reached and taught in a children's ministry. It is not a denominational network and theology is not the common focus. It is children's ministry and the children's leadership.

    Make a presentation of how the network could work. Most successful monthly meetings meet in local area churches with variations of either of these formats below, including the following ingredients:

    Registration and name tags for all
    Welcome and introductions of guests
    Food and table talk
    Prayer in small groups
    Topic of interest to membership
    Brainstorming and sharing of ideas
    Announcements and current events

Tour of host church
Resource table for sharing of printed ideas and programs.

Suggested brunch format:

9:00   Registration

9:30   Brunch

10:00   Meeting starts at tables or another room

        Introductions, announcements, and prayer time

10:30   Topic presentation (presenter/facilitator/speaker)
        Brainstorming/Discussion

12:00   Tour of host church (optional)

Suggested lunch format:

9:00   Registration, coffee, donuts or refreshments

9:30   Meeting starts (at tables or another room)

10:00   Meeting starts: introductions/announcements, prayer time

10:30   Topic presentation—presenter or facilitator

12:00   Lunch

12:35   Tour of host church (optional)

Encourage key individuals to volunteer for leadership. Suggest what officers you might want to provide some structure and framework for planning and fellowship. This spreads the leadership load and allows you to include others to cross denominational lines. (President, Vice Pres. of Membership, Vice Pres. of Programming, Secretary, Treasurer)

Schedule a Network Planning Session with these leaders. This is a key to launching a long-term networking effort. Plan a year's worth of meetings from the beginning. The year is so much easier to manage when you are busy. Decide on a brunch or a lunch-time schedule.

Select topics of interest to all (poll your group for suggestions). Brainstorm for ideas for speakers, discussion panels, presentations from vendors and suppliers. Invite publishing company representatives and experienced specialists that have expertise in a given area of interest common to most of your network. Note: that every subject will not fit everyone, all the time, but sooner or later everyone will get something really helpful. If your brainstorming is effective, good ideas will be stimulated every time. In the beginning, it is the interesting topic or speaker, which attracts members and visitors. Eventually, it is the friendship and fellowship within the network that becomes more dominant and significant to the members.

Children's leaders soon become your very best friends and this is when you will meet–once a month for lunch! (The "muncha-lunch bunch")

4. Announce the monthly meeting schedule to get your network up and running.
   • Plan your monthly meetings for the entire year and secure host churches.
   • Schedule the speakers/program for the whole year.
   • Create a yearly brochure complete with times, places and program.
   • Distribute this brochure to all the children's leaders in your area.
   • Share the leadership for key parts of the meeting.
   • Charge members and visitors $5 for lunch when catered or prepared.
   • Charge annual membership dues to cover mailing, brochures, and speakers.

Another Kid Helper Resource from…
Creative Children's Ministries
www.Kidhelper.com

Teaching Preteens Made Easy:
How to Connect with 5th & 6th Graders

By Pat Verbal

The PT Cruiser's retreat had been planned for months. Rustic lodge rented. Permission and medical forms signed. Bags packed with everything from ball gloves to curling irons. Huge boxes loaded into vans filled with food, volleyballs, nets, rackets, inflatable hockey sticks, cards games, puzzles, videos, Play-Do, water balloons and fishing gear. Speakers were prepared to talk about "Radical Faith." Nineteen fifth and sixth graders and six adults finally headed out for three days in the great outdoors.

Then, the RAINS came!

As challenging as that sounds, it was no problem for the energetic staff at the Richardson Church of the Nazarene in Richardson, Texas. Director Valerie King and her team knew preteens. They understood these wonderful creatures caught between the magical years of childhood and the awesome challenges of youth. The success of the retreat (and other exciting events throughout the year) is based on a solid approach to discipleship preteens and ground them in prayer.

Valerie admits the task is one that she daily turns over to God. "Each week as I get in my car and head for church, I worry about the kids. Will Ethan be there? What will it take to get Colin involved? I haven't seen Bryce since our play night. Should I send more cards in the mail? Should I change the program? Then I sense the gentle voice of God reminding me that it's my job to pray for these kids. God will bring them to us so we can love them, be genuine with them, and share the message of Jesus Christ."

Valerie encourages her leadership team to stick to the basics. "We try to live what we teach the kids about seeking God's kingdom and righteousness first in our lives. Then God will give us all we need to live for Him (Matthew 6:33)."

The Art of Abstract Thinking
By the time children reach fifth and sixth grade, they have moved from concrete thinking to abstract. This cognitive (mental) development allows them to understand religious words that never made any sense to them such as symbols and parables. Parables are stories Jesus told to teach specific principles. They are not true, but they teach about truth. The Easter story is filled with symbols of the Christian faith that become more precious as we mature such as the cross, the bread and cup of the Last Supper and the dove of the Holy Spirit. Children may learn about these things, but until they reach abstract thinking, it is difficult for them to apply them as part of their own religious experiences. If you watch carefully, you'll observe a window opening into the hearts of these young lives and begin to help them see God in new ways.

I observed this in a midweek club when we challenged the students to write their own parables. Michael, who was a bit of a trouble maker, surprised us with this parable about smoking. It clearly demonstrated his advanced reasoning skills.

The Chimney that Smokes
Once upon a time there was a house talking to the chimney.

The house asked, "Why do you smoke so much?" The chimney said, "I like to smoke and what I do isn't anybody's business."

The house said, "I don't think it is very good for you."

The chimney kept smoking. One day the chimney got clogged up and the smoke filled the house and ruined everything in it. The chimney asked, "How are you doing?" The house didn't answer, the house was dead.

The moral of the story is—the bad things you do to yourself can affect other people.

Michael continued to develop good Bible study habits. His class grew because they were challenged with age-appropriate activities.

If your preteen class isn't growing, there may be reasons you can identify and begin to change.

Keys to Shrinking Your Preteen Class
• Talk down to preteens.
• Ask preteens to sing children's songs.
• Give preteens busy-work.
• Call on them to read out loud.
• Encourage cliques.
• Keep discussion time to a minimum.
• Give them little or no free time in class.

Keys to Growing Your Preteen Class
Here are three keys for engaging your preteens and make teaching a lot easier.

1. The Purpose Key
• What is your purpose for working with preteens? What will your students remember as they leave your class and join youth ministries?

Valerie's desire for her students is that they know that salvation is not in attending church, being part of the group, or having godly parents. She plans activities for her class with a clear purpose.

"Daily I try to sit at the feet of Jesus," says Valerie, "and move forward under God's guidance and power. I study God's Word and pray for the fruit of God's Spirit to flow through me. I believe God wants us to share the complete gospel message, not a watered-down version that a young mind may find more appealing."

Valerie recommends the Evangecube to illustrate the Gospel to preteens. It also empowers them to share their faith with friends.
www.evangecube.org

2. The Tool Key

A gifted student asked me this question once, "Why can't it be as much fun to study the Bible as it is to study science or history?" He obviously enjoyed the science lab at his school and the history channel on television. I wanted to assure him that the Bible was more exciting than anything he could learn in a school textbook, but I realized this church kid would not believe me. Why? Because talk is cheap. So, I set out to show him that Bible study can be fun by introducing him to tools that would challenge his thinking. Students use similar tools at school and by this age they are beyond just hearing the story or doing a memory verse. Many students are ready to go deeper into God's Word.

Are these tools in your classroom?
>Junior Bible Concordance; verse references, subject texts
>Bible Dictionary; word meanings, origins, and usage
>Bible Atlas; maps, distance charts, typography
>Bible Bibliography; people in Scripture

Encourage questions in class, but don't hand out answers. Challenge students to research the person, place, or thing. Make wall charts, graphs, overheads or let students create a computer game centered around the lesson theme. Be sure to get reference tools designed for this age child.

Don't be guilty of pulling in old, dusty books from the church library—that could be a real turn-off.

3. The Action Key

Hang around the high school department for awhile. Preteens may not be ready for "Youth Culture," but they sure like to imitate it. That's not all bad. Like teens, fifth and sixth graders love animated lessons—hands-on stuff with a point. They don't like to be manipulated with busy work or meaningless tasks.

Get Fifth and Sixth Graders in Touch with the Word
1. Writing letters to missionaries.
2. Taking a field trip related to a lesson.
3. Solving mysteries and riddles.
4. Cooking a seder meal.
5. Creating Bible art murals.
6. Writing and performing Bible skits.
7. Serving in a kindergarten class.
8. Challenging pastors to a Bible quiz.

One fall the PT Cruisers decided to write a play just for fun. The drama centered around Christian foster family who opened their home to the tough kids no one else wanted. With the help of their teachers, the preteens created a wonderful three-act play that reflected the ups and downs of kids in difficult situations. The play evolved into a first-class Dessert Theater with a packed house of 350. Friends from school came. Family members bragged for weeks about the outstanding job they had done. Best of all they were given the liberty to be used by God to share His Gospel. The last scene climaxed in a country church with the homecoming of a young man's brother after the death of his parents. It left the audience with a strong message of God's power to answer our prayers and our need to care for one another.

Teaching the Word and instilling principles about life go hand in hand at this age level. It's a time for applying values the children have picked up in ten years of Sunday School.

Still wondering what you would do on a rainy preteen retreat? Good leaders are the best key for that situation. Valerie's leaders came equipped with a trick or two in case the weather turned bad. Ginger whipped out barrels of Play-Do and told the kids to each make a little person. They lined their clay people up on the edge of a table and introduced them to the group, telling their name and something about their personality. Next, they each chose someone else's figure and smashed it with a plastic bopper while shouting insults. Clay flew everywhere. Finally, they discussed the pride they experienced in making and introducing their little clay friends, and how it felt watching someone abuse them in light of Ephesians 4:29.

> "Do not let any unwholesome talk come out of your mouths, but only what is helpful for building others up according to their needs, that it may benefit."

Because these preteens understood how hurtful insults can be, they agreed to watch their own words and actions. It was a perfect, rainy day activity that won't soon be forgotten.

Bible Study Tools

The Student Bible Dictionary; A Complete Learning System to Help You Understand Words, People, Places and Events of the Bible by Karen Dockrey, Phyllis Godwin, Johnnie C. Godwin

The Student Bible Atlas by Tim Dowley, Richard Scott

What the Bible Is All About for Young Explorers; Based on the Best-Selling Classic by Henreitta Mears (Gospel Light Publishers)

International Children's Bible Dictionary by Lynn Waller

International Children's Bible Handbook by Lawrence Richardson (Sweet Publishers)

Patricia L. Verbal
8415 Pioneer Drive
Frisco, Texas 75034
972-377-0626
MTTC@aol.com

How to Really Help a Child Going Through a Difficult Time

By Vicki Wiley

More and more in our ministries we are called upon to show God's grace to children going through a hard time. Sometimes we have experience that tells us what to say and what not to say but more often than not we have no idea what to do or say when those around us are going through a crisis.

A crisis in the life of a child can be as intense as the death of a loved one, the death of a pet, moving, loosing a friend, the loss of a job for a parent or many other circumstances that affect our lives.

Dr. James Kok, Minister of Caring and Compassion at the Crystal Cathedral says "90% of caring is just showing up." But what about the other 10%? What can we say that will help and not hurt? Here are some things to keep in mind:

What to say and what not to say

As Children's Ministers and Sunday School teachers we are often at the forefront of where the ministry needs to be. But we don't know what we are doing, so typically when someone is experiencing a hard time we feel inadequate and do nothing so that we "don't interrupt his or her grief or make it harder."

The last thing that we want to do when someone really needs us is hurt the situation or make it worse. But if we don't know what to do, then that is sometimes the result. With a few simple rules to follow you can be sure that what you say will always help.

Each conversation that you have with a child that is hurting gives you the opportunity to make an impact. The problem is that every word that you say matters in these instances. So how can we be sure that what we say is for the good and not damaging to them?

Here is a short list of things to communicate with them:

- We grieve with them and feel very badly about what happened.
- We walk with them.
- We have time for them and we also want them to know that.
- God grieves with them.
- God walks with them.
- God has time for them.

Good things to say:
- How are you doing with all of this?
- Do you feel like talking?
- I'm so sorry about what happened.

Don't ever say:
- I understand (unless you have really been there).
- It's a blessing.
- You're lucky it wasn't worse.
- You now have an angel in heaven.
- You're young, it'll be OK.
- It's for the best.
- It was God's will.
- How does that make you feel? (too psychie).

When a child is going through something and telling us about it, we have a natural impulse to jump in, interrupt and tell about our own similar experience, what our neighbor went through, etc. Nothing could help LESS!

When a child is going through a hard time or a crisis, they need to talk. They do not need to listen to your story—They need you to listen to theirs.

In fact, even if you have been told the story of what happened by someone else, ask the child to tell you what happened. Let them tell the whole story no matter how long it might be. This helps them to sort the story out for themselves and at the same time lets you get the latest information first hand.

Saying things like "What happened?" "What did the doctor say?" "What do your parents tell you?" helps bring them to the facts of the situation. Be real with the amount of sympathy that you give—being overly sympathetic can make you seem fake.

When a child is experiencing a difficult time, you can be the one to help. But remember, for anyone to GET THROUGH pain, they must GO THROUGH pain. You are not there to take their pain away, only to ease the process of going through it.

What Kids Need

By Vicki Wiley

W/hat do you remember about being in Sunday School or Children's ministries while you were young? Most of you will remember a special teacher, performance, or class rather than great teaching. Why is that? Because children yearn for great relationships!

The whole world seems to be focused on the child in a way that I've never encountered before. Suddenly every market seems to cater to them; more stores are opening that have products for them, magazines such as *Sports Illustrated Jr, Time Jr,* etc. have surfaced. There are no fewer than ten cable TV stations just for kids as well as kids that are the focus of prime time TV.

During the last year *Time Magazine* featured an article on "young and bipolar" brain research is being done on how children learn, and time is being spent on many different diagnosis for behavior that psychiatrists now have for kids.

Our work is cut out for us! While the world around them is interested in them, fascinating and fast paced—we want them to settle down and learn to hear God's voice in their lives. As they are picking up things that are "spiritual" from all over the place, we want to teach them what is from God. So how do we accomplish this?

There are two things that we want to do as we work with children: educate them and let them experience God. Those two things together build faith.

Your church has probably already selected a good curriculum with age-appropriate education for the children. That's actually the easy part. The harder part is making yourself avaialble for a relationship with the child. A child experiences God first hand while watching you live out your life of faith.

How do you build a relationship with a child? Here are a few suggestions:

- Call them by name (you can't believe how important this one is!).
- Look them in the eye when you talk to them.
- Touch their hand or shoulder when you are listening to them talk.
- Always respect their answers.
- An occasional card means the world to a child that doesn't usually receive any mail!
- Show yourself to them—let them know that you pray all the time, that you love God and that you love and care about them.

Do you ever wonder what kids are wondering about when they think of God? I recently asked kids what they would ask God if they could. Here is what they said:

- How DO we really get to heaven, I mean, is it really true that we just believe in Jesus?
- When you die, what do you look like? How will your parents know that you are you?
- What does it mean to be born again? I know what you are going to say, but what does it really mean?
- Do angels ever fall through the clouds?
- Do angels come to get you to take you to heaven?
- Do you go through a cloud to get to heaven and when do you get your crown? Why do you have to wear a crown?
- If Adam and Eve did the first sin, would there be sin if they hadn't done it?
- How can God really be three people at the same time? I just don't get it. What does it really mean?
- How did God create without a wand?
- Does God try to change your thoughts so that you will do what He wants?
- How does God really know who you are going to marry?
- Is there really such a thing as a guardian angel?
- If you die young will you become an angel?
- If you die young do you automatically go to heaven?
- If you die young can you come back to earth as an angel and help your family?

What is the theme of these questions? What are kids wondering about?

One look at this list tells us that they wonder about death and what happens after death. They wonder how God will work things out in their lives. How can we reassure them that God is ever present for them? Here are a few suggestions:

- When facing problems and discussing solutions, remember to pray with the kids—reminding them that God has all things in His control.
- When you don't know an answer, don't be afraid to admit it! Kids love knowing that we are also mystified by the power of God.
- How do you explain bad things that happen to good people? Remind children that when bad things happen, God cries with us. Remind them that when people love God, bad things can happen but God works everything out for good.
- Most of all, let them know that ALL questions are GOOD questions and that you love to hear them talk and reflect about God!

Products and Services Directory

Bible Games

Bible Games Company
P.O. Box 237
Fredersicktown, OH 43019
1-800-845-7415
www.biblegamescompany.com

Child Abuse Prevention Resources

Strang Communication
The Guardian System
600 Rinehart Rd.
Lake Mary, FL 32746
1-800-451-4598
www.charismalife.com

Children's Bible Activities Online

Children's Ministry Today
8469 Seton Ct.
Jacksonville, FL 32244
904-777-3339
www.childrensministry.org

Communication Resources
4150 Belden Village St.
Fourth Floor
Canton, OH 44718
1-800-992-2144

Group Publishing Company
P.O. Box 481
Loveland, CO 80539
1-800-447-1070
www.grouppublishing.com

KidMo!
>
> 1113 Murfreesboro Road
> Suite 106-145
> Franklin, TN 37064
> 877-610-2935
> *www.kidmo.com*

Email: Bill@kidmo.com

LifeWay Church Resources
>
> One LifeWay Plaza
> Nashville, TN 37234
> 1-800-458-2772
> *www.lifeway.com*

One Way Street, Inc.
>
> P.O. Box 5077
> Engelewood, CO 80155-5077
> 303-790-1188
> *www.onewaystreet.com*

Picture This!
>
> Dan Peters, President
> 236 Castilian Ave.
> Thousand Oaks, CA 91320
> *www.bibledraw.com*

The Train Depot
>
> 2122 Palatka Rd.
> Louisville, KY 40214
> 1-800-229-KIDS
> *www.TrainDepot.org*

Children's Books

Augsburg Fortress Publishers
>
> 100 S. Fifth St., Suite 700
> Minneapolis, MN 55402
> 1-800-328-4648
> *www.augsburgfortress.org*

Barbour Publishing, Inc.
>
> 1810 Barbour Dr.
> Uhrichsville, OH 44683
> 1-800-852-8010
> *www.barbourpublishing.com*

Christian Book Distributors
  P.O. Box 7000
  140 Summit St.
  Peabody, MA 01961-7000
  978-977-5060 or 1-800-CHRISTIAN
  www.christianbook.com

Cokesbury
  201 Eighth Ave. S.
  Nashville, TN 37203
  1-800-672-1789
  www.cokesbury.com

Eerdmans Books for Young Readers
  255 Jefferson Ave., S.E.
  Grand Rapids, MI 49503
  1-800-253-7521
  www.eerdmans.com/youngreaders

Standard Publishing
  8121 Hamilton Ave.
  Cincinnati, OH 45231
  1-800-543-1353
  www.standardpub.com
Email: customerservice@standardpub.com

Tommy Nelson
  P.O. Box 141000
  Nashville, TN 37214
  615-902-3306
  www.thomasnelson.com

Tyndale House Publishers
  351 Executive Drive
  Carol Stream, IL 60188
  1-800-323-9400
  www.tyndale.com

Waterbrook Press, Inc.
  c/o Random House, Inc.
  1745 Broadway, 10th Floor
  New York, NY 10019
  212-782-9000
  FAX 212-940-7381
  www.randomhouse.com

Children's Bulletins

Children's Worship Bulletins
       Communication Resources
       4150 Belden Village St.
       Fourth Floor
       Canton, OH 44718
       1-800-992-2144
       www.ChildrensBulletins.com

Children's Church Supplies/Resources

Axtell Expressions, Inc.
       Dept. CM, 2889 Bunsen Ave. H.
       Ventura, CA 93003
       805-642-7282
       www.axtell.com

Betty Lukens, Inc.
       711 Portal Street
       Cotati, CA 94931
       1-800-541-9279
       www.bettylukens.com

Bible Candy
       1028 East Edna Place
       Covina, CA 91724
       www.biblecandy.com
       1-877-643-8922

Bring Them In
       P.O. Box 34564
       Houston, TX 77234
       281-922-6743
       www.bringthemin.com

Children's Music

Christian Book Distributors
       P.O. Box 7000
       140 Summit St.
       Peabody, MA 01961-7000
       978-977-5060 or 1-800-CHRISTIAN
       www.christianbook.com

Dean-O
>P.O. Box 3955
>Mission Viejo, CA 92690
>866-656-2328
>*www.Biblebeatmusic.com*

Integrity Music
>1000 Cody Rd.
>Mobile, AL 36695
>251-633-9000
>1-800-533-6912
>*www.integritymusic.com*

Mary Rice Hopkins
>P.O. Box 362
>Montrose, CA 91021
>818-790-5805 (or toll free 1-877-628-4532)
>*www.maryricehopkins.com*

Lillenas Publishing Company
>2923 Troost Ave.
>Kansas City, MO 64109
>1-800-877-0700
>*www.lillenaskids.com*

Tommy Nelson
>P.O. Box 141000
>Nashville, TN 37214
>615-902-3306
>*www.thomasnelson.com*

Word Music
>25 Music Square West
>Nashville, TN 37203
>1-888-324-9673
>*www.wordmusic.com*
Email: questions@wordmusic.com

Children's Themed Environments

Soft Play LLC
>12100 Vance David Dr.
>Charlotte, N.C. 28269
>704-875-6550
>*www.softplay.com*

Wacky World Studios
> 148 E. Douglas Rd.
> Oldsmar, FL 34677-2939
> 813-818-8277
> *www.wackyworld.tv*

Children's Videos/DVDs

Dean-O
> P.O. Box 3955
> Mission Viejo, CA 92690
> 866-656-2328
> *www.Biblebeatmusic.com*

Holy Bears, Inc.
> 12249 FM 529 Rd. Unit C
> Houston, TX 77041
> *www.holybears.com*

Integrity Music
> 1000 Cody Rd.
> Mobile, AL 36695
> 251-633-9000 or 1-800-533-6912
> *www.integritymusic.com*

Mary Rice Hopkins
> P.O. Box 362
> Montrose, CA 91021
> 818-790-5805
> *www.maryricehopkins.com*

Standard Publishing
> 8121 Hamilton Ave.
> Cincinnati, OH 45231
> 1-800-543-1353
> *www.standardpub.com*

Email: customerservice@standardpub.com

Tommy Nelson
> P.O. Box 141000
> Nashville, TN 37214
> 615-902-3306
> *www.thomasnelson.com*

Tyndale House Publishers
    351 Executive Drive
    Carol Stream, IL 60188
    1-800-323-9400
    www.tyndale.com

Choir/Choral Resources

Brentwood Benson Music
    741 Cool Springs Blvd.
    Franklin, TN 37067
    1-800-846-7664
    www.brentwoodbenson.com

LifeWay Church Resources
    One LifeWay Plaza
    Nashville, TN 37234
    1-800-458-2772
    www.lifeway.com

Lillenas Publishing Company
    2923 Troost Ave.
    Kansas City, MO 64109
    1-800-877-0700
    www.lillenaskids.com
Email: music@lillenas.com
Email: drama@lillenas.com

Christian Education Resources and Curriculum

Augsburg Fortress Publishers
    100 S. Fifth St., Suite 700
    Minneapolis, MN 55402
    1-800-328-4648
    www.augsburgfortress.org

Bible Visuals International
    P.O. Box 153
    Akron, PA 17501
    717-859-1131

Christian Ed. Publishers
    9230 Trade Pl. (P.O. Box 26639)
    San Diego, CA 92126
    1-800-854-1531
    www.ChristianEdWarehouse.com

Cokesbury
    201 Eighth Ave. S.
    Nashville, TN 37203
    1-800-672-1789
    www.cokesbury.com

Cook Communications Ministries
    4050 Lee Vance View
    Colorado Springs, CO 80918
    1-800-323-7543
    www.cookministries.com

Creative Teaching Associates
    5629 E. Westower Ave.
    Fresno, CA 93727
    559-291-6626 or 1-800-767-4282
    www.mastercta.com

Gospel Light
    1957 Eastman Ave.
    Ventura, CA 93003
    805-644-9721* or 1-800-4-GOSPEL
    www.gospellight.com
    *ouside the U.S.

Great Communications Publications
    3640 Windsor Park Dr.
    Suwanee, GA 30024-3897
    1-800-695-3387
    www.gcp.org

Group Publishing Company
    P.O. Box 481
    Loveland, CO 80539
    1-800-447-1070
    www.grouppublishing.com

Marketplace 29 A.D.
P.O. Box 29
Stevensville, MI 49127
1-800-345-12AD
Email: bjgoetz@marketplace29ad.com

Microframe Corporation
P.O. Box 1700
Broken Arrow, OK 74013
1-800-635-3811
www.nurserycall.com

Standard Publishing
8121 Hamilton Ave.
Cincinnati, OH 45231
1-800-543-1353
www.standardpub.com
Email: customerservice@standardpub.com

Strang Communications
Kids Church
600 Rinehart Rd.
Lake Mary, FL 32746
1-800-451-4598
www.charismalife.com

Upper Room Ministries
1908 Grand Ave.
Nashville, TN 37203-0004
1-800-972-0433
www.pockets.org

Christian School/Daycare Programs

Betty Lukens, Inc.
711 Portal Street
Cotati, CA 94931
1-800-541-9279
www.bettylukens.com

Cokesbury
201 Eighth Ave. S.
Nashville, TN 37203
1-800-672-1789
www.cokesbury.com

Gospel Light
    1957 Eastman Ave.
    Ventura, CA 93003
    805-644-9721* (or 1-800-4-GOSPEL)
    www.gospellight.com
    * Outside the U.S.)

Christian School Resources

Augsburg Fortress Publishers
    100 S. Fifth St., Suite 700
    Minneapolis, MN 55402
    1-800-328-4648
    www.augsburgfortress.org

Classroom Supplies

Church Ministries Distribution
    Free Shipping! All Publishers!
Email: john@churchministriesdistribution.com

Christian Ed. Publishers
    9230 Trade Pl. (P.O. Box 226639)
    San Diego, CA 92126
    1-800-854-1531
    www.ChristianEdWarehouse.com

Communication Systems

Jtech Communications, Inc.
    6413 Congress Ave., Ste. 150
    Boca Raton, FL 33487
    1-800-321-6221
    www.jtech.com

Long Range Systems, Inc.
    9855 Chartwell Dr.
    Dallas, TX 75243
    1-877-416-4050 (1-800-437-4996)
    www.pager.net

Microframe Corporation
P.O. Box 1700
Broken Arrow, OK 74013
1-800-635-3811
www.nurserycall.com

Seeker Nursery Paging Systems
3235 Satellite Blvd., Ste. 300
Duluth, GA 30096
1-866-575-3713
www.seekercommunication.com

Craft Resources

Guildcraft Arts & Crafts
100 Fire Tower Dr.
Tonawanda, NY 14150
1-800-345-5563
www.vbscrafts.com

S and S Worldwide
75 Mill St.
Colchester, CT 06415
1-800-243-9232
www.ssww.com

Curriculum

Big Idea Productions
230 Franklin Rd.
Franklin, TN 37064
800-295-0557
www.bigidea.com

Bring Them In
P.O. Box 34564
Houston, TX 77234
281-922-6743
www.bringthemin.com

Caring Hands Ministries
309 Hollyhill Ln.
Denton, TX 76205
940-367-4755
www.chministries.com

CharismaLife
  600 Rinehart Rd.
  Lake Mary, FL 32746
  1-800-451-4598
  www.charismalife.com

Christian Ed. Publishers
  P.O. Box 26639
  San Diego, CA 92126
  1-800-854-1531
  www.ChristianEdWarehouse.com

Cokesbury
  201 Eighth Ave. S.
  Nashville, TN 37203
  1-800-672-1789
  www.cokesbury.com

Cook Communications Ministries
  4050 Lee Vance View
  Colorado Springs, CO 80918
  1-800-323-7543
  www.cookministries.com

Gospel Light
  1957 Eastman Ave.
  Ventura, CA 93003
  805-644-9721* (800-4-GOSPEL)
  www.gospellight.com
  *outside the U.S.

Great Commission Publications
  3640 Windsor Park Dr.
  Suwanee, GA 30024
  1-800-695-3387
  www.gcp.org

Group Publishing Company
  P.O. Box 481
  Loveland, CO 80539
  1-800-447-1070
  www.grouppublishing.com

KidMo
    1113 Murfreesboro Rd. Ste. 106-145
    Franklin, TN 37064
    1-877-610-2935
    www.kidmo.com

KidzBlitz
    301 United Ct. Ste. 4
    Lexington, KY 40509
    1-800-467-1711
    www.kidzblitz.com

LifeWay Church Resources
    One LifeWay Plaza
    Nashville, TN 37234
    1-800-458-2772
    www.lifeway.com

Majesty Music
    P.O. Box 6524
    Greenville, SC 29606
    1-800-334-1071
    www.majestymusic.com

Marketplace 29 A.D.
    P.O. Box 29
    Stevensville, MI 49127
    1-800-345-12AD
Email: bjgoetz@marketplace29ad.com

Radiant Light/Gospel Publishing House
    1445 N. Boonville Ave.
    Springfield, MO 65802-1894
    1-800-641-4310
    www.GospelPublishing.com

Randall House Publications
    P.O. Box 17306
    Nashville, TN 37217
    1-800-877-7030
    www.randallhouse.com

Regular Baptist Press
    1300 N. Meacham Rd.
    Schaumburg, IL 60173
    1-800-727-4400 (Customer Service) 1-888-588-1600 (Home Office)
    www.rbstore.org

Standard Publishing
        8121 Hamilton Ave.
        Cincinnati, OH 45231
        1-800-543-1353
        www.standardpub.com
Email: customerservice@standardpub.com

The Train Depot
        2122 Palatka Rd.
        Louisville, KY 40214
        1-800-229-KIDS
        www.TrainDepot.org

WordAction Publishing Company
        2923 Troost Ave.
        Kansas City, MO 64109
        1-800-877-0700
        www.wordaction.com

Employment Resources/Services

Group Publishing's Available Church Positions Postings
        P.O. Box 481
        Loveland, CO 80539-0485
        1-800-635-0404 ext.4479
        www.cmmag.com
Email: swinter@grouppublishing.com

International Network of Children's Ministry
        P.O. Box 190
        Castle Rock, CO 80104
        1-800-324-4543
        www.incm.org

Event Planning Resources

Jtech Communications, Inc.
        6413 Congress Ave., Ste. 150
        Boca Raton, FL 33487
        1-800-321-6221
        www.jtech.com

Events for Children

Champions of Light
    Steve Geer
    www.championsoflight.org

Family Ministries Resources

Group Publishing Company
    P.O. Box 481
    Loveland, CO 80539
    1-800-447-1070
    www.grouppublishing.com

Flannelgraph

Betty Lukens, Inc.
    711 Portal Street
    Cotati, CA 94931
    1-800-541-9279
    www.bettylukens.com

Something Special for Kids
    Sam and Sandy Sprott
    1-800-Us 4 Kids

Gospel Magic and Performers

Dave and Jody
    Music that Matters
    708-479-8445

Dock Haley Gospel Magic
    P.O. Box 915
    Hermitage, TN 37076
    615-885-4800
    www.Gospelmagic.com
Email: dockhaley@gospelmagic.com

Ned and Joan Way
    P.O. Box 19229
    Louisville, KY 40259
    1-800-229-KIDS
    www.NoWay.org

One Way Street, Inc.
P.O. Box 5077
Engelewood, CO 80155-5077
303-799-1188
www.onewaystreet.com

Jeff Smith
Salt and Light Ministries
6420 Glebe Point Rd.
Chesterfield, VA 23838
804-748-9440
www.saltandlightmin.org

Steve Taylor
"Laughter That Uplifts!" Ministries
www.stevetaylorpro.com/gospel
1-888-473-7869

Mark Thompson
P.O. Box 2321
Redmond, WA 98073
800-867-6579
www.markthompson.org

Internet Resources

Children's Bible Activities Online

Communication Resources
4774 Munson St., Ste. 100
Canton, OH 44718
www.comresources.com

Childrensministry.com
www.childrensministry.com

Children's Ministry Today
8469 Seton Ct.
Jacksonville, FL 32244
909-777-3339
www.childrensministry.org
Email: info@childrensministry.org

Christianbook.com
P.O. Box 7000
140 Summit St.
Peabody, MA 01961-7000
978-977-5060 or 1-800-CHRISTIAN
www.christianbook.com

For Kids Only, Inc.
P.O. Box 10237
Newport Beach, CA 92658
1-888-646-9584
www.fko.org

Group Publishing Company
P.O. Box 481
Loveland, CO 80539
1-800-447-1070
www.grouppublishing.com

Leadership Training

Children's Ministry Magazine
6840 Meadowridge Ct.
Alpharetta, GA 30005
1-800-704-6562
www.cmmag.com

For Kids Only, Inc.
P.O. Box 10237
Newport Beach, CA 92658
1-888-646-9584
www.fko.org

International Network of Children's Ministry
Children's Pastors' Conference
P.O. Box 190
Castle Rock, CO 80104
1-800-324-4543
www.incm.org

Kidology Inc.
830 West Main Street #137
Lake Zurich, IL 60047
847-707-7552
www.kidology.org

Kids in Focus
>P.O. Box 1225
>Jamul, CA 91935
>Fax: 619-342-4474 or 1-877-932-4907 (toll free)
>*www.kidsinfocus.org*

Magazines & Periodicals

Children's Ministry Magazine
>P.O. Box 481
>Loveland, CO 80539-0481
>760-738-0086
>*www.cmmag.com*

Group Publishing Company
>P.O. Box 481
>Loveland, CO 80539-0481
>760-738-0086
>*www.grouppublishing.com*
>*www.groupmag.com*

LifeWay Church Resources
>One LifeWay Plaza
>Nashville, TN 37234
>1-800-458-2772
>*www.lifeway.com*

The Children's Pastor
>P.O. Box 190
>Castle Rock, CO 80104
>1-800-324-4543
>*www.incm.com*

Ministry Consultants

Kids in Focus
>P.O. Box 1225
>Jamul, CA 91935
>Fax: 619-342-4474 or 1-877-932-4907 (toll free)
>*www.kidsinfocus.org*

LifeWay Church Resources
> One LifeWay Plaza
> Nashville, TN 37234
> 1-800-458-2772
> *www.lifeway.com*

Ministry to Today's Child
> Pat Verbal
> 10472 Hay Meadow Drive
> Frisco, TX 75034
> 1-800-406-1011
> *www.ministrytotodayschild.com*

Email: MTTC@aol.com

Preschool Resources

Eerdmans Books for Young Readers
> 255 Jefferson Ave., S.E.
> Grand Rapids, MI 49503
> 1-800-253-7521
> *www.eerdmans.com/youngreaders*

Group Publishing Company
> P.O. Box 481
> Loveland, CO 80539-0481
> 760-738-0086
> *www.grouppublishing.com*

LifeWay Church Resources
> One LifeWay Plaza
> Nashville, TN 37234
> 1-800-458-2772
> *www.lifeway.com*

Lillenas Publishing Company
> 2923 Troost Ave.
> Kansas City, MO 64109
> 1-800-877-0700
> *www.lillenaskids.com*

Email: music@lillenas.com
> drama@lillenas.com

Randall House Publications
P.O. Box 17306
Nashville, TN 37217
1-800-877-7030
www.randallhouse.com

Safe Kids, Inc.
P.O. Box 4520
Beaufort, SC 29903
1-866-846-6339
www.churchnursery.com

WordAction Publishing Company
2923 Troost Ave.
Kansas City, MO 64109
1-800-877-0700
www.wordaction.com

Puppet Resources

Amaze Healing Wings
Puppets with a Heart
Darcy Maze
12470 Corkwood Lane
Victoria, CA 92395
760-245-4331
www.amazehealingwings.com

Axtell Expressions, Inc.
Dept. CM, 2889 Bunsen Ave. H.
Ventura, CA 93003
805-642-7282
www.axtell.com

Children's Ministry Today
8469 Seton Ct.
Jacksonville, FL 32244
904-777-3339
www.childrensministry.org

Maher Ventriloquist Studios
P.O. Box 420
Littleton, CO 80160
303-346-6819
www.maherstudios.com

One Way Street, Inc.
        P.O. Box 5077
        Englewood, CO 80155-5077
        303-790-1188
        www.onewaystreet.com

Plushpups—MT&B Corporation
        249 Homestead Rd.
        Hillsborough, NJ 08844
        1-800-682-1665
        www.plushpups.com

The Puppet Factory, Inc.
        904 W. 19th
        Goodland, KS 67735
        785-890-7143
        www.thepuppetfactory.com

Puppet Partners, Inc.
        1343 W. Flint Meadow Dr., Ste. 3
        Kaysville, UT 84037
        1-877-262-4117
        www.puppetpartners.com

Swanson Christian Supplies
        1200 Park Ave.
        Murfreesboro, TN 37129
        1-800-251-1402 or 615-896-4114
        www.swansoninc.com

The Train Depot
        2122 Palatka Rd.
        Louisville, KY 40214
        1-800-229-KIDS
        www.TrainDepot.org

Vacation Bible School Publishers

Augsburg Fortress Publishers
        100 S. Fifth St., Suite 700
        Minneapolis, MN 55402
        1-800-328-4648
        www.augsburgfortress.org

Big Idea Productions
  230 Franklin Rd.
  Franklin, TN 37064
  630-295-0557
  www.bigidea.com

Bring Them In
  P.O. Box 34564
  Houston, TX 77234
  281-922-6743
  www.bringthemin.com

Caring Hands Ministries
  309 Hollyhill Ln.
  Denton, TX 76205
  940-367-4755
  www.chministries.com

CharismaLife
  600 Rinehart Rd.
  Lake Mary, FL 32746
  1-800-451-4598
  www.charismalife.com

Christian Ed. Publishers
  P.O. Box 26639
  San Diego, CA 92126
  1-800-854-1531
  www.ChristianEdWarehouse.com

Cokesbury
  201 Eighth Ave. S.
  Nashville, TN 37203
  1-800-672-1789
  www.cokesbury.com

Cook Communications Ministries
  4050 Lee Vance View
  Colorado Springs, CO 80918
  1-800-323-7543
  www.cookministries.com

Gospel Light
>1957 Eastman Ave.
>Ventura, CA 93003
>805-644-9721* or 1-800-4-GOSPEL
>*www.gospellight.com*
>*outside the U.S.

Great Commission Publications
>3640 Windsor Park Dr.
>Suwanee, GA 30024
>1-800-695-3387
>*www.gcp.org*

Group Publishing Company
>P.O. Box 481
>Loveland, CO 80539
>1-800-447-1070
>*www.grouppublishing.com*

LifeWay Church Resources
>One LifeWay Plaza
>Nashville, TN 37234
>1-800-458-2772
>*www.lifeway.com*

Standard Publishing
>8121 Hamilton Ave.
>Cincinnati, OH 45231
>1-800-543-1353
>*www.standardpub.com*
>Email: customerservice@standardpub.com